FINANCE FOR
REAL ESTATE
DEVELOPMENT

Charles Long

**Urban Land
Institute**

T0350830

About the Urban Land Institute

The mission of the Urban Land Institute is to provide leadership in the responsible use of land and in creating and sustaining thriving communities worldwide. ULI is committed to

- Bringing together leaders from across the fields of real estate and land use policy to exchange best practices and serve community needs;

- Fostering collaboration within and beyond ULI's membership through mentoring, dialogue, and problem solving;

- Exploring issues of urbanization, conservation, regeneration, land use, capital formation, and sustainable development;

- Advancing land use policies and design practices that respect the uniqueness of both built and natural environments;

- Sharing knowledge through education, applied research, publishing, and electronic media; and

- Sustaining a diverse global network of local practice and advisory efforts that address current and future challenges.

Established in 1936, the Institute today has nearly 30,000 members worldwide, representing the entire spectrum of the land use and development disciplines. ULI relies heavily on the experience of its members. It is through member involvement and information resources that ULI has been able to set standards of excellence in development practice. The Institute has long been recognized as one of the world's most respected and widely quoted sources of objective information on urban planning, growth, and development.

About the ULI Center for Capital Markets and Real Estate

The ULI Center for Capital Markets and Real Estate focuses on real estate finance, real estate industry and investment trends, and the relationship between the capital markets and real estate. The mission of the Center is to promote understanding of the real estate capital markets and to provide leadership in fostering a healthy and productive real estate industry and capital markets sector that in turn promote thriving and sustainable communities worldwide. The Center pursues this mission through research, trend analysis, education, events, publications, web-based resources, advocacy, and thought leadership.

Copyright 2011 by the Urban Land Institute
1025 Thomas Jefferson Street, NW
Suite 500 West
Washington, DC 20007-5201

All rights reserved. No part of this book may be reproduced in any form or by any means, electronic or mechanical, including photocopying and recording, or by any information storage and retrieval system, without written permission of the publisher.

Catalog number: P100

Library of Congress Cataloging-in-Publication Data

Long, Charles,1947-
  Finance for real estate development / Charles Long.
    p. cm.
  ISBN 978-0-87420-157-4
1. Real estate development. 2. Real estate development--Finance. I. Title.
  HD1390.L66 2011
  332.7'2--dc22

                                    2011008977

Cover photo:
Codo 241, in York, Pennsylvania, was financed with long-term capital from local investors. It is a 70,000-square-foot adaptive-use project that includes rental apartments, offices, and a bistro.

J. David Allen and Son Photography

Author

Charles Long
Principal, Charles A. Long Properties, LLC
Oakland, California

Project Staff

Gayle Berens
Senior Vice President,
Education and Advisory Group

Dean Schwanke
Executive Director,
ULI Center for Capital Markets and
Real Estate; Senior Vice President,
Urban Land Institute

Anita Kramer
Senior Director, ULI Center for
Capital Markets and Real Estate

Adrienne Schmitz
Senior Director, Publications

James Mulligan
Managing Editor

Lise Lingo
Manuscript Editor,
Publications Professionals LLC

Betsy VanBuskirk
Creative Director

Anne Morgan
Graphic Designer

Craig Chapman
Senior Director, Publishing Operations

Reviewers

Ryan Beible
Student Reviewer
Johns Hopkins University,
    Edward St. John Department of Real Estate
Baltimore, Maryland

Stephen Blank
Senior Resident Fellow, Finance,
    Urban Land Institute
Washington, D.C.

David Blitz
Principal, Nebo Capital, Inc.
Los Angeles, California

Robert Feinberg
Senior Vice President, Grubb & Ellis
    New Mexico
Albuquerque, New Mexico

Terri Gumula
Workouts & Dispositions
    Vice President, Citigroup
New York, New York

Rebecca Rivard
Student Reviewer
Johns Hopkins University,
    Edward St. John Department of Real Estate
Baltimore, Maryland

Brent Smith
Associate Professor, Virginia Commonwealth
    University School of Business
Richmond, Virginia

Steven Spillman
Principal, Pacifica Companies
Mission Viejo, California

Roger Staiger III
Managing Director, Stage Capital, LLC
Fairfax, Virginia

About the Author

CHARLES A. LONG has had a long and varied career as a developer, development consultant, city manager, and educator, specializing in mixed-use infill and redevelopment projects, including acquisition, entitlement, development, and consulting. He has 36 years of diverse experience in local government and development with an emphasis on economic development, finance, and public/private partnerships. He served for eight years as city manager in Fairfield, California, a city with a national reputation as being innovative and well managed.

Since 1996 Long has worked as a consultant to public and private clients on development and management. He has held interim positions for several cities in finance, redevelopment and management, including interim town manager of Mammoth Lakes and interim city manager of Hercules and Pinole, all in California. His diverse assignments include writing redevelopment plans, working on development projects, conducting pro forma analysis, conducting strategic planning, representing public agencies in negotiations, marketing development opportunities, assisting with organizational development, conducting capital and financial planning, implementing budget reform, analyzing military base reuse, and promoting alternative energy development. He has overseen more than $600 million in public financing during his career. His work on development is focused in California, with an emphasis on public/private partnerships and mixed-use infill.

Long is a full member of the Urban Land Institute and, within ULI, a member of the Public/Private Partnership Council and a faculty member teaching the Real Estate Development Process II, Public/Private Partnerships, and Decision Making for Development Professionals courses. He has worked on 14 ULI Advisory Panels, most recently chairing a panel in Dallas, Texas. He is cochair of the Sustainability Committee for the San Francisco District Council and helped design and deliver seminars on implementing sustainable communities for public officials, sponsored by the Daniel Rose Institute. He has taught at the School of Public Administration at Golden Gate University and has conducted courses on real estate development, economic development, and organizational change internationally.

Long has a BA in economics from Brown University and a Masters of Public Policy from the University of California at Berkeley. He served in the U.S. Army as an infantry platoon sergeant.

Foreword

Financing a real estate development project is a challenging undertaking that requires sweat equity, working capital, market knowledge, financial experience, connections, and strong analytical and communication skills. It involves both art and science. In essence, a real estate developer must connect with and convince both equity and debt capital providers—who will likely put up most of the capital for a project—that the developer can successfully invest and deploy such capital, in an inherently risky business, and not only return that capital to the investor but also deliver promised returns on that capital.

Needless to say, investors and lenders expect to see a great deal of solid evidence that their capital will be well managed in this process. This book is intended to enhance understanding and provide a guide for developers and would-be developers looking to prepare that evidence and to successfully arrange and structure equity and debt financing for a real estate development project.

The book begins by putting finance into context within the development process, highlighting four dimensions for successful development—values, information, financial viability, and relationships. It then goes on to cover the basics of real estate finance, land valuation and acquisition, task management and budgeting, the capital markets for real estate, obtaining financing for development, the ownership entity and financing structures, managing risk in the entitlement process, public/private partnerships, and case studies and stories about how developers find capital and arrange financing.

Many books have been published on the subject of real estate finance or real estate development, but few actually focus on the nexus, the specific challenge of financing a project. Charles Long, the author of this book, brings a unique and practical perspective to this issue, drawing on his considerable development experience in both the private and public sectors. This is a book written not from an academic perspective but from a practitioner's perspective, on a topic that requires a practitioner's perspective. The book draws on that experience, as well as considerable research and the author's experience as an educator, to offer practical guidance and perspective on how real estate development finance works.

Dean Schwanke
Executive Director
ULI Center for Capital Markets and
Real Estate; Senior Vice President
Urban Land Institute
Washington, D.C.

Acknowledgments

This book, I hope, connects the practice of real estate development to its underlying concepts, a goal that I would not have been able to achieve without lots of help from colleagues who were generous in sharing their wisdom, experience, and encouragement. Among these are Rick Dishnica, Alex Rose, and Ehud Mouchly for patiently mentoring me; Anita Kramer at ULI for encouraging me to embark on this project; Dean Schwanke at ULI for pointing me in the right direction countless times; David Mulvihill at ULI for giving me great opportunities to engage with new teaching (and learning) experiences; Terri Gumula for conscientiously helping to make the book better; Stephen Blank, Steven Spillman, and Roger Staiger for patient and insightful reviewing; Adrienne Schmitz, the project director, for pulling everything together; and finally, to countless professionals in this wonderful business called real estate development who shared with me their projects and insights and who are cited in the book. I hope that I have conveyed at least a small part of the energy and creativity of this unique industry.

Charles A. Long

Contents

Chapter 1. The Development Process 2

Real Estate Overview.. 3

The Development Process and Risk............................... 6

Stages of Development... 8

    Predevelopment 8

    Development 9

    Close-out and Operation 10

Four Dimensions of Successful Development 12

    Values 12

    Information.. 12

    Financial Viability 13

    Relationships...14

Skills of a Successful Developer 14

Development Sectors 16

    Customer Issues 19

    Return, Absorption, and Risk 19

Case Study.. 22

Chapter 2. The Basics of Real Estate Finance 28

Basic Debt and Equity Structure 30

Project Valuation.. 33

    Capitalization Rates... 35

Measuring Project Return 38

    Internal Rates of Return 38

    Leverage 40

Funding a Project 41

    Funding Predevelopment Costs 41

    Debt Funding 41

    Equity Funding 43

The Typical Deal... 45

Financial Structuring for a Hypothetical Project........ 45

    Estimating Costs.. 48

    Evaluating Return 54

Chapter 3. Land Valuation for Acquisition 58

Determining a Valid Hurdle Rate for Evaluating
Project Viability 59

Calculating the Supported Investment and Residual
Land Value 62

    Costs 62

    Residual Land Value 63

Disciplined Acquisition: Site Selection, Negotiation,
and Due Diligence 66

    Information Inputs 67

    Negotiating with Site Owners 70

    Due Diligence 72

Example: Simple Pro Forma for a Mixed-Use Project 74

Chapter 4. Task Management and Budgeting 76

Task Management to Achieve Financial Viability 77

    Site 78

    Market 79

    Community 80

    Product/Project Design 80

    Cost and Construction Management................... 81

    Finance 84

    Personnel Selection... 84

    Other Services.. 90

Task Funding.. 91

Chapter 5. Capital Markets for Real Estate 92

Capital Market Conditions.. 93

Capital Sources 96

    Banks, Savings and Loans, and Mutual Savings Banks 99

    Commercial Mortgage–Backed Securities........................101

    Private Equity Capital 103

Fiduciary Principles 111

Investment Strategies 114

Property Characteristics 116

    Sector Risk 116

    Regional Strength 117

    Tenant Strength 118

    Value-Add Opportunities 118

Capital Markets and the Risk-Reward Evaluation................... 119

Chapter 6. Obtaining Financing for Development 120

Market Conditions..121

Connecting with Capital Sources................................123

    Accessing Predevelopment and Development
    Equity Capital 123

    Accessing Construction and Permanent
    Financing...126

    Finding a Buyer for the Property 126

Presenting to Financing Sources 126
    Experience, Credibility, and Financial Capacity
    of the Development Entity..................................127
    The Development Project and the
    Business Plan...127
    Entitlement Process and Role of Public/Private
    Partnerships 129
Conclusion..129

Chapter 7. The Development Entity, Joint Ventures, and the Financing Structure 130

Real Estate Entities..131
    Partnerships 132
    Limited Liability Companies (LLC).....................133
    S Corporations..133
    Real Estate Investment Trusts 133
    Corporations 134
Elements of a Joint Venture..................................134
    Business Plan 136
    Participants 136
    Governance 137
    Capitalization 137
    Revenue Distribution Among the Partners 138
    General Provisions 139
Financing Structure..139
Profit Distribution to the Development Entity 144
Example: Profit Distribution within a Development Entity 145

Chapter 8. Managing the Entitlement Process for Financial Viability 150

Mapping the Process...152
    Before Making an Offer 153
    After an Offer Is Accepted 153
    During Due Diligence 154
    As Circumstances Change 154
Managing Project Economics During Entitlement 154
    Density 155
    Parking 158
    Public Improvements 158
    Design...158

Managing the Process.................................159
Conclusion...161

Chapter 9. Public/Private Partnerships 162

Application 163
    Public Capital for Private Projects 164
    Entitlement Risk 166
    Site Access, Cleanup, and Reconfiguration......167
    Co-investment 168
Community Preparation 169
    Partnership Entity...170
    Financing Program for Infrastructure or Other
    Public Facilities 171
    Business Improvement Districts.........................171
    Stapleton Airport Redevelopment: An Example
    of Community Preparation 171
How Communities and Developers Work Together 172
    Negotiating a Deal..173
Public/Private Financing Tools 174
    Redevelopment Agencies 174
    Municipal Bonds 176
    Land Assembly and Conveyance 178
    Grants and Incentives 179
    Affordable Housing Subsidies 179
    Tax Credits...180
Deal Standards 182

Chapter 10. How Developers Get Capital 186

Getting Started...187
Building Relationships 192
Skills for Acquiring Capital in the 2010s.................194

Appendix A: Bios of Interviewees 198

Appendix B: Glossary 202

Index.................. 208

For supplemental materials, see http://www.uli.org/financered.

FINANCE FOR
REAL ESTATE
DEVELOPMENT

CHAPTER 1

The Development Process

R eal estate development requires diverse disciplines and activities to convert an idea into a completed project. The work up to completion must be paid for with invested time and capital supported by the property's finished development value, which results from either income or sales. Construction costs are the largest component of project costs, followed by land, architecture and engineering, legal, financial, environmental, management, marketing, and communications. Each discipline involves a different array of staff, contractors, and consultants who have different skills and roles. All these disciplines cannot function coherently without the skill of the real estate developer, who coordinates the different activities to create value. One of the most important skills that a developer brings to this process is the ability to obtain and manage appropriate equity and debt financing to fund these activities in a timely and cost-effective manner.

This chapter starts with a brief overview of real estate as a sector of the economy, its dependence on capital markets, and its dynamic nature. The chapter then describes the development process, its tasks, the overarching questions that a developer must address, the skills necessary to be a successful developer, and the role of finance in the development process. It concludes with an overview of the main sectors of real estate and their customer risk and absorption profiles.

Real Estate Overview

In 2007, private construction activity for commercial and residential real estate development in the United States totaled approximately $700 billion, according to the Bureau of Labor Statistics. With the addition of a reasonable estimate of 40 percent of this figure to account for land, design, financing, and other development costs, the real estate development sector contributed about 7 percent to gross domestic product (GDP) (Figure 1-1). Of this activity, about 71 percent was residential; the other 29 percent was nonresidential, including retail, office, industrial, lodging, education, and health care.

In addition to its contribution to ongoing economic activity, commercial real estate is an important investment category for major investors in their allocation of portfolio assets.

Commercial real estate has a relatively low total capitalization compared with U.S. stocks, according to the CME Group (figure 1-2). When combined with residential real estate, however, the value of U.S. real estate exceeds that of U.S. stocks and is approximately equal to that of the U.S. bond market.

Commercial real estate has grown in importance as an investment asset class over the past several decades, in part owing to new laws and new investment vehicles. The Tax Reform Act of 1986 substantially reduced tax rates for all taxpayers and eliminated accelerated depreciation

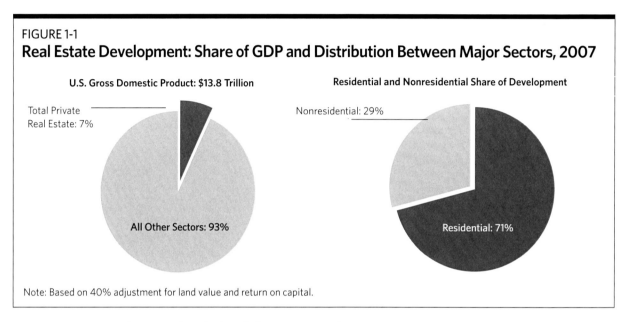

FIGURE 1-1
Real Estate Development: Share of GDP and Distribution Between Major Sectors, 2007

U.S. Gross Domestic Product: $13.8 Trillion

Total Private Real Estate: 7%

All Other Sectors: 93%

Residential and Nonresidential Share of Development

Nonresidential: 29%

Residential: 71%

Note: Based on 40% adjustment for land value and return on capital.

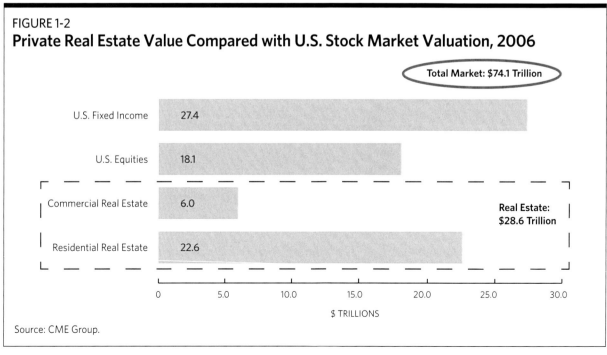

FIGURE 1-2
Private Real Estate Value Compared with U.S. Stock Market Valuation, 2006

Total Market: $74.1 Trillion

U.S. Fixed Income   27.4

U.S. Equities   18.1

Commercial Real Estate   6.0   Real Estate: $28.6 Trillion

Residential Real Estate   22.6

0   5.0   10.0   15.0   20.0   25.0   30.0

$ TRILLIONS

Source: CME Group.

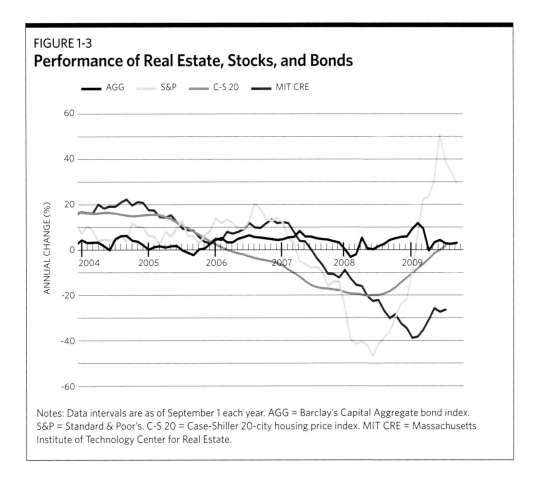

FIGURE 1-3
Performance of Real Estate, Stocks, and Bonds

Legend: ▬ AGG   ▭ S&P   ▬ C-S 20   ▬ MIT CRE

ANNUAL CHANGE (%)

Notes: Data intervals are as of September 1 each year. AGG = Barclay's Capital Aggregate bond index. S&P = Standard & Poor's. C-S 20 = Case-Shiller 20-city housing price index. MIT CRE = Massachusetts Institute of Technology Center for Real Estate.

for real estate, thus making real estate less of a tax shelter and more of an income-producing asset. (This change is discussed further in chapters 5 and 10.) The Act also broadened the investment scope of real estate investment trusts (REITs), making them development and management entities instead of merely lenders. These publicly traded investment vehicles made real estate investments accessible to many more investors. Then, in the early 1990s, following a disastrous real estate recession, the financial markets developed commercial mortgage–backed securities (CMBS), which sold securities backed by pools of real estate loans—resulting in substantially enhanced access to debt for the real estate sector. (Chapter 5 provides more detail on the effects of these two changes.) Private equity funds, backed by institutional money and high–net worth investors, also entered the landscape in the 1990s, often focusing on opportunistic investments. These changes together substantially transformed the real estate industry and increased the capital available for real estate investment, ultimately resulting in a far more sophisticated investment landscape with a broader set of participants and vehicles.

As these changes propagated through the industry, real estate competed more effectively with other asset classes for capital and attracted the interest of more investors. In the early 2000s, real estate performed better than equities and fixed income securities, largely because it was perceived as low risk; that is, as "always going up." Figure 1-3 compares the performance of bonds, stocks, commercial real estate, and residential real estate for the period from 2004 to 2010. Early in this period, real estate—both commercial and residential—outperformed both the equity and the fixed-income sectors; but in 2008, stocks and real estate collapsed and capital flowed out of real estate and stocks and into the safe haven of bonds. Then, while stocks recovered, real estate lagged as investors realized how much its performance correlates with jobs and capital availability.

More recently, the Great Recession of 2007 to 2008 highlighted not only the cyclical nature of the real estate industry but also its dynamic nature. Valuation losses in many markets and for many sectors placed property values below replacement costs, thus deferring development in these markets and sectors for some time, until valuations recovered to at least replacement levels. Investors redirected their energies toward new opportunities as distressed properties became available at much lower prices.

Inherently, real estate is a dynamic industry that adjusts to changing market and capital opportunities. The history of real estate development for the last two generations underscores this dynamic characteristic. Starting in the 1950s, with the baby boom and the mobility created by the automobile, the development industry responded with innovative housing production and auto-oriented suburban retail. Although some viewed this response with disdain (think of Malvina Reynolds' lyrics—"little boxes made of ticky-tacky"—or Joni Mitchell's—"They paved paradise and put up a parking lot"), it provided needed housing and created communities that reflected the sense of freedom of a nation with wheels. Throughout the 1960s and 1970s, as urban centers lost commerce and residents, the industry corrected many of its commodity-driven practices and responded to demand for new, higher-quality forms of retailing such as shopping malls and office parks. Gradually, in the 1980s and 1990s, suburbs became fringe cities and the concepts of business parks, lifestyle centers, and place making evolved. Beginning in the late 1990s, as people yearned for identity, the industry advanced the concept of smart growth and town centers, and mixed-use development evolved. Going forward in the 2010s, the development industry will continue to respond to evolving demands with more sustainable development, more infill, more revitalization, and more mixed-use products.

The dynamism in the industry relies on the capacities of the professional developer to recognize and harness market demand, to enable the creativity and practicality of architects, contractors, marketers, and financiers to produce value from ideas. Starting with an idea and a piece of land and, perhaps, a major tenant, the developer puts money and time at risk to design a project, obtain community support, buy land, and—if financing sources can see that it will work—to construct and close out the project. The developer is the conductor of a complex, multidisciplinary process that depends on exogenous forces, especially market demand and capital availability. No other industry creates a product that involves the collaborative effort of so many disciplines in such a publicly accountable process. Real estate development is unique. In this chapter we begin learning how to do it effectively.

The Development Process and Risk

Development involves putting increasing amounts of investment capital at risk over time. As more capital is invested, the risk to that investment should be reduced by the growing certainty that the project will be successful and provide returns to investors.

Figure 1-4 diagrams the risk and cost profile of a typical real estate development project. Costs increase with time, but the risk profile is the inverse of the cost profile. Risks from unknown and uncontrollable factors are high in the early stage, when uncertainty is high because of scarce information. Risk lessens as the project proceeds through design to entitlement and financing as more information is developed, uncertainties are resolved, and—most important—risk is controlled through competent management strategies.

At the initiation of a new development project, the developer evaluates two dimensions of economic viability. First, can the project pay a return on investment if it is actually built? Second, and equally important, does the developer have sufficient capital to fund the early project costs to bring the project to a stage where it can be financed and built? This second dimension highlights the risks that the developer takes to get a project to the point at which it can demonstrate viability and thereby attract capital from outside investors and lenders.

The early costs of a development project are relatively low; they involve investigatory work, market analyses, preliminary design, navigating the approval process, cost estimating, and site analysis—costs categorized as "soft costs" and typically paid from the developer's own capital, at least until project viability has been demonstrated to a financing source and outside funding becomes available. With time, these costs can accumulate to be quite significant—reaching into millions of dollars for larger projects and hundreds of thousands for smaller projects. The risks and funding of these predevelopment costs can constitute a major challenge to the economic viability of a real estate development project, especially in areas where the entitlement process is long, costly, and uncertain.

The first significant cost that a project incurs is, typically, acquiring either the land or an option to buy the land. Knowing how to evaluate what a project can afford to pay is crucial. Land value for a project must be evaluated on the basis of the "residual" of the project's value less all development costs (including an adequate return), not on the basis of comparables or appraisals. (Chapter 3 addresses this issue in detail.)

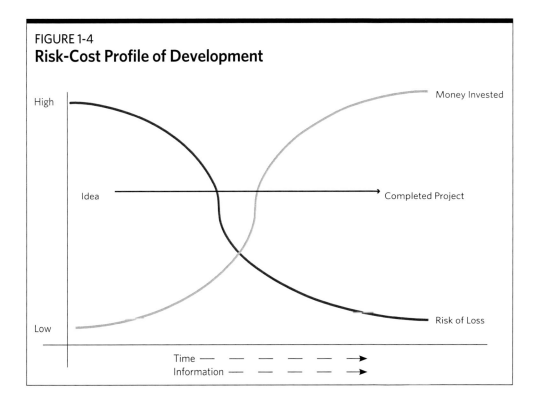

FIGURE 1-4
Risk-Cost Profile of Development

Costs grow as the project becomes more complete, as entitlement applications are filed, as community groups are engaged in the entitlement process, and as equity and debt financing sources are pursued. By the start of construction, the risks to project success are largely confined to managing construction, reacting to unforeseen market downturns, and executing the marketing, leasing, and management plan. Of these, only market conditions are beyond the control of the development team.

Any project faces the very real risk that the market could collapse during construction, resulting in reduced leasing or sales, and project failure. During construction, there is the risk that costs and construction time could exceed projections, resulting in funding short-falls or a higher carrying cost for capital. The developer's challenge at the beginning of a project is to identify the issues that represent future risk and to conceive of and implement competent management strategies to mitigate them. Market collapse and construction risks are easier and cheaper to mitigate if they are defined and anticipated before they happen.

In summary, the key management strategy for successful development is to continually monitor whether there is a likelihood of adequate return on investment and whether the project warrants the investment of additional time and money to proceed. The developer should resist the complacency induced by momentum, so that the discipline of monitoring key issues does not erode as more costs are incurred. The sooner an unviable project is abandoned, the smaller the loss. Many development projects are abandoned, some quite late in the process, when information about costs, markets, or entitlement conditions shows that they are not viable.

Stages of Development

Figure 1-5 shows the three stages of development and the tasks associated with each:

- The predevelopment phase, which has the highest risk of loss, consumes a relatively small 5 to 15 percent of project costs.
- The bulk of project expenditures, 80 to 90 percent, occur during construction in the development phase.
- Close-out, involving marketing, selling, leasing, and managing the project after completion, also consumes a relatively small 5 to 8 percent of project costs.

Figure 1-5 groups the tasks, showing how they evolve over the three phases from information gathering and planning into implementation. The effective implementation of construction and close-out depends on the quality of work done on the predevelopment tasks. The following subsections describe the primary focus of each of the three phases. (Chapter 4 describes in detail the management and funding of each task in the three phases.)

PREDEVELOPMENT

The predevelopment phase is when all the most important ideas behind the project concept and plan are created and refined, and the time when the most important decisions are made. Notes Dan Rosenfeld, a mixed-use developer based in Los Angeles formerly with Urban Partners, LLC, "Eighty to 90 percent of project value is created during predevelopment." During predevelopment the developer conceives the project, acquires land, designs

FIGURE 1-5

Stages and Tasks of the Development Process

Stages	Predevelopment	Development	Close-out
Share of Total Project Budget (%)	5–15%	80–90%	5–8%
TASKS	Site selection	Close on land purchase	
	Negotiate terms of land acquisition and execute purchase constract		
	Due diligence on land		
	Market analysis	Continue to monitor market conditions and financial viability	Leasing or selling
	Preleasing and presales planning	Initiate marketing and lease-up/sale	
	Site analysis	Construction: Implement construction management strategies	Construction close-out, punch list, and tenant move-in
	Design development		
	Project design		
	Preconstruction planning		
	Financing analysis Financing commitments	Comply with financing source requirements	Provide return to financing sources
	Entitlement	Set up property management	Ongoing project management

the project, secures financing commitments, and obtains the entitlements. In other words, the tasks in this stage shape what occurs in later phases, including the strategies used to respond to changes in market and financing conditions.

The tasks in predevelopment focus, first, on designing a product that responds to the market, that can be entitled, and that can be built at a cost that allows an adequate return on investment. To accomplish this, predevelopment must necessarily address implementation steps to achieve project viability. Each task in predevelopment, then, generates an implementation strategy for later phases. Only after a high degree of certainty is achieved about project value, cost, and entitlement, can the project obtain financing commitments from lenders and investors. (Chapters 3 and 4 discuss task management and funding in more depth.)

DEVELOPMENT

Although the development phase involves high project costs, the success of this phase depends largely on the quality of the work done in the predevelopment phase. Notes Richard Dishnica, a developer in the San Francisco Bay Area, "Things go wrong in the development phase because somebody didn't spend the money or didn't communicate key information early enough. Things going wrong early are cheaper than [things going wrong] later." Assuming that the developer has competently managed the predevelopment tasks, the risks in the development stage are mostly controllable through competent management and funding of the construction process.

The following are examples of issues in the development stage:

- *Unexpected site conditions:* Conditions such as poor soils, hazardous waste, or archeological artifacts are discovered after the start of construction, because of inadequate site analysis. These conditions can cause expensive delays for remediation or archeological research, and may require redesign of the project, resulting in higher-than-expected costs and a threat to project viability.

- *Unexpected increases in material costs:* Depending on market conditions for materials, the timing of orders for construction materials such as steel or concrete may make a significant difference in costs. Monitoring material costs to capture the best pricing enables an optimal ordering strategy. If costs are escalating rapidly, early ordering may be advantageous; in a declining market, waiting may be the optimal strategy. Of course, the ordering of materials also must take into account the degree of certainty that the project will not change or be cancelled.

- *Unwieldy and costly design:* Design affects costs. As an example, if a high-rise residential condominium project has many unit floor plans, construction costs may be higher than expected and delivery of the units for sale will be delayed because of longer construction time. This kind of problem could be avoided if the contractor, architect, and marketing consultants work closely during predevelopment to streamline the design with fewer floor plans, thus streamlining the construction process and lowering costs.

- *Change in market conditions:* Markets are dynamic. If the market for buyers or tenants drops dramatically or capital markets deteriorate, the project can fail. Changes in the market are hard to anticipate, but taking another look at market conditions before the start of construction and making contingency plans to respond to possible changes in market conditions can help a developer mitigate the risk of a deteriorating market.

- *Changes in the local political dynamics:* For example, a supportive zoning board member quits a less supportive one joins the board, or a neighborhood group becomes vocal in its disapproval of the project.

To avoid these types of problems, a developer must engage the services of competent professionals, including architects, contractors, engineers, attorneys, marketing experts, property managers, and financial experts. Creating and managing a team with a sense of common purpose is critical to success. The developer serves the role of motivator, team leader, and trusted expert, and elicits the best from each member of the team. Engaging the members of this team early is important and is worth the cost. (The selection of team members is discussed in more detail in chapter 4.)

CLOSE-OUT AND OPERATION

How the marketing, sale, or lease-up of a project occurs depends very much on its sector type, its physical configuration, its size, and its capital funding requirements. Some projects must be presold or preleased for capital sources to fund it and construction to start; others simply can be built "on spec" (speculation) and marketed to customers as a completed project. Some projects can be phased, with capital invested only for each phase; others must be entirely built before lease-up or sale can occur, resulting in a much larger carrying cost for the capital invested through project completion.

Close-out strategies focus on minimizing the time and the capital carrying costs from project completion to lease-up or sale, either through preleasing or presales or through aggressive marketing campaigns that begin as soon as possible. The following examples give a sense of how customer profiles, project characteristics, and capital funding requirements create different close-out conditions with different implications for marketing to minimize capital costs:

■ A project of single-family, for-sale homes is typically phased at the rate at which sales occur. The developer first builds model homes (if the project is large enough to absorb the costs) and then builds units to be delivered after buyers contract to purchase. By phasing the construction and delivery at the rate at which contracts for sale are executed, the developer minimizes the cost of capital and reduces the risk of having to pay capital carrying costs on unsold units in inventory.

■ For-sale, high-density housing (condominiums) must be delivered as completed buildings before sales can close. For projects selling to buyers who must obtain Federal Housing Administration–qualified mortgages, the project must meet a minimum percentage level of presales (50 percent in 2010) before any such mortgages will be funded. Both these conditions mean that the developer has high capital carrying costs for all the units in a building. Mitigating these costs requires conducting an aggressive marketing program, to minimize delays in closing units after buildings are completed.

■ Apartments for lease are typically marketed shortly before the entire building is completed, with move-in at building completion, shortly after tenants sign leases. As with a high-density condominium project, the developer pays capital carrying costs for completing the entire project before lease-up starts—again requiring an aggressive marketing program so as to minimize delay between project completion and lease-up.

■ Retail projects typically must have leasing commitments for the large or "anchor" tenant spaces before capital sources fund the project and construction starts. This approach reflects the nature of the retail market, where the ability to lease the smaller, "in-line" shop spaces depends on the flow of customers that the major tenants attract to the center. If the large tenants are "credit tenants"—recognized by capital sources as low-risk sources of income for the project—the developer's cost of capital will be lower. Depending on its configuration, a retail project may be amenable to phasing as a way of reducing capital carrying requirements. For instance, developers frequently delay the construction of separate building pads in a retail center until they have tenants with executed leases. As these examples illustrate, the close-out strategy for a retail project depends on the amount of space preleased to major tenants, the project phasing, and the rate of lease-up of the in-line space.

■ In many markets, large office projects may require leasing commitments for all or a significant portion of their square footage before capital sources fund and construction starts. In strong markets, preleasing may not be a requirement but, as with condominium and apartment projects, the close-out strategy must minimize the time between project completion and lease-up.

■ Small retail and office projects, as well as the uncommitted small-space components of large projects, may obtain funding without preleasing commitments, but marketing to obtain quick lease-up should begin as soon as possible after the start of construction.

■ Industrial projects of up to moderate size usually get built with minimal preleasing because the relatively small unit size of the tenant spaces does not attract commitments until after the project is ready to occupy. Larger industrial projects usually require preleasing or presale commitments before capital sources fund the project and construction starts.

Four Dimensions of Successful Development

A project does not spring into being; it is the result of a process that engages all the stakeholders and frequently produces a project that differs from the original concept. James Graaskamp, a respected and insightful teacher and writer on real estate development, observes, "Real estate development is the common ground of developers, consumers, and communities: Equilibrium is reached through appreciation of joint objectives rather than confrontation and pursuit of total victory."

As a real estate development project proceeds, the developer is always pursuing this equilibrium of joint objectives. In pursuing this goal, the successful developer focuses on four fundamental dimensions throughout the development process. They can be summarized in the following four statements:

- Development is a values-driven business in which the developer creates a project that manifests core values.
- Development is an information-driven process in which the accumulation of information reduces uncertainty.
- Development is a capital-intensive enterprise with large up-front costs and risks, requiring continuous testing and evaluation of the financial viability of a project as information accumulates.
- Development is a relationship-based business in which integrity and trustworthy behavior is critical to success.

VALUES

Development is, above all, a values-driven process. It should begin and end with the question, "Is this a development that I will be proud of?" Patrick Kennedy, a mixed-use developer in Berkeley, California, offers this advice to new developers just starting out: "Start with what you admire." Every project reflects the values of its developer. Does the developer strive to create community ownership? Do the developer's projects embody the responsible long-term use of land? Does the developer treat people with respect?

Inevitably, good intentions bump up against reality. Financial exigencies may erode a developer's values-driven intent, for example. An experienced developer, though, is always aware of the relationship between values and product, and as a project evolves continually asks the question, "Is this project turning out to be what I intended when I started? Is this a project that I will be proud to be associated with?"

INFORMATION

Obtaining information and resolving uncertainty lies at the heart of achieving success in a real estate development project. But information usually has a cost—if not in money, at least in time. So, the developer is constantly asking the question, "Is the cost of obtaining more information to reduce risk worth the risk of incurring loss?"

Because every development project is its own enterprise, much of the information that the developer needs is unique to that project. Each project has its own site, market, design, costs, and development conditions. Each project requires time and money to obtain this information. Five areas of inquiry occupy the developer throughout the project:

■ *Site analysis:* What are the physical, environmental, and legal conditions of the site?
■ *Market support:* What are the prices, rate of absorption, and product mix that the market will support?
■ *Community support and development conditions:* What is the level of community support, how long will it take to get a development approved, and what requirements will the community impose as a condition of approval?
■ *Product and project design:* What product configuration, site design, and project design fit the site, respond to the market, are consistent with community requirements, and can be constructed cost-effectively?
■ *Construction costs:* How much will it cost to construct the project as designed, and what is the best way to shape the design so it can be constructed cost-effectively?

Chapters 3 and 4 discuss how to manage the tasks that inform these areas of inquiry.

FINANCIAL VIABILITY

Because most projects cannot be built without loans and investment capital from outside sources, developers must demonstrate to funding sources that a project has sufficient profitability to repay its lenders and investors. Few, if any, projects can make this demonstration until after they have proceeded a considerable way through the information gathering in the predevelopment process and resolved most of the uncertainties about viability, leading to answers to the following questions:

■ What is the profitability of the project if it is built, and what are the costs of getting the project ready to present to financing sources?
■ What are the potential sources of financing (including equity and debt, construction and permanent, private and public)?
■ What are the costs for obtaining capital, both debt and equity, and how are the costs and availability of capital likely to change over the time frame of development?

To answer these questions, developers prepare a financial pro forma that models a project's financial performance, including the costs of capital and the sources and application of funding to project phases over time. (Chapter 4 describes this application of capital sources to project phasing.)

Capital for a real estate project can come from three basic sources:

■ The developer's own capital and asset resources, which fund all or a portion of the predevelopment expenses, the "coinvestment" requirements, and any recourse requirements (the last two are described in chapter 2);
■ A lending source such as a bank or other source of a loan, which is secured by a lien on the property; and
■ An outside equity source, which invests in the project to achieve a return based on project performance.

Good developers learn how to assess the financial viability of a project right from the start as part of land acquisition and due diligence, and they continue to evaluate that viability as new information emerges and as decisions are made throughout the development process.

How the developer estimates and communicates findings regarding the viability of a real estate project determines whether it can attract the capital necessary to proceed.

RELATIONSHIPS

Development is, at its core, a relationship-based business. A developer works with financing sources, architects, contractors, consultants, community representatives, and customers, and succeeds only to the extent that these stakeholders trust the developer. So the developer's question in this dimension is, "Will I maintain and enhance relationships of trust with other stakeholders in my actions on this project?"

The needs of stakeholders in a real estate project are diverse and may conflict. Lenders and investors expect a return on capital and a return of capital, creating pressure to reduce costs and maximize income. The land owner expects performance on the purchase contract, creating pressure to take the risk of closing on the land before all the approvals are granted. Communities impose increasingly broad development conditions, creating pressure to increase costs. Project team members, such as architects and contractors, expect to contribute their expertise to achieve a common vision. A developer with the skills and vision to develop high-quality projects understands how to build relationships of trust with all these stakeholders, even though their needs may conflict.

None of the four dimensions—values, information, financial viability, and relationships—operates in isolation. Value-driven developers attract relationships with those of similar values. Information-driven decisions are reliable and, therefore, enhance the financial viability of the project. Financially viable projects succeed and increase the developer's reputation for trustworthiness. The synergy of all the dimensions produces success.

Skills of a Successful Developer

Success in real estate development relies on a broad range of skills, as illustrated by the following examples of what a developer must accomplish to succeed with a project:

- Understand the market and match a vision to the market possibilities.
- Negotiate effectively with landowners to obtain land.
- Persuade and negotiate with a community to own the developer's vision.
- Ensure that financing sources understand the project and provide both debt and equity at reasonable rates.
- Manage a broad range of disciplines, especially design and contracting, to work effectively together to achieve a common vision.

To be effective, a developer needs the following skills:

- *Visualization*: Experienced developers have the ability to walk onto a piece of land and see how the site can be developed. Although this skill does not replace or supersede those of the architect, it does enable the developer to identify opportunities and constraints on a "first cut" basis, equipping the developer to initiate the land acquisition and design processes effectively.

- *Negotiation:* Good developers are good negotiators, not in the hard-bargaining mode of getting the best deal, but as good problem solvers. They prepare for negotiation by knowing the project's economics and, consequently, knowing what the project can and cannot afford. They listen first and propose after. They anticipate issues and raise them in a timely way to give stakeholders who are affected the opportunity to engage issues rationally. They control emotions and try to ensure that outcomes are not clouded by anger or stress. They understand that solving problems is not about winning and losing, it is about creating outcomes that are better than lack of agreement.
- *Trust building:* Trust sounds like a personal characteristic, but it is actually a set of personal behaviors. Research shows that these three behaviors, consistently practiced, are the essence of trustworthy behavior:
  - First, do what you say you are going to do. By implication, then, never make a commitment that you are not sure you will keep.
  - Second, explain. A developer who explains motives illuminates the underlying thought process and creates understanding among a project's many stakeholders.
  - Third, be information-driven. This means responding to reality as described by data, not preconceived notion. It means, if the information changes, the developer's opinion or actions change.
- *Presentation (and communication and marketing, in general):* Explaining a project to a project team, community members, financing sources, local officials, and others requires that developers know how to make effective presentations. Even though members of the project team may take the lead on presenting or explaining some parts of a project, a developer's ability to explain and present is, almost always, critical to the presentation's success.
- *Technology application:* Since at least the late 1990s, being computer- and Internet-savvy has been a basic skill of most businesses—and particularly the development business. In addition to having basic computer skills and being competent at using spreadsheet software, it is important for developers to understand the potential for new applications of technology to critical tasks: for gathering information, for communicating with large groups, for communicating effectively among team members. Technology constantly evolves and presents opportunities to become more effective. One example is the now standard use of digital project simulations to create realistic renderings of a project from any angle. Another is project management and design software that speeds communication between design and construction team members on complex issues, leading to quick resolution of problems and more cost-effective routing of mechanical, electrical, and plumbing systems.
- *Finance:* Developers must understand financial analysis and projections as well as capital markets and sources. They must be able to explain a project's basic economics, including costs, income potential, value, and management approach from a financial perspective. Increasingly, developers must also understand the tools and process for obtaining public financing. They must have the skill to work with financial sources in a way that builds trust and responds to their financial interests and fiduciary parameters.
- *Legal:* A real estate development project is as much a fabric of legal contracts and governmental regulation as it is bricks and mortar, so understanding and being able to make decisions about basic contract and property law are critical skills for success as a developer.

■ *Political:* For most development projects, the right to build results from a vote by a local government body to approve the project. The ability to map a community's political power structure and understand community politics are critical skills for effective developers.

■ *Management:* Development is a team process, and effective developers are good managers of people. Development is also a production process; so effective developers also understand how to manage complex processes. And in the case of income-producing property, developers must know how to promote and operate the property effectively.

Development Sectors

Real estate development can be described as having eight primary sectors, each with its own customer and financial profiles:

■ *Land development:* This sector involves planning large land areas, frequently involving multiple uses. The land developer then sells portions of the development to those who specialize in building the designated use for the land.

■ *Single-family, detached residential:* The for-sale, single-family product type is most commonly associated with low-density suburban development, typically up to eight units to the acre. At the high-value, low-production end of the market are speculative homebuilders, who purchase lots and build a small number of high-value homes for sale. At the high-production end of the market are national homebuilders, who build a diversity of product types, from high-end luxury homes to lower-cost production homes in a variety of settings, including master-planned communities, resorts, and retirement communities.

■ *Attached and multifamily residential, for-sale:* This sector, which differs from the multifamily rental apartment sector, involves higher-density, for-sale homes, including townhomes with densities from 12 to 30 units to the acre and condominiums in multistory buildings with densities over 25 units to the acre, mid-rise buildings with up to 100 units per acre, and high-rise buildings with up to 200 units per acre or more.

■ *Multifamily apartments:* This sector involves moderate- and higher-density residential apartments available for rent, with densities ranging from 20 units per acre to over 200 units per acre.

■ *Retail:* The retail sector includes small, single-user buildings (such as fast-food restaurants), grocery-anchored neighborhood centers, community shopping centers, power centers, regional malls, and a variety of specialty types, including lifestyle centers, outlet centers, and town centers. Each project is targeted to a specific customer base, so tenant mix is critical.

■ *Office:* This sector involves both low-density suburban office buildings, with floor/area ratios (FAR, the ratio of building floor area to land area) of 0.25, and high-density urban high-rise office buildings with FARs as high as 30 or more.

■ *Industrial:* This sector includes suburban warehouse and distribution facilities, research and development facilities, and business parks—sometimes including in their mix some office or retail space.

■ *Lodging:* This sector, which is quite broad, generally includes two categories—limited-service hotels and full-service hotels. It tends to experience booms and busts, with periods of heavy production followed by periods of retrenchment.

Although these categories would seem to cover most development types, the variation in product types and the complexity of contemporary development has blurred distinctions among sectors. Development today is inherently more complex, more urban in character, and more mixed-use in type. Sectors are only a starting point for evaluating contemporary project characteristics because more and more development today contains multiple uses, especially because of the increasing emphasis on urban infill, place making, and the revitalization of "edge cities." Mixed-use development is now considered its own sector, even though it still faces significant financing, design, and operational challenges in many

FIGURE 1-6
Examples of Multifamily For-Sale Product Types

Product Type	Typical Density (Units/ Acre)	Building Cost/ Sq. Ft. ($)	Additional Floor Area[a] (%)	Parking		
				Configuration	Spaces/ Unit	Additional Cost/ Space ($)
Townhomes, on-grade (wood frame)	11–22	130	0	Surface or direct-access garages within building footprint with additional surface or carport parking	1.5–2.5	Garage: 0 Surface: 3,000
Townhomes, 3- to 4-story, on grade (wood frame)	25–40	140	0	Attached direct-access garages within building footprint with additional surface or carport parking	2–2.5	Garage: 0 Surface: 3,000
Multifamily, 2- to 3-story, on grade (wood frame)	18–25	130	10–20	Surface and detached garages or carports (wood or steel frame)	1–2.5	Garage: 12,500 Surface: 3,000
Flats, 2- to 4-story over podium (wood frame)	35–65	140	15–20	1-level concrete podium structure	1–2.5	Garage: 15,000
Flats, 3-and 4-story (wood frame) with separate parking structure	40–65	145	15–20	Separate above-grade parking structure	1–2.5	Garage: 25,000
Flats, 4-story (wood frame) with 2 levels of below-grade parking	50–90	145	15–20	2-level semi-subterranean garage	1–2.5	Garage: 30,000
Medium density mid-rise, over 4 stories	>60	160	15–20	Above- or below-grade structure	1–2.5	Garage: 30,000
High density mid-rise, over 6 stories	>75	170	15–20	Above- or below-grade structure	1–2.5	Garage: 30,000

a. Includes corridors, common areas, and activity rooms. Higher percentage associated with higher amenities.

locations. Market forces are driving much of this trend, but changing land use regulations are also encouraging it. Increasingly, cities are adopting zoning codes that go beyond the historical one-use zone to enable or even require mixed use as part of policies to encourage more sustainable development. (Chapters 8 and 9 discuss the challenges of mixed use in more detail, in the context of sustainable development and public/private partnerships.)

To give a specific example of the blurring of distinctions among sector categories, figure 1-6 describes eight product types in the residential for-sale sector. For the last six product types, the residential units are sometimes configured to be part of a project that also

---

FIGURE 1-7
Customer Characteristics by Sector Category

Category	Primary Customer	Customer Characteristics
Land Development	Residential or commercial developers for each project phase	Desire to purchase fully entitled, ready-to-go sites
Single-Family	Homebuyers	Purchase financed through home mortgages Desire customized units, minimized HOA costs
Multifamily For-Sale	Homebuyers	Purchase financed through home mortgages Desire customized units, minimized HOA costs
Multifamily Apartments	Tenants	Early move-in desirable Desire to minimize deposits, lessen lease period
Retail	Anchor, whose commitment to rent or own is usually necessary for project financing Smaller tenants who will commit after project starts construction	Anchors: seek limits on CAM charges and control of center layout Control of scope and cost of tenant improvements important
Office	Large tenants, whose commitment may be necessary for project financing Smaller tenants, who will commit after start of construction	Large tenants: usually desire customized space and signage Tenants: seek limits on CAM charges
Industrial	Large tenants who will contract for build-to-suit Smaller tenants who will commit after start of construction	Specialized utility and building configuration needs for some users
Lodging	Hotel franchise and operations companies, who will control project specifications. May have for-sale units as well as nightly occupancy units	Project owner frequently separate from brand franchisor/operator Branding and networking increasingly important for project success
Mixed-Use	Homebuyers, retail and office tenants, hotels	Customer-specific characteristics Frequent conflicts over parking and operations among customer groups

Notes: HOA = homeowners association. CAM = common area maintenance.

has retail or office, with the result that the residential products are actually mixed use. The retail sector has other examples of this blurring of sector distinctions. Retail product categories include entertainment retail, town center, lifestyle center, neighborhood retail, and community retail. All these product categories now are being developed with residential, office, or lodging integrated into the project. Similarly, contemporary high-rise or mid-rise office and business parks now typically have multiple uses.

The market and regulatory trends for mixed-use projects create an evolving challenge for developers, who in the past tended to specialize in single-use product types. Developers now must understand the customer issues as well as the return, absorption, and risk characteristics of multiple sectors.

CUSTOMER ISSUES

A developer operating in an unfamiliar sector must learn about the important issues of the customers of that sector. For example:

■ For-sale residential customers, including buyers of single-family, townhomes, or condominiums, finance their purchases with home mortgages and a downpayment. The availability of financing, then, is a major factor in close-out. Many residential developers partner with a mortgage source. Residential customers also put demands on the developer at move-in for completing "punch list" items—such as leaking faucets, missing light fixtures, or defective appliances. Residential developers, as a consequence, must staff a punch list team to follow up on customer issues immediately after move-in.

■ Retail tenants focus on parking, signs, tenant improvement allowances, location, and center operations before committing to lease in a retail project. They also tend to ask for some developer contribution toward tenant improvements; depending on market conditions and their desirability to the developer in creating synergy in the tenant mix, they may receive such concessions. Retailers also have strong preferences about the control of storefronts and fixtures and may require that their own contractors install tenant improvements.

■ Industrial customers, a diverse group of users, require building and site layout specifications (such as loading docks, floor strength, ceiling height, or clean rooms) that reflect the particular operational needs of their businesses.

■ Office tenants are concerned about floor-plate sizes and configuration, tenant improvement allowances, lease terms, and—increasingly—green building features and energy costs.

Figure 1-7 summarizes customer profiles for nine broad sector categories.

RETURN, ABSORPTION, AND RISK

Understanding the differences in return, absorption, and risk profiles among sectors is also important. Here are four examples:

■ A retail project usually needs preleasing commitments from major tenants before it can be built. Once these commitments are secured, investors are likely to feel more comfortable that the prospects for attracting other, smaller tenants to the project are good—thus reducing perceived risk. As risk is reduced, the cost of capital to finance the project can also be reduced.

■ A single-family home developer with a large enough project typically builds model homes as the means of marketing the residential units. The market risk in this type of

FIGURE 1-8
Return, Absorption, and Risk Characteristics of Real Estate Sectors

Sector Category	Target Return (%)	Absorption	Risk
Land Development	20–30	Sale of project phases	High risk of not receiving entitlement
Single Family	8–15	Pre-orders for units by phase	Possible change in market from start of construction to occupancy
Multifamily For-Sale	8–15	Sales and occupancy upon completion	Possible change in market from start of construction to occupancy
Multifamily Apartments	7–12	Lease and occupancy upon completion	Possible change in market from start of construction to occupancy
Retail	7–12	Preleasing by major tenants usually required for financing Major tenants needed to ensure smaller tenant interest	Possible market change for small shops, although anchor tenants are committed
Office	7–12	Depending on market, may require leasing precommitments	Possible change in market from start of construction to occupancy
Industrial	7–12	Leasing precommitments required only for larger projects	Possible change in market from start of construction to occupancy
Lodging	10–15	Occupancy upon completion	Possible change in market from start of construction to occupancy
Mixed-Use	10–20	Sales, leasing, and occupancy upon completion	Possible weak market for some sectors Operational risks from conflict of uses

Note: Return is annual unleveraged return on total project costs.

project is that the initial investment in model homes will not be returned if the market turns bad and orders for houses do not come in. Consequently, investors demand a high rate of return on the upfront investment in models but accept a lower rate of return on capital advanced for the actual construction of units for which orders have been taken. One industry that grew during the mid-2000s when prices were increasing was model-home financing. GMAC Mortgage and private individuals would provide such financing to defer the cost to the developer. The idea was that the capital provider would own the model home, enjoy the run-up in prices for a development, and earn a return of and a return on capital as the models were sold at the conclusion of the project. In a market with stable or declining prices, the capital carrying cost for model homes becomes a challenge to overall project viability.

■ A high-density condominium project also delivers units on the basis of customer orders. In contrast to a single-family home project, the developer must finish almost the entire building before units can be occupied. Depending on the size of the project, capital may need to be invested for 24 months or longer, creating a substantial risk that conditions may change by the time those units are ready for delivery. Consequently, investors demand a relatively high rate of return.

■ A land development project typically takes a very long time between the contract to purchase land and the sale of developable parcels or finished lots. The developer may spend substantial sums to entitle the property and then may install some basic infrastructure, such as arterial streets and water and sewer mains. The project is then sold in phases to other developers, who build components of the total project. The developer attempts to minimize the capital invested in land acquisition by contracting for a phased take-down of the land tied to the construction schedule or a close of purchase only upon entitlement. Although entitlement costs may be modest compared with overall project costs, these investments are likely to be tied up for quite a long time with a high risk of loss, depending on the nature of the community and its attitude toward growth. As a result, investors demand a very high rate of return on capital invested in a land development deal.

These different risk profiles and absorption characteristics mean that the capital necessary for producing a project is invested for different periods of time at different levels of risk. As a consequence, different real estate sectors tend to have different return-on-investment parameters. Figure 1-8 lists nine major real estate sectors and shows the range of annual rates of return and the absorption and risk characteristics for each.

800/900 North Glebe Road, Arlington, Virginia

DEVELOPER:
The JBG Companies
Chevy Chase, MD
www.jbg.com

ARCHITECT:
Cooper Carry
Alexandria, VA
www.coopercarry.com

CONTRACTOR:
Clark Construction
Nashville, TN
www.clarkconstruction.com

This project, on a 3.9-acre site, began construction in late 2008. It has four major components:

- Approximately 144,000-square-foot office building developed by JBG for the Virginia Tech Foundation to house administration and technology uses;
- A 316,000-square-foot, 10-story trophy office building, with a dramatic exterior design and state-of-the-art building systems, built to achieve LEED Gold certification;
- 89 affordable housing units; and
- 28 townhome sites to be developed by another developer.

   Other important project characteristics:

- Underground parking serving all four uses, with three floors and approximately 800 parking stalls to serve all four project components;
- Close proximity (less than 1/4 mile) to Metro subway system;
- Immediately accessible to I-66 and Route 50, major routes serving the region;
- Easy access to Reagan National and Dulles airports; and
- Immediate access to biking and running trails.

Rendering of the project, as viewed from the corner of Wilson Boulevard and North Glebe Road.

Site acquisition was completed in the spring of 2006; the entitlement process was completed in February 2008. When the property was acquired, JBG intended to develop the entire site for residential and mixed-use office. In 2007, JBG reached agreement with Virginia Tech foundation to develop and sell the northern portion of the site to the foundation as a build-to-suit research center with computational laboratories, offices, and conference space to accommodate executive programs, training programs, and workshops. During entitlement, JBG agreed with county officials to expand the development program to include parking and foundation for a separate affordable housing project, to include land owned by Arlington County adjacent to the original site. JBG also paid $6 million toward the cost of the affordable housing project.

This project highlights the importance of monitoring market conditions and gearing the development phase to changing market conditions. It also highlights the importance of engaging the development team early, both to ensure an effective entitlement process and to resolve many of the construction issues. JBG engaged the services of Cooper Carry and Clark Construction immediately upon completing the acquisition. This team met at least weekly throughout the entitlement process.

During the process, Arlington County and the community expressed concerns about several issues:

- Impacts of high-density development on adjacent residential uses;
- Preservation and enhancement of affordable housing supply displaced by the project;
- Preservation of the sign for a closed auto dealership that previously occupied the southeast corner;
- Height and massing of the structure and their effect on adjacent neighborhoods;
- The need to put all utilities serving the site underground;
- Site circulation and public access through the site; and
- Construction effects on the surrounding neighborhoods, especially crane swing and power interruptions from putting utilities underground.

To deal with entitlement concerns, the development team used several strategies and approaches:

- The land was tied up under an option, so that close of escrow would not occur until the start of construction.
- The team included experienced consultants, including civil engineers who were familiar with the public process in Arlington County.
- The team established a high level of community involvement, spending considerable time talking with the community early on.
- The team mapped the length of time for the project to get through entitlements and come on line, and monitored progress in meeting the planned schedule.
- The team cultivated strong working relationships with county staff and policy makers, and worked with key people in the jurisdiction.
- The team engaged in behind-the-scenes briefings for citizen groups and county officials on the project to obtain informal feedback before the official public hearings.
- The project achieved a density bonus as a result of building to LEED (Leadership in Energy and Environmental Design) standards.

■ Recognizing the challenges and scheduling issues associated with relocating utilities underground, the team engaged in extensive planning meetings with the Virginia Department of Transportation, the utility company, and neighbors affected by the relocation to schedule and obtain encroachment permits for utility work.

■ Early on, the team identified the issue of the effect of construction cranes on neighbors and worked to mitigate concerns before the start of construction.

■ To help the community understand and comment on the project, the team used extensive project modeling tools, including a complete physical model of the site and extensive computer simulations of the completed site with the ability to view the project from different perspectives.

The community was very concerned about the overall appearance of the project, so the team provided highly detailed skin, landscape, and hardscape plans—beyond those typically required of a project during entitlement. These details usually are presented later, during the building plan check; however, by addressing these issues upfront as part of entitlement, the team was able to work through neighbors' concerns so that they were addressed before the start of construction.

The county's concern about preserving the auto dealership sign was handled in a fairly innovative way. A design feature evoking the old sign was added to the front of the south

Project site plan, showing mix of uses.

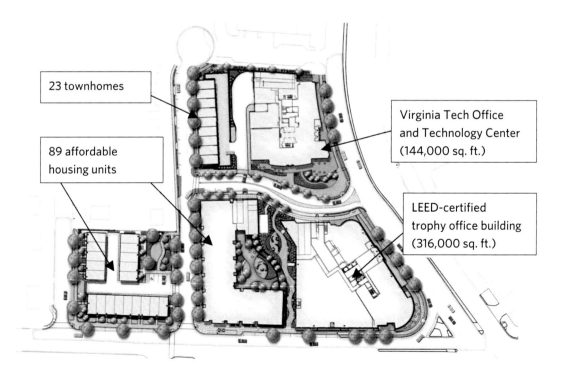

23 townhomes

89 affordable housing units

Virginia Tech Office and Technology Center (144,000 sq. ft.)

LEED-certified trophy office building (316,000 sq. ft.)

building, creating the added benefit of distinguishing the building from generic office buildings in the area. County concerns about public circulation through the site were addressed by connecting Glebe Road to Wakefield Road to the west with an east–west public street.

The northern portion of the site was presold to Virginia Tech as an office and technology center at a price reflecting the cost of development plus a developer's fee. This portion of the site faced a contractual delivery date of February 2011. Construction delays would incur penalties and loss of income.

One of the team's key decisions was to construct the foundations and garage underlying all four project components as a single piece and pro-rate the costs among the components. The timing of the construction of the office buildings and the two housing sites was separated from that of the foundation and parking garages. This decision had several benefits:

■ Constructing the foundation and garages as one piece produced a cost savings of about 12 percent compared with constructing the foundation and garages separately for each project component.

■ The project needed only one foundation permit and one set of encroachment permits from the county instead of four, resulting in considerable time and cost savings.

■ Installing the foundation and garage for all four components first minimized disruption to existing uses as later project components were constructed.

The team also gave considerable thought to the phasing of the excavation and garage construction. The timing required juggling three issues: overhead power line removal, installation of a transformer in the garage structure, and the effects of the overhead crane operation on adjacent neighborhoods. All these issues were resolved before construction started, resulting in no construction delays.

The planned start of construction for the office building on the south site was November 2008, but when that time came, the market had collapsed, the national financial crisis was at its height, and no office tenant was signed up for the building. JBG decided to delay the start of construction of the office building. JBG continued with construction of the foundation for all four components and continued as the fee developer for the Virginia Tech Center but deferred incurring the cost of the south office building.

In June 2010, JBG lost a competition for a major office user to locate on the south office site. In the meantime, the delivery of the Virginia Tech Center and the two housing sites remained on schedule. JBG will construct the office building on the south site when debt financing is obtained, which, depending on evolving market conditions, may or may not entail having a committed major tenant.

In a presentation on this project in June 2010, the development team reported that the project demonstrated the worth of the following principles:

■ The team process resulted in an early understanding of design concepts and priorities.

■ Early identification of what could be changed and what could not helped avoid wasted efforts.

■ Contractor feedback offered a great opportunity to refine the design in a way that affected pricing positively (glass size, garage configuration).

800/900 North Glebe Road, Arlington, Virginia

- The contractor worked on a negotiated bid situation instead of a competitive one, resulting in an open book on the general conditions, the fee, and the few contractor-provided components. (Note: The remainder of the construction components beyond those provided by the general contractor were subcontractor competitive bids.)
- The team had the opportunity to involve subcontractors in the resolution of several design issues.
- The entitlement and construction process involved weekly team meetings before construction started. The team identified project milestones and fostered active participation in the meetings.
- No design feature of the project was shown publicly before the team confirmed that it was something that the project could afford. There was an ethic of validating pricing against other projects and reaching out to other contractors for comparables.

In their presentation, team members articulated the principles they believe contributed to success:

- Work together to solve the problem instead of pointing fingers.
- Know the personalities involved and how they respond.
- Understand goals and expectations (date for completion, budget, etc.).
- When problems occur, come to the table with solutions.
- Be willing to ask a team member to change personnel if necessary.
- Create understanding among all team members on how the project is being funded.
- Get paid in a timely manner.
- Keep the momentum of the project rolling forward.
- Get everyone's goals aligned.

Rendering of public open space at 900 North Glebe Road.

CHAPTER 2

The Basics of Real Estate Finance

R eal estate development financing falls into two primary categories: debt and equity. Debt financing receives a return based on fees and an interest rate, either fixed or variable; equity financing receives a return based on project performance. Although equity investors are technically the owners of a development project, lenders are actually in a senior position in the financing "capital stack," because their interest in the project is senior to the interest of the equity investor and is secured by the underlying real estate. If the owner fails to pay debt service, the lender can foreclose on the property, resulting in the lender obtaining ownership of pledged real estate assets. The risk to the lender in any development deal is lower than the risk to the equity investor, so the lender's returns (the interest rate and fees that it charges for the mortgage) are lower as well. Thus, the cost of debt capital is generally much lower than the cost of equity capital because the lender is in a far more secure position than the equity investor. For this reason, developers tend to use as much debt as possible when financing a project.

To minimize their risk, lenders establish underwriting criteria that—varying with market conditions—limit the percentage of project cost or value that they will fund; these limits are expressed as loan-to-value (LTV) or loan-to-cost (LTC) criteria. They are established so that if the project stops performing well enough to pay its debt service, lenders can recover all or most of the debt principal through foreclosure. Foreclosure gives the lender sole ownership of the project, wiping out the value held by the equity investors.

Equity investors receive their return from the project revenues available after paying operational costs and debt service—in other words, from profits. These profits are usually distributed hierarchically in a "waterfall" to a series of equity investor "pools," each of which has a different rate of return and position in the capital stack. In addition, profit on a sale or refinancing of a project has its own formula for distribution.

A higher debt percentage means higher "leverage"—that is, a higher percentage of the project financed with debt. Higher leverage means lower financing costs on a greater percentage of project costs; thus, after paying debt service, profits produce higher returns to both the developer and the smaller amount of capital required from equity investors. As a consequence, developers and equity investors usually seek high leverage; however, doing so also raises the risk for the investors. Consequently, many equity investors, such as pension funds and high–net worth individuals, avoid high leverage and accept lower rates of return on equity for the reduced risk of losing a highly leveraged project to the lender if the project performs below expectations and cannot pay debt service.

The financial viability of a real estate project is based on how its value compares with its costs. Both of these factors are influenced by ever-changing conditions in the capital markets that affect several aspects of financing and viability: the amount of leverage available to a project; interest rates; the loan terms, such as guarantees and recourse provisions; capitalization rates; and the returns needed to attract capital to real estate over competing investment classes such as stocks and bonds.

A word about terminology: Like other areas of human endeavor, real estate financing has its own terminology or buzzwords. Shorthand terms of the industry include waterfall, "pari passu," capital stack, "recourse," "cap rate," "DCR," LTV, LTC, "mezzanine," and "promote," as well as many more. They can be bewildering and intimidating to a beginning developer. This book attempts to explain as many terms as possible and includes a glossary for reference. But in the real world different terms are frequently used for the same concept. So as you read this chapter, understand the concepts and pick up as much of the terminology as you can, but do not be intimidated when you encounter terminology in the real world that you do not understand. Ask what it means! The concepts are not that complicated, and you should never allow unfamiliar financial terminology to obscure your understanding of the concepts.

Basic Debt and Equity Structure

In a typical development project, debt will fund from 50 to 80 percent of project costs or value, with equity paying for the remainder. Some developers and investors prefer debt to remain below this range, while others look for higher levels—in some cases achieving 100 percent debt financing when conditions are right. Figure 2-1 shows the basic financing structure for a real estate development project or investment.

Debt for a development project occurs in two stages:

■ Construction loans—part of a category of loans called "acquisition, development, and construction" loans, or ADC—are short-term; they are usually adjustable rate loans tied to the prime rate and often require developer guarantees that are secured by recourse to the developer's assets. Although acquisition and development are two purposes for which these types of loans are made, their most frequent use is for construction. Most construction loans are provided by banks and are based on a percentage of project costs. Not all project costs are eligible for inclusion, however; usually, only on-site costs associated with the primary collateral for the loan are eligible; off-site costs, such as a traffic signal, generally are not.

■ A permanent loan repays the outstanding construction loan based on the lender's underwriting criteria for adequate debt coverage and/or the LTV percentage. Permanent loans are generally nonrecourse, so the lender looks only to the property value as security for the loan. These loans may have a fixed or adjustable rate, may be interest only, or may even involve negative amortization. They typically have a required payoff, usually within five to ten years, and a longer amortization, usually 30 years. This structure creates term risk—when the developer may not be able to arrange an appropriate new loan sufficient to repay the old loan and to provide a return of excess financing proceeds to equity investors.

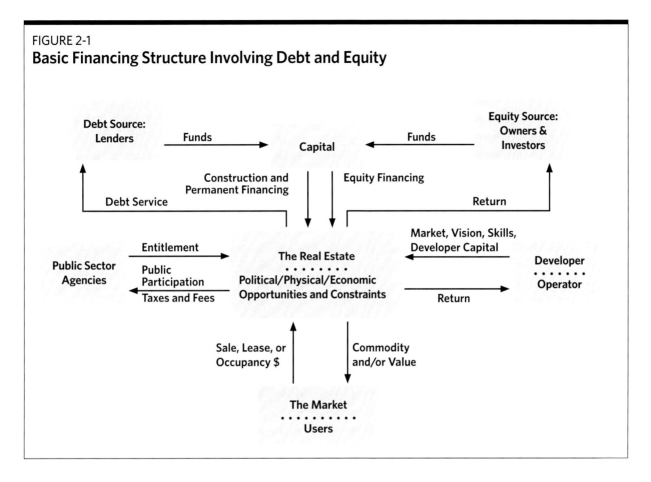

FIGURE 2-1

Basic Financing Structure Involving Debt and Equity

After a project is built, if it is a for-sale project, the debt and equity capital used for building is repaid from sales proceeds, with debt repaid first and equity investors receiving a distribution of the remaining sales proceeds. For an income-producing project, the permanent loan replaces the construction loan and is usually repaid in monthly installments. Equity investors receive their return from the revenues that are available after paying these installments and operating costs.

As a rule, the equity portion of funding for a development project pays its share of the project costs first, before the construction loan starts funding. This ensures, right from the start, that the lender is insulated from risk exposure by the equity investor. It also ensures at the outset that the lender does not fund the project to a higher share of project value than the lending criteria allow.

After the project is completed and either sales are completed or the permanent loan is in place, the project profit after debt service and operating expenses is distributed in a waterfall. The first pool pays the equity investors a high percentage of profit, first, to repay principal (return of equity) and, then, to pay a "preferred" annual return on equity—typically 9 to 12 percent, depending on market conditions. After the requirements of return of equity and preferred return have been met, subsequent distributions pay a "promotional" return to meet the investors' target return rates. After those targets are met, the percentage distribution between the developer and equity investors shifts to give a higher percentage distribution to the developer.

Usually, the developer is required to "co-invest" with the equity investors. This co-investment, which ranges from 5 to 15 percent of the equity amount, ensures that the interests of the developer and equity investors are aligned. The developer receives a return on this amount when the equity investors do, separately from the developer return that is paid in the waterfall distribution of profits. Developers may also be paid fees apart from returns; these fees become part of the overall development costs.

Some projects that have existing debt and equity are financed with an intermediate category of capital that adds to the capital stack; it is called, variously, "performing debt," "gap financing," "subordinated debt," "junior debt," or "mezzanine debt." This financing funds a gap that neither the primary debt nor equity covers. It typically finances a component of project costs associated with a change in future project value that results from a fundamental conversion of the project. For instance, mezzanine debt might finance a major renovation and retenanting of a shopping mall.

Mezzanine debt can be structured purely as "junior debt" that increases leverage and receives only an interest rate return to the lender. As leverage resulting from the mezzanine debt increases, it receives both an interest rate return and a return based on project performance. So mezzanine debt combines features of debt and equity. The mezzanine lender may also secure its loan by becoming a participant in the joint venture that owns and controls the project or require an "inter-creditor" agreement to make the loan that provides some access to the property value in the event of foreclosure. Some mezzanine loans are also secured by the project owner's assets.

Returns to mezzanine debt can vary widely depending on the degree of leverage and the degree of risk assumed by these investors. Because mezzanine debt's priority of payment is lower than that of the primary debt, mezzanine investors expect rates of return somewhere between those of debt and equity. Those rates may vary from 8 to 20 percent or greater, depending on the risk investors assume. Figure 2-2 shows the conceptual capital stack, including mezzanine debt.

The amount of debt that a project qualifies for varies with its financial viability, the financial strength of the developer, and conditions in the capital markets. The following sections discuss these three parameters of financing, starting with project valuation.

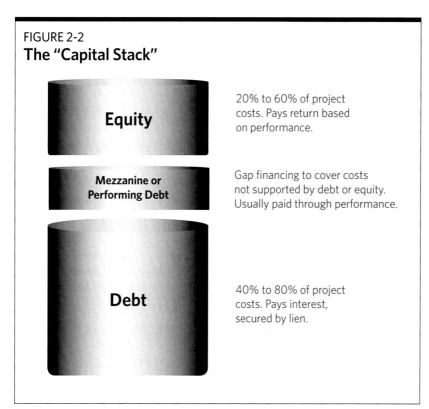

FIGURE 2-2
The "Capital Stack"

Equity
20% to 60% of project costs. Pays return based on performance.

Mezzanine or Performing Debt
Gap financing to cover costs not supported by debt or equity. Usually paid through performance.

Debt
40% to 80% of project costs. Pays interest, secured by lien.

Project Valuation

To evaluate whether a project is financially viable, a developer begins with an assessment of the project's projected net income and, thus, its ultimate value. Subsequently, the developer estimates the project's development costs and whether the difference between value and cost is sufficient to provide a return that is sufficient to pay lenders and investors and to provide the developer an adequate profit. (Chapter 3 explains in more detail how the financial viability analysis affects the price that a developer can afford to pay for land, a key decision by the developer in creating financial viability.)

Project value comes from one or both of two sources: sales and income. Here is how each type of project is valued:

■ A for-sale project, such as single-family homes, townhomes, or condominiums (residential or office), will generate value equal to its net sales value after marketing costs. The value of a for-sale project results from its total units multiplied by the net sale price per unit.

■ Retail, apartments, and most office and industrial projects primarily generate annual income in the form of rent from tenants. The valuation of an income-producing project depends on the application of a capitalization rate (discussed later in this chapter).

Sometimes a project has a mix of uses or income types. For instance, a mixed-use project with residential and retail generates value from both the sale of the residential units and the leasing of the retail space. Or sometimes income derives from the sale of development sites, called pads, to larger anchor tenants in a retail project or to other outlying users. These sales can be credited immediately against costs.

For an income-producing project, value is determined using estimates of net operating income and capitalization rates. Figure 2-3 shows the basic economics of an income-producing project's development and operation. After such a project is built, it generates a total income called "effective gross income." After operating expenses for maintenance, management, taxes, insurance, utilities, and replacement are deducted, the resulting net amount is called "net operating income" or NOI. NOI is a basic metric for evaluating the value and amount of debt that an income-producing project can support.

The permanent financing for a project depends on the NOI. Lenders look at three basic criteria to determine how large a loan a project can support:

■ *Debt Service Coverage Ratio (DSCR or, more simply, DCR):* The DCR is the ratio of stabilized NOI to debt service. Most lenders lend only when the DCR meets an underwriting criterion in the range of 1.10 to 1.40. Depending on general conditions in the capital markets, a strong project sponsored by a strong development entity may qualify for a DCR at the lower end of the range.

■ *Loan to Cost (LTC):* The LTC ratio measures the amount of the loan relative to the validated project costs; it is used primarily as a criterion for the construction loan. Lenders look closely at these costs and may not allow all costs to be counted when determining the ratio. Unless a development entity is very strong, the lender usually does not allow the loan to exceed 80 percent of costs; during the mid-2000s period of exuberance, however, LTC ratios got as high as 1.05.

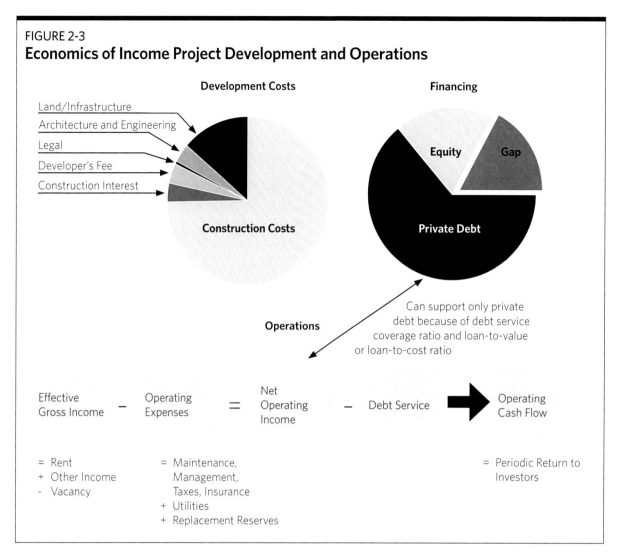

FIGURE 2-3
Economics of Income Project Development and Operations

Development Costs

- Land/Infrastructure
- Architecture and Engineering
- Legal
- Developer's Fee
- Construction Interest

Construction Costs

Financing

Equity   Gap

Private Debt

Can support only private debt because of debt service coverage ratio and loan-to-value or loan-to-cost ratio

Operations

Effective Gross Income − Operating Expenses = Net Operating Income − Debt Service ➡ Operating Cash Flow

= Rent
+ Other Income
− Vacancy

= Maintenance, Management, Taxes, Insurance
+ Utilities
+ Replacement Reserves

= Periodic Return to Investors

■ *Loan to Value (LTV):* The LTV is the ratio of the loan to the project value. The determination of value for an income-producing project is described later in this chapter. Again, unless the developer or the market is very strong, the lender is unlikely to allow the loan to exceed 80 percent of costs.

Since the Great Recession, a fourth criterion has emerged—the debt yield ratio. It measures the "coverage" of a loan by comparing the amount of the NOI with the size of the loan. This ratio is used primarily by money centers and investment banks that originate loans that are securitized as commercial mortgage–backed securities. Other commercial lenders that originate and hold loans usually do not use this ratio. The underwriting criterion for the debt yield ratio is usually 10 percent or greater, although for strong properties in core markets it can drop below 10 percent.

When underwriting a loan, lenders usually evaluate a project on all three of the basic ratios. Equity investors fund the remaining project costs; however, the combination of loans and equity may still leave a gap. To fund any gap, the developer must locate additional capital sources, from mezzanine financing or perhaps a public/private partnership. Repayment of these additional sources depends on project performance, which may exceed that projected by the lenders and the primary investors.

After paying debt service, the annual cash flow remaining is called "operating cash flow" (OCF) or "net cash flow"; this amount is available for distribution to investors and the developer. For a proposed project to be viable, the OCF must be sufficient to provide a return of equity and a return on equity that are sufficient to attract investors and to provide an adequate return to the developer.

The following describes how the NOI is used to determine project value. In this discussion the term "value" means the price at which the project could sell, which is estimated on the basis of a market parameter called a capitalization rate.

CAPITALIZATION RATES

The NOI used to determine value is that which can be projected to continue, that is, the "stabilized" NOI with a stable roster of tenants. This ongoing NOI is the starting point for the valuation of an income-producing project.

The conventionally accepted way of evaluating the value of an ongoing NOI is to apply a "capitalization rate" or cap rate. The cap rate is an indicator of current market conditions for the availability of capital and the perceived price appreciation of a project. The cap rate is generally defined as the NOI divided by the value of the property. Prevailing cap rates in the market at any given time are a composite of data on the ratio of NOI to sale price for actual property transactions.

Theoretically, a capitalization rate is equivalent to the "discount rate" that results from calculating the present value of an equal annual stream of cash flows over an infinite period. Arithmetically, the present value of an equal annual periodic cash flow at a specified discount rate over an infinite period is expressed as follows:

$$\text{Present Value} = \frac{\text{Annual Cash Flow}}{\text{Discount Rate}}$$

As an example, a cash flow of $1,000 per year discounted at a rate of 8 percent has a present value of $12,500 over an infinite period.

The cap rate is a term of art in the real estate business that is, in effect, an "all-in" reflection of project value, taking into account current market conditions for borrowing costs, requirements for return on equity, reliability of the income stream, and the project's potential for appreciation. Conceptually, the cap rate derives from the formula for calculating the present value of an infinite stream of equal annual cash flows; it differs technically from a discount rate in that it is a much broader measure of the investment attractiveness of the income stream of a project based on its NOI. In general, projects that have an increasing or low-risk NOI trade at low cap rates, while those with riskier, less reliable NOIs trade for high cap rates in comparable market conditions. In addition, investors realistically expect that a project's cash flow will change over time with project depreciation, a reality that is reflected in the capital market's practice of assessing project valuation using two cap rates: an "initial rate" and a "terminal rate" (described more fully later in this chapter).

Cap rates also vary with the investment climate and reflect market conditions for competing investments and liquidity of capital. In general, higher cap rates are associated with capital markets that have high costs of capital, low perceived appreciation potential, and low relative demand from investors for the asset class, thus resulting in lower property values. Low cap rates characterize the inverse circumstances: namely, low costs of capital, high perceived appreciation potential, and relatively high demands from investors for the asset class.

Another way to look at a cap rate is that it is the inverse of the price-to-earnings multiplier, or P/E, that is used for evaluating stocks; for instance, a cap rate of 5 percent is the inverse of a P/E of 20. Looking at the P/Es for stocks, you will see a range of, say, 8 (or a cap rate of 12.5 percent) for stocks that are priced with little expectation of growth in earnings to as high as 50 (or a cap rate of 2 percent) for stocks that are priced with significant expectation of growth in future earnings. Higher cap rates mean lower earnings multiples and lower property values, and lower cap rates mean higher earnings multiples and higher property values.

Applying this discussion of cap rates, the fundamental formula for valuing a rental project based on a stabilized NOI is expressed as follows:

$$\text{Project Value} = \frac{\text{Stabilized NOI}}{\text{Cap Rate}}$$

To get a sense of how the cap rate market indicator affects market value, figure 2-4 compares project values with the same NOI and different cap rates. As the cap rate increases by 40 percent from 5 to 7 percent, the project value declines to a level that is the inverse of the ratio of the cap rates, or 71.4 percent; in other words, whereas the ratio of 7 to 5 is 1.4, the ratio of 5 to 7 is 0.714.

Cap rates also reflect property type, geographic conditions, and capital market conditions, which means they vary with use, location, and time. To get a sense of the variation over time, consider the change in cap rates that occurred in the 1990s and early 2000s with the emergence of commercial real estate as an asset class. For most income-producing sectors in the 1990s (office, apartments, and industrial), cap rates ranged from 8 to 12 percent, depending on the region, the quality, and the property sector. In the mid-2000s, cap rates reflected the greater liquidity in capital markets and investors' expectations of increasing property values for real estate, as they dropped to the range of 6 to 8 percent for most categories of income properties, with rates for some sector types in strong markets falling to the range of 4 to 5 percent. The stock market mirrored the capital market conditions with

FIGURE 2-4
Project Values with Various Cap Rates

NOI ($)	Cap Rate (%)	Increase in Cap Rate (%)	Project Value ($)	Share of First Property Value (%)
2,000,000	5.0	—	40,000,000	—
2,000,000	6.0	20.0	33,333,333	83.3
2,000,000	6.5	30.0	30,769,231	76.9
2,000,000	7.0	40.0	28,571,429	71.4

Note: — = not applicable.

FIGURE 2-5
Cap Rates from a Sample of Retail Sales Transactions, 2004 to 2008

Center	Location	Date	Sq. Ft.	Sale Price ($ Millions)	Cap Rate (%)
Sierra Center	Milpitas, CA	January 2008	106,934	43.9	4.76
St. Helena Plaza	St. Helena, CA	September 2007	10,800	6.2	6.00
Tahoe Truckee Factory Stores	Truckee, CA	March 2007	38,049	12.3	5.90
Garin Ranch Shopping Center	Brentwood, CA	January 2007	55,797	22.1	7.25
Southwest Pavilion	Reno, NV	January 2004	80,137	11.5	8.30
Fremont Hub RECAP	Fremont, CA	2005	510,372	119.2	5.70
Beacon Retail	San Francisco, CA	2007	86,000	42.0	5.50
Aurora at Yerba Buena	San Francisco, CA	2006	157,636	66.0	4.10

Source: Grubb and Ellis, Walnut Creek, CA.

an increase in P/E ratios in stocks. The average P/E ratio for stocks in the S&P 500 index in 1995 was about 15. By 1999 it had increased to more than 34 and by March 2002 it had reached almost 47. Its long-term historic average is about 15.

More recently, in 2007, cap rates reached very low levels but then moved up considerably with the financial crisis that followed. In March 2007, the $39 billion leveraged buyout of Equity Office Properties by the Blackstone Group was evaluated at a cap rate of 4.33 percent. However, market conditions changed almost immediately thereafter. With the financial liquidity crisis that began to manifest itself in earnest in August 2007, cap rates edged up considerably, with a significant spread among properties depending on location and tenant quality, and considerable uncertainty in the market on valuations.

Figure 2-5 shows cap rates for several retail shopping center sales in northern California and Nevada in 2007. Locations closer to the San Francisco Bay Area had much lower cap rates than those farther out or in Nevada. In addition, cap rates for later sales are lower.

Figure 2-6 provides an example of differences in cap rates over time and by geographic area. It charts retail cap rates for the Bay Area (a relatively strong market) compared with those for the entire United States from 2001 through 2008. Note the dramatic decline in cap rates over this period. In the overall U.S. market, the decline from a 9.5 percent cap in 2002 to a 6.2 percent cap in 2008 resulted in an increase in project valuations of more than 53 percent. For the Bay Area, the decline was even more dramatic, from 9.5 percent in late 2001 to 5.8 percent in early 2007—almost a 64 percent increase in valuations. These data show that investor confidence in the Bay Area increased more over this time period than in the broader U.S. market.

Information on current market cap rates is available from numerous public sources such as market newsletters and private sources such as the Appraisal Institute, Real Estate Research Corporation (RERC), Real Capital Analytics, and the National Council of Real Estate Investment Fiduciaries (NCREIF). Current market data is also available from some of their Web sites:

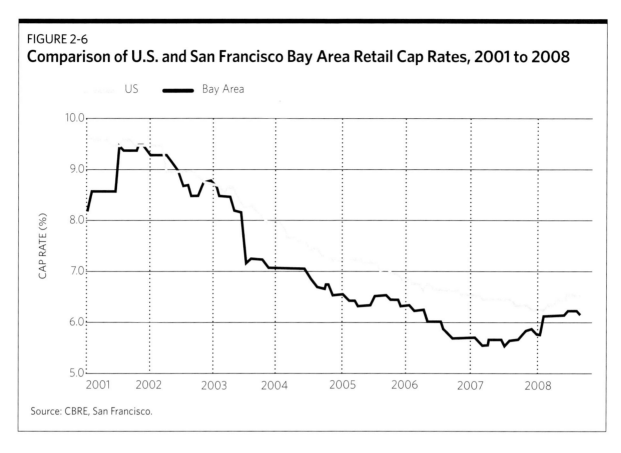

FIGURE 2-6
Comparison of U.S. and San Francisco Bay Area Retail Cap Rates, 2001 to 2008

US ▬▬ Bay Area

Source: CBRE, San Francisco.

■ RERC, http://www.rerc.com

■ Real Capital Analytics, http://global.rcanalytics.com

■ NCREIF, http://www.ncreif.org

Although cap rates are a fundamental metric of real estate transactions, they are also a snapshot because they measure valuation on the basis of one year's stabilized NOI. A more comprehensive measure of viability involves a multiyear projection of cash flow to determine a project's internal rate of return. The next section discusses this concept.

Measuring Project Return

The internal rate of return (IRR) measures the total profitability of a project over its entire holding period, taking into account the variation in periodic cash flow. The unleveraged IRR measures the return on total project costs. The leveraged IRR measures the return on equity investment and developer capital using debt, which will increase the projected IRR.

INTERNAL RATES OF RETURN

The IRR is the discount rate which, when applied to the income flow of the project, results in a present value equal to the amount of the investment. In other words, it is the discount rate (d) solved for in the following equation, where the time periods run from period 1 through *i* and cash flow (CF) is measured broadly to include both OCF and non–OCF, such as refinancing or sale proceeds:

$$\text{Amount of Investment} = \frac{CF_1}{(1+d)} + \frac{CF_2}{(1+d)^2} + \frac{CF_3}{(1+d)^3} + \dots \frac{CF_i}{(1+d)^i}$$

Solving for the IRR is an iterative algorithm which calculates and recalculates present value by trying higher and lower values of *d* in smaller increments until the present value of the stream of OCF and proceeds from capital events (explained below) equals the amount of the investment.

Calculating an IRR is sometimes exotic, in that—because it uses a polynomial equation—there are cases of multiple solutions when future inflows of capital are mixed with outflows. In addition, an IRR calculation for large-scale projects is sometimes misleading when comparing the results with those for smaller projects. Finally, an IRR may be inapplicable to financing projects that accumulate cash for payout later. So it is important to recognize the limitations in comparing IRR calculations across different project types. Nonetheless, an IRR calculation is still the most relevant for comparing the returns of similar project types.

Calculating IRR with a modern financial calculator is relatively simple. With a spreadsheet program such as Excel or any of a variety of commercially available real estate analysis packages such as Argus it is simpler still. Figure 2-7 shows a simple calculation of an IRR that can be duplicated in a spreadsheet program.

In calculating the internal rate of return on a project, the developer makes assumptions about how long the project will be owned and whether it will be sold or refinanced. Sales and refinances, called "capital events," are similar to selling or to taking equity out of a house through a refinancing. As the NOI becomes established, or if it increases, the project can support more debt. Refinancing permits the owner to potentially pull cash out of the project if it has performed well. A capital event may also be the source for repayment of any mezzanine financing in the capital stack.

FIGURE 2-7
Simple Calculation of IRR

Initial Investment	Income for Each Period			
	1	2	3	4
($100)	$6	$7	$8	$110

Internal Rate of Return: 7.63%

Sale of the project is usually planned to occur at the end of a holding period. Because most outside equity investors do not want their investment tied up indefinitely, the developer plans a holding period by the end of which the investment is liquidated.

In projecting a future sale for a planned holding period, the assumed cap rate for that sale is usually higher than the current market rate. In general, financial viability is measured based on two cap rate assumptions: an initial (or going-in) cap rate and a terminal (or going-out) cap rate. The initial rate reflects the value of a project under current market conditions in its current physical condition with its current rent roll. A newly built project is assumed to be in excellent condition, and the stabilized NOI is valued at the initial cap rate. The terminal rate is usually projected as higher than the initial rate—not necessarily because the market is projected to deteriorate, but primarily because the project will have depreciated and may have some characteristics of obsolescence as a result of its age. Many information sources on cap rates provide market survey results for current initial and terminal rates.

LEVERAGE

To minimize the share of the project financed with equity investment, a developer normally attempts to get as large a loan as the project will support. This strategy, called "leveraging," involves minimizing the at-risk equity investment requirement so that profits provide return to a smaller investment. Higher leveraging results in a higher return on equity because a greater percentage of the project financed with debt means more of the capital stack carries a lower interest rate and a longer repayment period, leaving more cash flow available for equity investors. As mentioned earlier, some equity investors that are particularly risk-averse, such as pension funds, often avoid high leverage for two reasons: to minimize the potential for loss of the project to foreclosure and to minimize the risk of having to put cash into the project to service a loan if the income should drop and become insufficient to service the debt.

Figure 2-8 shows an example of how leverage affects returns on equity. The project costs $10 million to construct and generates a project value at the end of two years of $12 million, for a 20 percent cash-on-cash return. With the "profit" of $2 million at the end of two years, the unleveraged annual rate of return on the project is 9.5 percent. The advantage of leverage becomes clear when comparing 80 percent leverage to 60 percent. For the 80 percent leverage, the return on equity is 31.1 percent. For the 60 percent leverage, the return on equity is 18.1 percent.

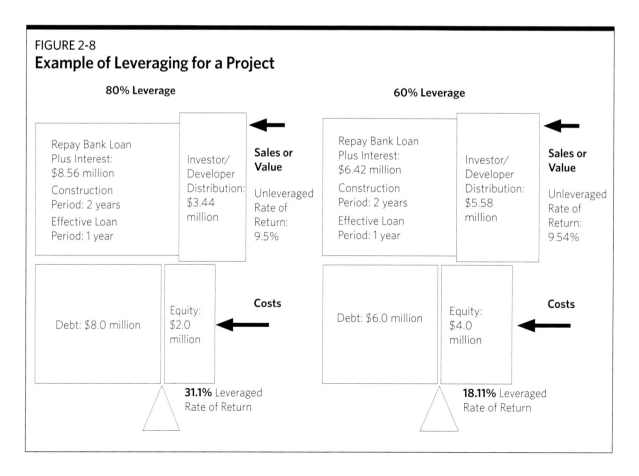

FIGURE 2-8
Example of Leveraging for a Project

Funding a Project

A developer needs to focus particularly on three areas of project funding: funding predevelopment costs, terms for debt, and terms for equity.

FUNDING PREDEVELOPMENT COSTS

As discussed in chapter 1, predevelopment costs are costs incurred for the project before construction starts. These costs are the most at-risk expenditures that a developer or investor makes on a project because they are incurred before the project is deemed to be viable, before approvals are obtained from the city or county, and before funding for construction has been secured. They include architect fees, consultant fees, entitlement processing (design, special studies, community outreach, etc.), nonrefundable land deposits, developer staff time, and preconstruction management. Even for a moderate-sized project in today's regulatory environment, these costs can easily reach $500,000 to $1 million. Larger projects easily can incur many millions in cost for predevelopment and can take years to entitle. (Two recent projects in California took 20 years and over $20 million.)

Outside capital to fund these costs is expensive and difficult to obtain until the developer achieves two viability objectives:

■ It becomes clear that the project has a high likelihood of approval from the land use authority.
■ The project's economic viability is established through verified market and cost analysis.

Until these two objectives are achieved, outside investors require a high rate of return (25 percent or more), depending on the track record of the developer and the nature of the project.

Obtaining capital for the acquisition of development property is another challenge in predevelopment funding. Equity investors usually need to see that the two viability objectives have been achieved before they will fund payments for site acquisition. Lenders for development property base loans on the "as is" condition of the property, which may not reflect its acquisition price or development value. In this circumstance, the developer must be able to pledge additional assets to cover any LTV requirements. The developer also must show a source of income to support interest payments before development starts; most banks require the developer to fund an "interest reserve" upfront on loans for development property. These loans are relatively short term (two to four years) and provide for repayment at the funding of the construction loan for project development. In rare instances, lenders may subordinate a loan on development property to the construction loan and wait for payment from sale proceeds or permanent financing of the completed project.

DEBT FUNDING

The only thing a developer needs in order to borrow money is the ability to pay it back; to put it another way, lenders are not in the business of making loans that are not secured by both verified cash flow and assets. Unlike investors, lenders are not looking for an upside; they just want to make sure that the project will pay principal and interest on time and that it has sufficient value to cover the loan balance from the proceeds if they need to foreclose.

As previously described, an acquisition, development, and construction loan almost always requires performance guarantees and recourse provisions. "Non-recourse" loans made a brief appearance in the early 2000s and came with much lower LTC ratios, but since the onset of the Great Recession, recourse provisions are back, probably to stay. These guarantees require that the developer provide a completion guarantee on items such as project construction, budget performance, and lease-up. To secure these guarantees, the lender has recourse to the developer's assets, usually secured by a lien on the assets as security for the pledge. Assets of the developer that are not included as security for the guarantee are identified in a "carve-out agreement."

The developer seeks the permanent loan commitment as soon as practicable, usually after there is a demonstrated cash flow. Permanent lenders on most income-producing projects usually require a significant portion of the project to be leased as a condition of funding. This gives "credit tenants"—those that are strong financially and on which the lender can base the creditworthiness of the project—significant leverage in negotiating rents, special requests, and concessions on deal terms such as tenant improvement allowances. Permanent lenders may also require the loan to meet underwriting criteria that allow them to sell the loan to a commercial mortgage–backed security pool, a process that is available with larger, more creditworthy projects (and described in chapter 5).

As a risk mitigation strategy, developers may purchase "forward commitments" for a permanent loan, including commitments on funding amount and rate. When markets are liquid and loan sources plentiful, shopping for a loan is common, but in tighter markets lending is less a commodity service and more relationship based. In such markets, lenders limit their business to developers who have a strong performance record and developers seek permanent funding through lenders with whom they have a relationship.

Construction lenders require several conditions to ensure that a project's value is sufficient to secure the loan. Investors must put their money into the project first. Lenders may also require preleasing commitments to ensure that the conditions necessary for a permanent loan are met. As "draws" are made by the developer to pay contractors, the lender ensures that the value of the project always exceeds the loan value outstanding. The lender also monitors mechanic's liens (liens by contractors, subcontractors, and consultants who have not been paid) to ensure that they are all released (or paid and cleared).

The best way to ensure a smooth relationship with a construction lender is through competent construction management. This entails a lot of documentation of what is completed and management of relationships between contractors and subcontractors to ensure smooth draws and timely funding. To ensure timely decisions, a streamlined dispute resolution process is also usually a loan condition.

Lenders secure their loans with a first deed of trust (a lien) on the project's value, giving them the right to foreclose on the project if loan payments are not made. Sometimes a lender syndicates a loan and segments loan components into different levels, or tranches, based on their priority of payment in case of default. A two-tiered segmentation, for example, would have "A" and "B" notes; the A lender would have a first deed and the B lender would have a subordinate lien or second deed of trust. Additional segmentation beyond A and B tiers is also a possibility.

Part of the lender's security will be a Subordination, Non-Disturbance, and Attornment (SNDA) Agreement. This agreement gives the lender the right to foreclose if the developer defaults, while preserving the rights of the tenants to remain as long as they pay rent. Working out the provisions of a SNDA Agreement may involve reconciling standard provisions required by the lender with conditions required by the major tenants.

EQUITY FUNDING

Investment capital usually flows to a project under some form of joint venture or partnership agreement (a limited-liability corporation or LLC, or a limited partnership) that stipulates the use of the funds, the roles of the parties, the business plan, and the decision-making process. (These structures are described in chapter 7.) In general, the equity funding mechanism gives equity investors oversight of and transparency into the development transaction.

Equity investors operate on the same principle that governs all successful transactions in real estate. As Jerome Gates of Citibank observes, "Financings are about relationships. Recognize that 'who' you partner with is just as important as the property you buy. The trustworthiness and reliability of the developer is just as important as the merits of the particular project."

To align the interests of the developer with those of the investors, equity investors usually require a developer to co-invest on a project. A typical co-investment requirement is 10 percent of the total equity. In the high-liquidity capital markets during the mid-2000s, this requirement was waived for developers who had a strong record of performance, but that was highly unusual. A developer who puts more money into a project has more control over key project decisions and can negotiate lower borrowing rates.

Equity investment is repaid from OCF and capital events—in other words, after debt repayment. The order of equity investment repayment is, first, return of principal and then a tiered distribution of return on principal in the form of preferred return and then promotional return; the distribution is divided using some formula negotiated between the equity investor and the developer. The promotional return, or promote, is the accrued obligation for distribution from OCF after payment of return of principal and preferred return.

Preferred return is a rate applied to the principal equity balance outstanding that accrues as a first-priority obligation of the project after repayment of debt and investment (or equity) principal. Preferred return can vary in most markets from 8 to 12 percent, depending on prevailing interest rates and what is negotiated between the investor and developer. Developers always seek a low preferred return, because any delays in project opening compound a preferred return obligation on the equity balance outstanding and consume profits that would otherwise be available for distribution between the developer and investor.

Promotional return distribution formulae vary widely and depend on the relationship between the investor and developer. After repayment of principal and preferred return targets have been met, the next pool of the waterfall distributes a majority of the promote to the equity investors until the return targets of 15 to 25 percent are met. This distribution to equity is usually "pari passu" (of equal steps); that is, proportional to the capital actually invested. After the equity investor's return targets are met, the subsequent distribution pools provide the developer a much larger share.

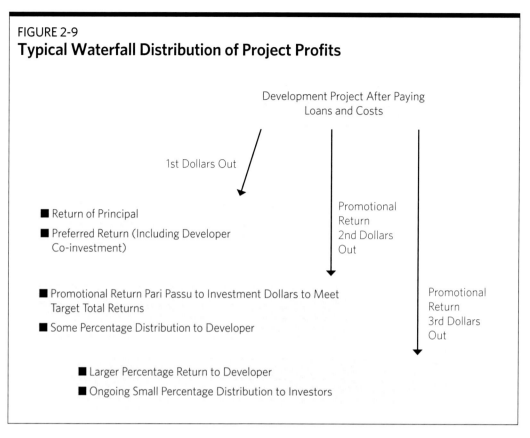

FIGURE 2-9
Typical Waterfall Distribution of Project Profits

Development Project After Paying Loans and Costs

1st Dollars Out

- Return of Principal
- Preferred Return (Including Developer Co-investment)

- Promotional Return Pari Passu to Investment Dollars to Meet Target Total Returns
- Some Percentage Distribution to Developer

  - Larger Percentage Return to Developer
  - Ongoing Small Percentage Distribution to Investors

Promotional Return 2nd Dollars Out

Promotional Return 3rd Dollars Out

Capital events (refinancings or sales) may have different distribution formulae that allow the developer a higher percentage distribution. The objective of these formulae is to encourage the developer to position a project to capitalize on these opportunities.

Figure 2-9 generically diagrams the waterfall distribution of profits for a real estate project in which each pool has a different distribution formula. The higher pools distribute more profits to equity investors; the distribution to the developer increases in the lower pools.

Although figure 2-9 shows a generic waterfall distribution, it assumes a payout within each pool proportional to investment (pari passu). Sometimes the funding for a project puts some investors in a subordinate payout position to others. For instance, a land owner or lender could seek a higher return based on project performance and attribute an at-risk

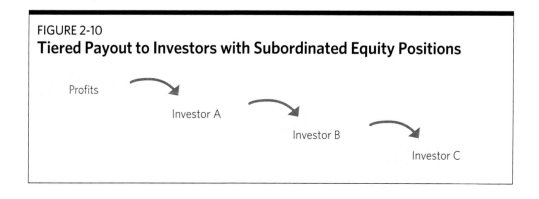

FIGURE 2-10
Tiered Payout to Investors with Subordinated Equity Positions

Profits

Investor A

Investor B

Investor C

principal amount to a subordinated equity position. These subordinated positions result in a tiered payout to investors that is based on passing profitability hurdles. Figure 2-10 diagrams a payout regime in which investor A earns a specified return (a preferred rate) and additional return is shared with investor B. When investor B has earned a stated minimum, investor C, sometimes referred to as the residual tranche, earns the remaining amount. The details of each project's waterfall are specific to the group of investors and the circumstances associated with the project funding and costs.

The Typical Deal

To summarize, the capitalization of a typical development project has the following basic structure:

- Debt constitutes 50 to 80 percent of the financing, depending on developer guarantees and recourse provisions. Recourse loans, which are the norm in most capital market conditions, result in higher leverage—that is, a higher percentage of cost financed with debt.
- Equity investment constitutes 20 to 50 percent of the financing, with a co-investment required from the developer, or operating partner, of 10 percent of the equity requirement.
- Distributions provide first, a return of equity investment, and second, a preferred return to equity investors. Thereafter, a waterfall distributes the promotional return to investors on the basis of a formula that gives the developer an increasing share as profits increase. When a capital event occurs, profits are distributed to reward success by the development entity and the investor group after the IRR hurdle (that is, the targeted internal rate of return) is met.

Capital is usually invested in a project through a joint venture entity, which provides for joint control by the investors and developer on major decisions. Negotiating the agreement to establish this entity is time-consuming; one practitioner noted, "You spend 95 percent of your time negotiating 5 percent of the issues that never occur." The goal is to make sure that all the parties are like-minded and that all interests are aligned. The agreement stipulates the waterfall provisions and compensation provisions for the developer. It provides for a holding period, usually three to seven years, so that the investors have a defined period of time for which their funds will be in the project. (Chapter 7 describes the numerous variations of joint venture agreements in more depth.)

Example: Financial Structuring for a Hypothetical Project

This example shows how a typical income project (in this case, a retail project) would be analyzed and financed. We follow this project through the steps to evaluate its financial viability and show a profit distribution scenario based on a possible financing structure.

Because retail is so tenant dependent, the process of conceptualizing a project is frequently an iterative communication loop that connects a market (the extent and nature of demand for particular goods and services, as well as for particular shopping center environments and experiences), a location, and retailer preferences. Ultimately, the developer's talent and skill in conceptualizing at this early stage determines whether a project is possible.

Because merchandising mix is so critical to the success of a retail project, responding to the market means envisioning the tenant mix. Who are the major tenants? What is the product mix of the smaller tenants? What is the customer profile? To answer these questions, the developer needs good communication with retailers and understanding of their preferences for customer profile, location, and co-tenancy. The developer needs firsthand familiarity with the local market, its customer characteristics, competitors, and prices. All this knowledge goes into determining the merchandising mix of the project, which then leads to a determination of its location and scope, square feet of leasable space, amount of parking, and configuration on the site. The process of envisioning draws on the talents of brokers and market experts as well as architects and site planners, though it is also important to minimize the cost of outside services at early stages, as discussed in the section on predevelopment costs.

After determining the scope, the developer looks at total rental income for each category of space. Larger spaces with anchor or major tenants usually have lower rents per square foot or are pad sales. Income comes in the form of minimum or base rents, percentage rents, and recoverable operating expenses; it is expressed initially in the form of the first year of stabilized income—that is, the first year of full occupancy by long-term tenants. Figure 2-11 shows a typical income statement format for a hypothetical retail project of 60,000 square feet.

For financial viability purposes, the assumptions must avoid using speculative income or income based on favorable conditions that may or may not occur. Such income may provide "upside opportunity" to investors and to the developer but should not be considered as part of the initial determination of viability. They may be the basis of "gap financing" or mezzanine financing in the capital stack. In other words, upside revenues, such as percentage rents, are listed as a line item but not included in the projection for the

FIGURE 2-11
Hypothetical Project: Retail Revenue Estimate, Stabilized Year 3

Revenue	Sq. Ft.	Rental Rate ($/Sq. Ft. or % Participation)	Annual Revenue ($)
Major A	22,000	$24	528,000
Major B	18,000	$24	432,000
In-Line Shops	20,000	$33	660,000
Total Base Rental Revenues	60,000	$27	$1,620,000
Participation Rents	60,000	5% over $300/sq. ft.	0
Common Area Maintenance (CAM)	60,000	$9	540,000
Gross Scheduled Annual Income			**$2,160,000**
Less Vacancy/Collection Loss (7.0% of line shops' rent and CAM)			(50,400)
Effective Gross Income			**$2,109,600**

purpose of determining the primary debt and equity portions of the capital stack. Rents in this example are expressed in dollars per square foot per year. In many markets they are expressed in dollars per square foot per month.

Minimum rental revenues are shown after subtracting leasing commissions and occupancy costs; in general, they need to reflect the income available to the project owner to pay expenses that are the owner's responsibility. Unlike the prevalent practice in office development, the vast majority of retail projects quote rents as "triple net rents" (frequently shortened in pro formas to NNN), which do not include the three major occupancy costs:

■ Taxes,

■ Maintenance, and

■ Insurance.

This concept is frequently expressed as "gross rents" (which include property taxes, insurance, and maintenance) versus "net rents."

Many retail projects recover a portion of the project's operating expense by charging an additional rent as "recoverable operating expenses." In this hypothetical project, these charges are shown as a separate revenue category paid by tenants as additions to their base rents. These charges typically include property taxes, property and liability insurance premiums, and CAM charges. They could also include such items as utilities sold or furnished to tenants, and security. All these charges must be evaluated from the point of view of the market and tenant acceptability. Frequently, tenants do not all pay the same CAM charges; some larger and more desirable tenants receive discounts.

Most retail projects also charge an additional category of rent called "overage or percentage rent," where "percentage" means an additional rent over the base rent that is a percentage of retail sales over a certain level, expressed in dollars per square foot. In 2010, the average retail center had sales in the range of $300 to $400 per square foot. Usually, for sales over a specified level, the project owner charges an additional rent of 5 to 10 percent, with higher percentages for higher levels of sales. This percentage rent is beneficial to tenants because it gives the project owner an incentive to help them succeed. Because percentage rents depend on favorable conditions which may or may not occur, they are not included in the financial analysis for viability or capital funding, so this hypothetical project does not include percentage rents in the first year of stabilized income.

Also not included in the income estimate are individual deals with tenants for tenant improvements, or TIs. These are individual store improvements such as counters, racks, and carpeting, beyond the basic "shell" cost of a tenant space, which the developer funds as part of the project construction costs, usually at an amount of $10 to $15 per square foot as tenant improvement allowances. Restaurants usually have a much higher TI cost—as high as $75 per square foot for very desirable restaurants

TIs usually are the responsibility of individual tenants. Sometimes an individual tenant that is important to the tenant mix may negotiate for a higher developer contribution to TIs. Retailers with good credit ratings can also negotiate for more or ask the development entity to serve essentially as a financing source for TIs. Under these circumstances the developer installs the TIs and then amortizes some or all of the extra costs with a higher rent. This arrangement adds to the capital requirements of the developer, but the income associated with the extra rent should cover the cost of this additional financing.

This income source is not included in this hypothetical project because it is usually a self-funding component. TIs also are usually financed with a layer of financing that is separate from the basic project financing.

Included in the income estimate is a 7 percent "vacancy and collection allowance" for the in-line shops; that is, a reduction of 7 percent in estimated income for the portion of the project composed of the smaller tenants. Usually, no vacancy is assumed for the income associated with the major tenants because they are larger, more creditworthy, and more reliable in meeting their long-term lease obligations. This allowance is a judgment call based on market conditions and may be higher or lower, though 7 percent is somewhat of an industry standard.

Note that the estimate is for stabilized year 3; that means there are some higher vacancy levels in the first two years of the project's operation for which there will probably be negative cash flow that will need to be financed. Finally, note that the revenue estimate in year 3 does not include rent increases scheduled for later years. The complete cash flow pro forma for later years is discussed later. For now, we focus on the first stabilized income year as the basis for evaluating project value.

ESTIMATING COSTS

Two kinds of costs must be estimated: first, all the costs of building the project (land, construction costs, soft costs, etc.) and second, the annual operating expenses. Figure 2-12 shows an initial estimate of development costs for the hypothetical project for which income was estimated in figure 2-11. Figure 2-12 shows numerous categories of costs, with direct construction costs accounting for only 59 percent of the total development costs and the remainder accounted for by land, indirect costs, and financing costs.

The developer must make sure that all costs categories are addressed, including site development, parking, design, marketing, and construction financing. Beware of the all-in estimate. Because every source of information includes different categories in its estimates, the developer cannot assume that all the categories are addressed. In putting together the estimate, developers include the major players, such as the contractor and the architect. A considerable amount of research and knowledge goes into making these estimates, including knowledge of construction, financing, services, and governmental fees and exactions.

Note that the project costs show a "lease-up reserve" of $427,000, which is equal to the negative cash flow associated with the year after construction is complete, during which the project is leased up. The developer can finance this deficit from permanent project financing only to the extent that funders approve including this first-year deficit in project costs.

Developers must recognize that "you cannot cut the board longer," so in the early stages of project feasibility, they err on the side of higher costs rather than lower. This means including an adequate contingency in the budget at the early stages to protect the viability analysis from coming up short. Figure 2-12 shows contingency both in the "hard cost" (direct cost) category and in the "soft cost" (indirect cost) category. These line items are important to maintain in the budget because funding sources will monitor expenditures against the budget as the project proceeds. The contingency amount in the budget can be reduced as the project proceeds and more reliable estimates are obtained. As the project goes to financing, it is important to recognize that cost overruns in the budget will most likely be the developer's responsibility. Estimating costs too low can be very expensive.

FIGURE 2-12
Hypothetical Project: Development Cost Estimate

	Leasable Sq. Ft.	60,000		
	Land Area at $12/Sq. Ft.	240,000		

	Total Cost ($)	Cost/Sq. Ft. ($)	Share of Direct Cost (%)
Land Acquisition[a]	2,880,000	48.00	30.4
Subtotal	**$2,880,000**	**$48.00**	**30.4**
DIRECT COSTS			
Building Construction	5,400,000	90.00	56.9
Tenant Improvements	900,000	15.00	9.5
Land Development and Offsites	1,370,000	22.83	14.4
Overhead	500,000	8.33	5.3
Parking (240 Stalls @ $3,500)	840,000	14.00	8.9
Contingency on Construction	474,200	7.90	5.0
Subtotal	**$9,484,200**	**$158.07**	**100.0**
INDIRECT COSTS			
Design and Engineering	700,000	11.67	7.4
Development Fees and Exactions			
Impact Fees	256,852	4.28	2.7
Municipal Fees and Permits	190,587	3.18	2.0
Long-Range Planning Fees	20,000	0.33	0.2
School Fees	18,765	0.31	0.2
Water District Fees	93,241	1.55	1.0
Insurance	113,296	1.89	1.2
Marketing and Leasing	210,960	3.52	2.2
Contingency on Indirects	474,200	7.90	5.0
Subtotal	**$2,077,901**	**$34.63**	**21.9**
FINANCING COSTS			
Construction Interest/Other Financing	1,000,000	16.67	10.5
Legal and Financing Fees	300,000	5.00	3.2
Lease-Up Reserve	427,000	7.12	4.5
Subtotal	**$1,727,000**	**$28.78**	**18.2**
TOTAL DEVELOPMENT COSTS	**$16,169,101**	**$269.48**	**170.5**

a. Allocation based on leasable square feet.

Figure 2-13 shows estimates of annual operating expenses and net operating income for the hypothetical project. Operating expenses include all maintenance, management, taxes, and insurance—some of which are recoverable from tenants and some of which are not. Because of inevitable tenant turnover, the project also estimates re-leasing expenses, which are the cost of replacing tenants that leave with new tenants. The budget also estimates an annual set-aside replacement for periodic major maintenance (usually at $0.50 to $0.75 per square foot), such as rerooofing a building or resurfacing a parking lot, and ongoing additional marketing costs. Frequently, the CAM charges amortize some portion of major maintenance and marketing costs.

Subtracting the annual expenses in figure 2-13 from the effective gross income from figure 2-11 yields the NOI, the fundamental parameter of financial viability for a real estate project. This can be expressed generally as follows:

(Effective Gross Income) – (Operating Expenses) = Net Operating Income (NOI)

The NOI is distributed between repayment of debt and return to the equity investors and developer. The adequacy of NOI to meet these two demands is evaluated by comparing the project valuation at a cap rate with the costs of the project.

In the case of the hypothetical project, figure 2-13 shows an NOI of $1,434,600. Figure 2-14 shows the project value calculation, which is based on the assumption that market conditions are valuing similar projects at a cap rate of 6 percent. In other words, market conditions at this cap rate are such that if the project were built and leased as planned, then it could, theoretically, be sold at a price of about $23.9 million. Compared with the costs of development in figure 2-12, which are about $16,169,100, this project looks like it could produce a "profit" upon sale of about $7,740,900, as shown in figure 2-14. In other words, if this project were built at the assumed cost, leased at the assumed rates, and sold

---

FIGURE 2-13

Hypothetical Project: Calculation of Net Operating Income

	Sq. Ft.	Cost/Sq. Ft. ($)	Total Cost ($)
Effective Gross Income (from figure 2-11)			**$2,109,600**
Operating Expenses			
Nonrecoverable Expenses	60,000	0.75	45,000
Recoverable Expenses	60,000	9.00	540,000
Marketing Costs			30,000
Replacement Reserves		0.50	30,000
Re-leasing Costs (25% of in-line every five years)	1,000	30.00	30,000
Total Annual Expenses			**$675,000**
Net Operating Income			**$1,434,600**

FIGURE 2-14

Hypothetical Project: Surplus/Gap Analysis

		Cost/Sq. Ft. ($)
Supported Investment at Cap Rate of 6%	$23,910,000	398.50
(Less) Total Development Costs	($16,169,101)	(269.49)
Surplus (Gap)	**$7,740,899**	**129.01**
Surplus (Gap) Share of Development Costs (%)	**47.9%**	

at the cap rate in the current market, as shown in the figure, it would produce a return on costs of about 47.9 percent.

Figure 2-15 shows a funding program of debt and equity for the hypothetical project based on the development costs and NOI calculations in the previous figures. The loan is constrained to be the lesser of 1) debt supported by a DCR of 1.25, 2) an 80 percent LTC ratio, and 3) a 75 percent LTV ratio. Because the LTV and DCR ratios result in higher loan amounts than the LTC ratio, the loan is constrained to 80 percent of costs. The remaining project costs are funded with an equity investment and developer capital.

Note the debt repayment terms assumed in figure 2-15. The interest rate is 6.75 percent with a 30-year amortization of the loan. Even though it is typical for such a loan to have a ten-year repayment requirement, the amortization period and interest rate are much less

FIGURE 2-15

Hypothetical Project: Project Loan and Equity Funding

Market Interest Rate on Debt	6.75%				Loan Amount
Loan Amortization Period (Years)	30		Ratio Applied to		Loan Amount
Supported Debt Based on DCR of	1.25	$1,434,600	NOI from figure 2-13		$14,606,701
Supported Debt Based on LTC of	80%	$16,169,101	Project Costs from figure 2-12		$12,935,281
Supported Debt Based on LTV of	75%	$23,910,000	Supported Investment from figure 2-14		$17,932,500
Lesser of DCR or LTC or LTV = Supported Debt		-->			$12,935,281
Annual Debt Service on Supported Debt	$1,016,353				
Share of Costs Financed with Debt	80%				
Equity Investment and Developer Capital to Finance Remaining Costs	$3,233,820				

FIGURE 2-16
Hypothetical Project: Project Cash Flow and IRR

Year--->		Construction	1	2	3	
Income Growth Rate				See assumptions below		
Expense Growth Rate				See assumptions below		
Vacancy/Delinquency, Line Shops			75%	40%	7%	
Base Rents			$1,620,000	$1,620,000	$1,620,000	
Recoverable Expenses			$510,000	$510,000	$540,000	
Participation Rents			$0	$0	$0	
Total Gross Revenue			**$2,130,000**	**$2,130,000**	**$2,160,000**	
(Less) Vacancy, Line and Majors	(Major B opens in year 2)		($964,500)	($284,000)	($50,400)	
Effective Gross Revenue			**$1,165,500**	**$1,846,000**	**$2,109,600**	
(Less) Nonrecoverable Expenses			($36,000)	($36,000)	($45,000)	
(Less) Recoverable Expenses			($510,000)	($510,000)	($540,000)	
(Less) Major Maintenance Reserve			($30,000)	($30,000)	($30,000)	
(Less) Marketing Costs			$0	$0	($30,000)	
(Less) Re-leasing Costs			$0	$0	($30,000)	
Net Operating Income			**$589,500**	**$1,270,000**	**$1,434,600**	
(Less) Debt Service			($1,016,353)	($1,016,353)	($1,016,353)	
Operating Cash Flow			**($426,853)**	**$253,647**	**$418,247**	
Gross Sale/Refinance Proceeds						
(Less) Closing Costs at 2.5%						
(Less) Loan Balance						
Net Sale/Refinance Proceeds						
Return Calculations	Initial investment and rate of return					
Leveraged Cash Flow	($3,233,820)	$0	($426,853)	$253,647	$418,247	
IRR on Equity (Leveraged)	21.7%					
Unleveraged Cash Flow	($16,169,101)	$0	$589,500	$1,270,000	$1,434,600	
IRR on Project (unleveraged)	9.7%					

Note: Based on 60,000 square feet of leaseable area.

		Income and Expense Growth Assumptions				
		Base Rents Per Sq. Ft.		Recoverable Operating Expense		
		Leasable area	60,000			
		Year 1	stabilized year	Year 1	$8.50	
		Year 2	stabilized year	Year 2	$8.50	100%
		Year 3	stabilized year	Year 3	$9.00	106%
		Year 4	103%	After Year 3	103%	
		Year 5	103%			
		Year 6	103%	Notes: Marketing in first three years included in Development Costs. Re-leasing costs based on 25% turnover every five years. Sale at year 10 based on a cap rate 1% higher than current cap rate.		
		Year 7	103%			
		After 7	103%			

	4	5	6	7	8	9	10
	7%	7%	7%	7%	7%	7%	7%
	$1,668,600	$1,718,658	$1,770,218	$1,823,324	$1,878,024	$1,934,365	$1,992,396
	$556,200	$572,886	$590,073	$607,775	$626,008	$644,788	$664,132
	$0	$0	$0	$0	$0	$0	$0
	$2,224,800	$2,291,544	$2,360,290	$2,431,099	$2,504,032	$2,579,153	$2,656,528
	($51,912)	($53,469)	($55,073)	($56,726)	($58,427)	($60,180)	($61,986)
	$2,172,888	**$2,238,075**	**$2,305,217**	**$2,374,373**	**$2,445,605**	**$2,518,973**	**$2,594,542**
	($46,800)	($48,672)	($50,619)	($52,644)	($54,749)	($56,939)	($59,217)
	($556,200)	($572,886)	($590,073)	($607,775)	($626,008)	($644,788)	($664,132)
	($30,000)	($30,000)	($30,000)	($30,000)	($30,000)	($30,000)	($30,000)
	($30,000)	($30,000)	($30,000)	($30,000)	($30,000)	($30,000)	($30,000)
	($30,000)	($30,000)	($30,000)	($30,000)	($30,000)	($30,000)	($30,000)
	$1,479,888	**$1,526,517**	**$1,574,525**	**$1,623,955**	**$1,674,847**	**$1,727,245**	**$1,781,193**
	($1,016,353)	($1,016,353)	($1,016,353)	($1,344,645)	($1,344,645)	($1,344,645)	($1,344,645)
	$463,535	**$510,164**	**$558,173**	**$279,310**	**$330,202**	**$382,600**	**$436,548**
			(REFINANCE)				**(SALE)**
			$17,113,502				$25,445,616
			($427,838)				($636,140)
			($11,351,069)				($14,768,857)
			$5,334,595				$10,040,618
	$463,535	$510,164	$5,892,768	$279,310	$330,202	$382,600	$10,477,167
	$1,479,888	$1,526,517	$1,574,525	$1,623,955	$1,674,847	$1,727,245	$24,809,475

Nonrecoverable Operating Expense						
Year 1	$0.60					
Year 2	$0.60	100%				
Year 3	$0.75	125%				
After Year 3	104%					

costly than the return to equity requirement of 15 to 20 percent or greater, where the principal repayment terms require return of equity out of OCF as the first priority.

Applying this typical deal scenario to the hypothetical project, assuming a recourse loan, the funding program would look like that shown in figure 2-15, namely a loan of 80 percent of project costs ($12,935,281), with a 20 percent investment equity requirement ($3,233,820). The development entity would be investing 10 percent of the equity requirement, or $323,380.

EVALUATING RETURN

Now let us examine how total project return is evaluated. Figure 2-16 shows an IRR calculation for the hypothetical project and shows, based on the assumptions, a leveraged IRR of 21.7 percent. The leveraged IRR is the return on the equity investment ($3,233,820), which is shown in figure 2-15 as 20 percent of costs, where costs include the first-year deficit in OCF.

Figure 2-16 illuminates some additional concepts typical of an income-producing project. First, note that part of the leveraged return is based on a "refinancing" of the project at year 5. This capital event is expected to occur as a result of the NOI becoming established and being able to support more debt, thus allowing the owner to pull cash out of the project through refinancing. A second capital event occurs when the project is sold in year 10, or at the end of a planned holding period. Most equity investors want a project to have a planned holding period by which time their investment is liquidated. Note that construction is assumed to take one year and is included as a period in the calculation, recognizing that the investment needs to provide returns for this period as well as when the retail center is operating.

Also note that the assumed cap rate for which the sale occurs at the end of the holding period is 7 percent, a full percentage point higher than the current rate of 6 percent. The initial rate reflects the value of a project under current market conditions in its current physical condition. The hypothetical project is new and consequently in excellent condition. The terminal rate is projected as higher, not necessarily because the market is projected to change but primarily because the project will have depreciated and may have some characteristics of obsolescence as a result of its age.

The unleveraged IRR on the project is 9.7 percent. This is the return on the total project costs, treating NOI as OCF—in other words, as if the project were financed with all equity and no debt. The unleveraged return is based on NOI through year 9 and the capital event of a sale in year 10. Sales proceeds are net of commissions. The unleveraged IRR on projects is the rate of return that is usually quoted by market data services and is usually available from the same market data services that provide information on interest rates and cap rates.

In the example, the 9.7 percent unleveraged IRR and the 21.7 percent leveraged IRR on investment are probably sufficient to attract equity and developer capital in 2010–2011, depending on the credibility and reliability of the development entity. Although modest rent increases of 3 percent per year after year 3 are included in the projection, the upside potential of percentage rents is not projected in these cash flows. If the project succeeds and hits percentage rents, the returns could be higher.

Figure 2-17 shows a possible distribution scenario for this hypothetical project over a ten-year holding period. In this scenario, the distribution of the preferred return and the waterfall promote return to equity results in an IRR for the equity investors of 15.2 percent. The example shows a scenario (one of many possibilities) in which equity investment principal is returned first and the preferred return obligation accumulates through the fifth year, when a refinancing pays off both the principal and the preferred return obligation. A likely distribution scenario is that full return of principal for the equity investors would occur only on such a capital event. The promotional return is then distributed, 50 percent of the first $200,000 of leveraged cash flow and 30 percent of the remaining leveraged cash flow to the investors, with all remaining leveraged cash flow going to the developer. Remember that the developer is also an equity investor by virtue of the co-investment requirement, so the developer receives 10 percent of the return on equity in addition to the approximately $9,446,360 of developer return, for a total return of $10,402,490.

As an example of the difference between static and cash flow valuations, compare the total leveraged cash flow available for distribution with the surplus/gap analysis of figure 2-14. Note that total leveraged cash flow over the 10-year period, including capital events, is about $19 million, while the valuation surplus for the project in the first stabilized year of NOI was estimated at about $7.7 million. Remember that percentage rental income has not been included in the projections, so there could be additional upside to this deal. Remember also that the return shown for the developer does not include fees that are funded as part of project costs and that increase developer return. This comparison gives a sense of the difference between the static valuation metric of a cap rate versus the cash flow analysis from capitalizing growth in rental rates and capital events as part of the cash flow return.

FIGURE 2-17

Hypothetical Project: Project Return to Equity Investment and Developer

	Year-------->	Construction	1	2	
Total Cash Flow	($3,233,820)	$0	($426,853)	$253,647	
Return of Capital					
Annual Payment		$0	$0	$253,647	
Total Returned		$0	$0	$253,647	
Preferred Return	9.00%				
Preferred Return Obligation		$291,044	$608,282	$931,242	
Repayment of Preferred Return Obligation		$0	$0	$0	
Return to Equity from Promotional Return					
Promotional Return Available for Distribution					
50% of First $200,000 Per Year and 30% of Remainder		$0	$0	$0	
Total Payments to Equity Investors	($3,233,820)	$0	$0	$253,647	
Total IRR to Equity Investors	15.2%				
Distribution to Developer of Remaining Promote		$0	$0	$0	

Total payments to equity investors (includes return of capital)	$9,561,282
Total payments to developer (does not include return on co-investment, which is 10% of payments to equity investors)	$9,446,359
Total distribution of OCF	$19,007,640

Notes:
First-year negative cash flow is funded with equity.
Totals do not include equity investment or first-year negative cash flow.
Total return to developer: $10,402,487. (Includes payment to developer and return on developer co-investment.)

	3	4	5	6	7	8	9	10	TOTALS
	$418,247	$463,535	$510,164	$5,892,768	$279,310	$330,202	$382,600	$10,477,167	$19,007,640
	$418,247	$463,535	$510,164	$1,588,227					
	$671,894	$1,135,429	$1,645,593	$3,233,820	capital returned				$3,233,820
	$1,245,628	$1,546,589	$1,828,723	$1,993,308					
	$0	$0	$0	$1,993,308	preferred return paid				$1,993,308
				$2,311,233	$279,310	$330,202	$382,600	$10,477,167	$13,780,512
	$0	$0	$0	$733,370	$123,793	$139,061	$154,780	$3,183,150	$4,334,154
	$418,247	$463,535	$510,164	$4,314,905	$123,793	$139,061	$154,780	$3,183,150	$9,561,282
	$0	$0	$0	$1,577,863	$155,517	$191,142	$227,820	$7,294,017	$9,446,359

Land Valuation for Acquisition

A greeing to business terms for land acquisition is the first and, some would say, the most important decision a developer makes that affects project viability. If the project cannot support the price or timing of payment for land, the developer should not acquire the site and should look elsewhere for development opportunities.

How does a developer know whether the project can afford a particular piece of land? To answer this question, think about this principle: "Land's value comes from its use." Land valuation for a development project results from an economic determination of "residual land value," the price at which the difference between total project value (discussed in chapter 2) and total project costs (including land) provides a return on the project sufficient to attract investment and compensate the developer.

This chapter discusses three dimensions of effective land valuation for the acquisition process:

■ Determination of a valid hurdle rate for project viability;

■ Calculation of the supported investment and residual land value; and

■ A disciplined acquisition process of site selection, negotiation, and due diligence before finalizing a commitment to purchase a site.

Determining a Valid Hurdle Rate for Evaluating Project Viability

A project's "hurdle rate" is the minimum expected rate of return that a developer requires for a project to show that it will be economically viable. Economically viable means it produces sufficient profit to repay capital sources and provide adequate compensation to the developer for the time and skill invested. Equity investors and lenders also have hurdle rates for minimally acceptable return, but these rates are for components of the project, not the project as a whole. For the developer to evaluate overall project viability in the early stages of a project, it is important to use a hurdle rate that measures overall project viability, including debt and equity, and to contract for a land price that contributes to viability.

For this purpose, most developers use a simplified approach by establishing a minimum "cash-on-cash project hurdle rate," which is the minimum return on costs that a project must meet to be considered viable. Before discussing how to determine that rate, however, consider the myriad ways that return is expressed—as return on costs, return on sales, and return on equity, among many others. As noted in chapter 2, the rigorous way to measure the return on a project is to calculate its IRR on both a leveraged and an unleveraged basis. Doing so requires looking at the cash flow of the project (which is difficult to determine in the project's early stages) and calculating the discount rate at which the present value of the income equals the present value of the costs or, if the calculation is of the leveraged return, of the equity investment. If the IRR is sufficiently high to meet the investment criteria of lenders, investors, and the developer, then the project is financially viable. Although readily available financial and spreadsheet software programs make calculating the IRR much easier than in the past, the level of detail necessary to chart expenditures and income by time period requires estimating too many unknowns, making it impractical to apply to a site that a developer is investigating for possible acquisition. Hence, developers use the shortcut of the cash-on-cash approach.

To determine the cash-on-cash hurdle rate, a developer must accurately estimate the leverage, the cost of capital, and the time to deliver a completed project based on the characteristics of that project. The hurdle rate, then, is based on an assessment of three factors:

■ The time from the start of construction to project close-out, which is either the time for completing all the sales of a for-sale project or the time to achieve a stabilized rent role for an income-producing project;
■ The percentage of the project financed by loans and the interest rate on the loans; and
■ The percentage of the project financed by equity and the target rate of return necessary to attract the equity.

Here is an example of a cash-on-cash hurdle rate calculation:

■ A for-sale residential project requires two years from the start of construction to completely sell all the units.
■ The financing package will be
  ▮ A bank loan for 65 percent of project costs at a 6 percent interest rate, and
  ▮ Equity investment for 35 percent of project costs at a 20 percent target rate of return on equity.
■ The cash-on-cash hurdle rate is calculated as the weighted cost of capital over the time period to create the entire project value, as follows:

$$(1 + (0.65 * 0.06 + 0.35 * 0.2))2 - 1 = 0.229, \text{ or approximately } 23\%$$

Rounding up the hurdle rate makes the assessment of project viability easier and is appropriate given that the other determinants are also estimates. Using safe assumptions protects against overpaying for the land.

A project with the absorption and financing characteristics given in this example must generate a 23 percent return on costs to provide sufficient profitability to cover all costs, including loan costs and return to investors. Because developers tend to specialize in projects that have similar characteristics and because they look at several possible sites for a project, using the same cash-on-cash hurdle rate for different sites accurately estimates the required return. Figure 3-1 shows how the hurdle rate changes with different absorption,

FIGURE 3-1
Cash-on-Cash Hurdle Rates for Different Project Parameters

Months to Achieve Project Value	Debt		Equity		Hurdle Rate (%)
	Share of Funding (%)	Interest (%)	Share of Funding (%)	Annual Return (%)	
36	60	6	40	20	39.0
36	65	6	35	20	36.4
36	75	7	25	20	34.0
24	60	6	40	20	24.5
24	65	6	35	20	23.0
24	75	7	25	20	21.6
18	60	6	40	20	17.9
18	65	6	35	20	16.8
18	75	7	25	20	15.8
12	60	6	40	20	11.6
12	65	7	35	20	10.6
12	75	7	25	20	10.3

debt, and equity parameters. Note that when the leverage increases—that is, when the debt component increases—the cash-on-cash return needed to meet project viability declines.

The cash-on-cash hurdle rate sets the threshold level of the return on costs needed to achieve a viable project, but it is only one element of the analysis. This rate relies on estimates of construction time, the absorption period for sales or lease-up, the probable mix of debt and equity, and the interest rate and rate of return on equity. As these estimates change, the hurdle rate changes.

In addition, the hurdle rate should be adjusted based on the developer's judgment about circumstances unique to a particular site. For instance, if a site will require extra time for entitlement processing or will have extraordinary predevelopment expenses associated with special studies, then the risks and cost of funds will be higher and the hurdle rate should be adjusted upward. Similarly, if the land purchase contract requires significant nonrefundable deposits before the granting of an entitlement, the hurdle rate should be adjusted upward. The precise amount of the adjustment is a judgment call. As described in the next section, the adjustment also depends on how the developer estimates costs in the initial project pro forma. The next section describes how to estimate that pro forma and how to use the concept of supported investment to estimate residual land value.

Calculating the Supported Investment and Residual Land Value

After a hurdle rate is determined, it can be applied to calculate the "maximum supported investment" for the project. Maximum supported investment is the total amount that the developer can afford to spend, including land, and still achieve the hurdle rate of return on costs. The calculation is as follows:

$$\text{Supported Investment Hurdle Rate} = \frac{\text{Project Value}}{(1 + \text{Hurdle Rate})}$$

Chapter 2 discussed in some detail how to estimate project value and advised that the evaluation of project viability starts with that estimate. The developer must then evaluate whether the costs of producing the project, including acquiring the land, are within the limits of the maximum supported investment. To do this, the developer needs a valid estimate of what the project will cost to develop.

COSTS

Before contracting to purchase a site, the developer estimates costs drawn on his or her familiarity with current construction costs and techniques. The developer should know the market for construction services and should conduct a considerable amount of research on site conditions and adjust costs accordingly. After obtaining control of the site, the developer can engage the services of a contractor to prepare a more detailed cost analysis. In the early stages, however, cost estimates are divided into fairly broad categories:

■ Building costs,
■ Site development (demolition, grading, utilities, and landscaping),
■ Parking (may be included in building costs for some types of projects),
■ Connection and impact fees,
■ Off-site costs (such as traffic signals or road improvements),
■ Design (architecture, engineering, consultants, etc.),
■ Marketing (brokers, advertising, etc.),
■ Construction management,
■ Taxes during construction, and
■ Contingency costs.

It is important not to lump costs, a practice that obscures categories that need special attention for further analysis and research.

Site and entitlement conditions play a significant role in the initial estimates. If the site has grading challenges or requires extensive demolition of existing structures, this category should show expected costs that are higher than normal. If the entitlement process looks challenging and time-consuming, the estimate for the design category should be adjusted upward to reflect a longer and more complex design period.

The contingency category should receive special attention in the early stages of a project. For normal conditions, a contingency of 10 to 15 percent of construction costs is usually adequate. But if the construction looks complex or the predevelopment process uncertain and time-consuming, then the contingency estimate should be higher to reflect these potential costs. Follow the admonition, "You cannot cut the board longer. Avoid wishful thinking." If costs come in lower than estimated, the developer is a hero. If they come in higher than estimated, the developer may lose a lot of money. When estimates of costs (other than for land) reflect the circumstances for a site, the calculation of the residual land value will automatically incorporate these circumstances.

RESIDUAL LAND VALUE

Having determined a hurdle rate, the project value, and the maximum supported investment and created a pro forma of development costs, the developer can now determine how much a project can afford to pay for land and still meet project viability requirements. Land is a component of the project costs identified in the maximum supported investment, but it is the only cost that the developer determines whether to incur on the basis of the other costs of development. It reflects the residual capacity to pay. Here is the formula for residual land value:

Maximum Supported Investment – All Project Costs Without Land = Residual Land Value

The result of this calculation tells the developer what the land is worth at the point when it is fully entitled and construction can start. If the developer must pay for all or a portion of the land before reaching this point, there will be additional carrying costs for capital on the land. To obtain an accurate estimate of residual land value, the developer must estimate all these extra carrying costs in the project pro forma to ensure that they are subtracted from the maximum supported investment and that the return is sufficient to attract capital to pay these costs. In addition, the risk that the entitlement will not be achieved could result in the developer (along with lenders or investors who may have participated in funding these early land payments) holding land that may be worth less than the purchase price.

The following three examples show how these concepts are applied.

- *Example 1:* A residential project on one acre of land will produce 25 townhome units selling for $480,000 each, producing $10 million in project value. The buildout and sale period is 12 months from the start of construction. The financing for this project is 75 percent debt at 7 percent interest and 25 percent equity with a 20 percent rate of return. From figure 3-2, the hurdle rate on this project is 10 percent.
- *Example 2:* A commercial developer is producing 50,000 square feet of retail on a 4.5-acre site which will develop over two years and produce annual net rental income (NOI) of $1.5 million. Cap rates for this quality of retail center in today's financial markets are typically 6.0 percent, resulting in a project value of $25 million. The financing for this project is 65 percent debt at 6 percent interest and 35 percent equity with a 20 percent rate of return. From figure 3-2, the hurdle rate is 23 percent.
- *Example 3:* A mixed-use developer is producing 50 condominium flats in three stories built on a podium over 10,000 square feet of retail and parking on a 25,000-square-foot site. The flats will sell for an average price of $350,000, for a sales value of $17.5 million, and the retail will produce $350,000 of NOI valued at a cap rate of 7 percent, for a value of $5 million. Total project value from both components is thus $22.5 million. The project will take 24 months to build and absorb both the residential sales and the retail leasing. The financing for this project is 65 percent debt at 6 percent interest and 35 percent equity with a 20 percent rate of return, resulting in a required 23 percent hurdle rate of return.

Figure 3-2 shows the supported investment and residual land value calculation for these three examples.

This analysis does not tell the developer what to pay for the land; it provides information about what the developer can afford to pay. The price and terms that the developer agrees to are the result of a site selection and negotiation process in which the developer carefully

FIGURE 3-2

Supported Investment and Residual Land Value Calculation, Three Development Scenarios

	Example 1	Example 2	Example 3
Site Area (acres)	1	4.5	0.57
DEVELOPMENT PLAN			
Residential Units	25	0	50
Sq. Ft./Unit	1,600	0	1,000
Value/Unit	$480,000	0	$350,000
Total Sales	**$12,000,000**	**$0**	**$17,500,000**
Retail			
Sq. Ft.	—	50,000	10,000
Net Rental Rate ($/Sq. Ft./Year) (NNN)	—	$30	$35
Net Operating Income (NOI)	**—**	**$1,500,000**	**$350,000**
Parking			
Number of Surface Stalls	25	150	0
Number of Structured Parking Stalls	0	0	130
Total Parking	**25**	**150**	**130**
Cap Rate	—	6%	7%
Finance and Absorption	65% at 6%, 12 months	65% at 6%, 24 months	65% at 6%, 24 months
Hurdle Rate (from figure 3-1)	10.9%	23.0%	23.0%
Project Value	**$12,000,000**	**$25,000,000**	**$22,500,000**
Maximum Supported Investment	**$10,820,600**	**$20,327,200**	**$18,294,500**
COSTS			
Building Construction			
Residential ($/Sq. Ft.)	$120	—	$120
Retail ($/Sq. Ft.)	—	$110	$110
Total Building Construction	**$4,800,000**	**$5,500,000**	**$7,100,000**

avoids committing to closing on the land until the uncertainties associated with its use are resolved. The next section discusses how a developer approaches site selection, negotiates with land owners, and implements due diligence in a way that ensures that the land price contributes to project viability.

FIGURE 3-2 (continued)

	Example 1	Example 2	Example 3
Site Development ($20/Sq. Ft.)	$871,200	$3,920,400	$496,600
On-site Parking			
Surface	$4,000	$4,000	—
Structure	—	—	$25,000
Total Parking Costs	**$100,000**	**$600,000**	**$3,250,000**
Total Construction Costs	**$5,771,200**	**$10,020,400**	**$10,846,600**
City Development Fees			
Residential Development Fee ($/Unit)	$25,000	$0	$25,000
Retail Development Fee ($/Sq. Ft.)	$0	$5	$5
Total City Development Fees	**$625,000**	**$250,000**	**$1,300,000**
Indirect Costs			
Residential Liability Insurance ($10,000/Unit)	$250,000	$0	$500,000
Design and Engineering (5% of Construction Costs)	$288,600	$501,000	$542,300
Real Estate Brokerage Fees (5% of Value)	$600,000	$1,250,000	$1,125,000
Financing Fees and Taxes (2% of Construction Cost)	$115,400	$200,400	$216,900
Contingency (10% of Construction)	$577,100	$1,002,000	$1,084,700
Total Indirect Costs	**$1,831,100**	**$2,953,400**	**$3,468,900**
Total Costs of Development Without Land	**$8,227,300**	**$13,223,800**	**$15,615,500**
Residual Land Value (Maximum Supported Investment Less Total Cost of Development Without Land)	$2,593,300	$7,103,400	$2,679,000
Cost ($/Sq. Ft.)	$59.00	$36.24	$107.90
PROFIT (Maximum Supported Investment Less Total Cost of Development Including Land)	$1,115,600	$4,672,800	$4,205,500

Disciplined Acquisition: Site Selection, Negotiation, and Due Diligence

Site acquisition entails three important steps that lead to the final commitment to purchase:

■ Site selection occurs before the developer starts negotiation.

■ Negotiation leads to an offer and, if successful, the execution of a purchase contract that sets terms and conditions for purchase.

■ After executing the purchase contract, the due diligence takes place in a stipulated period of time, enabling the developer to conduct more detailed research to validate the information that was used to determine the acquisition price.

The site acquisition process is, at its heart, an information-gathering process that informs these three steps. Each step involves gathering more and more information on the six areas of focus described in chapter 1 and below, leading to a final purchase and sale agreement and site control by the developer.

At the beginning, the information-gathering step relies primarily on what the developer already knows, but as acquisition proceeds to identifying viable candidate sites, it moves toward researching a particular site. Research on a site occurs before the developer makes an offer and continues through the negotiation process. After a purchase contract is signed, the developer has a period of time, called the "due diligence period," to hire outside experts and verify the information that was the basis of the original offer.

After due diligence validates the assumptions used to arrive at the land price, the developer then has a binding "purchase and sale agreement," or PSA. Thereafter, the developer proceeds with the full scope of the predevelopment tasks including finalizing the design, managing the entitlement, estimating costs more precisely, continually monitoring market conditions, and addressing future implementation issues.

Brokers can help with information gathering, but not all developers look to brokers as a primary source of leads for viable sites. Some developers view listed properties as a primary source of development sites; others view listed properties as overpriced, picked over, and lacking in opportunity to create true value. Regardless of which approach a developer uses to identify viable sites, though, brokers can help with at least some aspects of site selection and negotiation, so it is important to maintain good working relationships with the brokerage community.

It is important to recognize that brokers know a lot about a market and can uncover opportunities that may not be listed. They may have "pocket" listings—listings for which property owners have negotiated lower fees with the direction of bringing only offers from suitable buyers. Or they may have a history of working with a property owner but have no listing. So brokers can provide help and information on property and property owners, regardless of whether a property is listed. Maintaining relationships with brokers can be a significant advantage to a developer. That advantage means that when a broker helps make a deal happen, it is important for the developer to provide a fee commensurate with the scope of the assistance.

INFORMATION INPUTS

Figure 3-3 illustrates the six information areas of focus discussed in chapter 1 as the inputs to site acquisition. Before attempting to purchase a site, a developer must have an in-depth understanding of these six areas, based on experience and on research conducted through ongoing professional relationships across a wide spectrum of disciplines.

SITE ANALYSIS

Site analysis starts with information about the site's area, boundaries, circulation, utility availability, prior uses, and surrounding uses. A title report should be ordered to identify loans, easements, and deed restrictions. The developer should also gather as much information as possible about the owner's likely circumstances and motives.

During negotiations, the developer should continue to gather information from the owner. The title report should be reviewed with the owner and more information obtained on prior uses, to assess the probability of the site containing hazardous waste. The developer should also explore other questions:

- Does the owner have a recent survey of the site?
- Has there been any investigation of hazardous waste?
- Is there a possibility of unstable soils or flooding on the site?
- What is the history of the development of the site, and how has this development been viewed by those involved with surrounding uses?
- Is the title for the site clear?
- What are the encumbrances on the site, and who is responsible for clearing them if the purchase proceeds?
- Are adequate utilities and traffic capacity available?

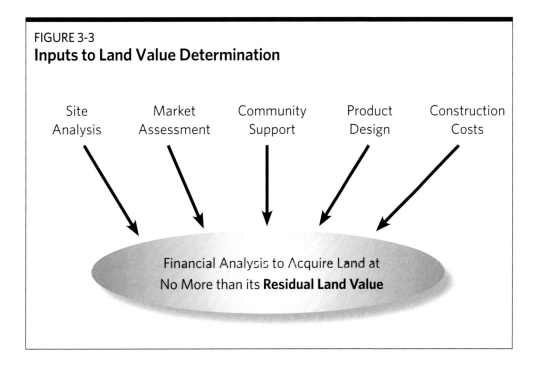

FIGURE 3-3
Inputs to Land Value Determination

Site Analysis → Market Assessment → Community Support → Product Design → Construction Costs →

Financial Analysis to Acquire Land at No More than its **Residual Land Value**

During due diligence, the developer spends money to hire outside experts to verify the property owner's representations and to investigate areas of uncertainty. Some of the expenditures during due diligence may be billed back to the property owner as a credit against the purchase price (the site survey, for example); others will be the developer's expense. Finally, the developer should attempt to include in the purchase contract a requirement that close of escrow is conditioned on receiving the project entitlement. Some developers refuse to sign a purchase contract without this condition.

MARKET ASSESSMENT

Before making an offer, the developer should have conducted an "in-house" market survey to document transactions near the site. This survey informs the developer about pricing and provides some guidance for configuring the product for the development.

During due diligence, the developer should hire an outside market analyst to address the question, "What is the best market-driven development plan for the site?" This study will confirm, dispel, or modify the developer's initial instincts about the site and may change the project value calculation that was the basis for determining the residual land value.

Although hiring outside market analysts costs money, their impartial analysis and advice can provide huge benefits, aiding the developer in configuring a project that responds to market opportunities in terms of product type, physical connection to the surrounding community, and target market and approach. Their analysis can inform the design team about how to configure the project to attract maximum market acceptance.

COMMUNITY SUPPORT

A developer needs to become immersed physically, politically, and socially in the community to really understand the likelihood of community support for the project.

- Physical immersion involves driving, biking, walking, and riding transit; some developers sit in a supermarket parking lot and watch the customers. The developer needs to understand how the transportation system connects a site to the community and region.
- The Internet provides a huge window to information. Google maps, parcel map data services, and Internet market data have dramatically increased the precision and scope of information available.
- Political immersion means, of course, talking to staff at City Hall. It also involves attending council meetings, tracking the local media, and monitoring local blogs on community affairs. This immersion leads to an understanding of the politics behind the regulatory framework and of the community's readiness to respond to development proposals.
- Social immersion involves identifying community groups. One developer and his wife join the local historical society. They both like history and they connect with a segment of the community that has ownership and is likely to be vocal on development issues.

Ultimately, this immersion helps answer the question, "What configuration of uses and conditions of development will the community permit, and what is the process by which the community will approve the project?" Several specific issues must be addressed:

- The preferences and influence of neighbors;
- The effects of zoning and development regulations on potential development;

- The cost of meeting development conditions; and
- The cost of and time needed to get the entitlement.

PROJECT/PRODUCT DESIGN

In the early stages of site acquisition, the developer may have only a preliminary sketch of a site plan to use in estimating how much development can occur. These preliminary estimates, though, are the basis for estimating project value for the purpose of determining residual land value.

Before completing the due diligence, the developer should engage the services of a design team to create a more considered configuration of the development plan that responds both to the market opportunities and to community preferences. This plan should then be valued, its costs estimated, and the residual land value recalculated.

After due diligence, the design evolves as the community reviews it. The early layout and development plan should be on the conservative side for estimating project value. The cost of the final design that is entitled may differ significantly from the early estimate.

CONSTRUCTION COSTS

The developer should prepare a preliminary pro forma to estimate the residual land value as the basis of the offer. This pro forma should identify areas of uncertainty—areas where the developer perceives potential problems or construction risks.

During due diligence, the developer should hire a contractor to provide preconstruction services and a more reliable cost estimate for the preliminary design. Again, this estimate should be on the conservative side because, as design proceeds, issues will be discovered that can significantly affect project cost.

FINANCIAL ANALYSIS

With information from the five other input areas, the developer is able to prepare a preliminary financial analysis as the basis for determining the estimated residual land value. Throughout the acquisition process and continuing through the entire predevelopment process, the analysis should be informed by several principles:

- Forecast on the basis of current market conditions for prices and costs—avoid wishful thinking.
- Identify sensitive numbers and focus attention on reducing risk in these areas.
- Incorporate the time and cost of capital in the cost estimate to ensure that the maximum supported investment is calculated using a pro forma that reflects true project risks.

After due diligence is completed, as predevelopment proceeds, the financial analysis must be updated continually to monitor how changes resulting from entitlement, market conditions, and costs affect project viability.

The primary challenge that a developer faces in determining the right land price is that most of the information needed to determine residual land value has not been fully researched before a deal with the landowner must be negotiated. Only after a site is under contract, during the due diligence period, can the developer risk spending the sums necessary to obtain more reliable information. Site selection, then, is a process in which the developer must start by being pessimistic about the inputs to the analysis and become optimistic only as information justifies it. The old admonition in the development business is "don't fall in love with the real estate"; that is, pay attention to the uncertainty of early information and the risks it creates for purchasing a site at too high a price.

NEGOTIATING WITH SITE OWNERS

When a promising site has been identified, the developer begins further research and creates a preliminary site development plan. At this step, the developer calculates a residual land value based on estimated project value and cost estimates and begins the process of determining what to pay for the site.

The process of negotiating with a property owner requires the developer to understand the owner's circumstances, including the owner's expectations and sophistication in real estate, and the site's history. A property owner is likely to be involved in a development-related land transaction for a considerable time, depending on the terms of the purchase contract. The goal of the negotiation, in addition to achieving an affordable price, should be to create a business relationship that is responsive to the expected risks associated with the site.

In contacts with the property owner, the developer should gather as much first-hand information as possible about the owner's outlook and circumstances before deciding what to offer. Among the questions to pursue:

- What are the owner's concerns about a possible sale, and what does the owner consider a viable means of addressing these concerns?
- Has the owner been approached by other developers in the past, and what was the owner's experience, good or bad, with those developers?
- Are other developers currently interested in the site?
- What is the owner's understanding of the development process, and could the owner assist in the process?
- What is the owner's preference about putting land into the project as equity?
- Has the owner gathered critical information on the site such as a survey, an environmental analysis, and the title?

When the developer has learned as much as can be learned about the site, an offer can be prepared. It must be prepared with an anticipation of how the property owner will respond. Will the negotiation be a hard-bargaining situation involving offers and counteroffers, or will it be a sharing of information leading to an outcome in which both parties feel comfortable that the price fairly reflects the residual land value? The developer should anticipate these dynamics and attempt, where possible, to avoid the win-lose of a hard-bargaining situation.

Managing the chemistry of the negotiations involves managing the channels of communication. Will personal meetings with the property owner enhance trust and communication, or will they intimidate the property owner? Does the owner have trusted representatives? Is a broker involved, and how is the broker contributing to making a deal? Is there an understanding of markets and real estate finance, and if there is not, how does the property owner evaluate whether a deal is a good deal?

For some property owners, it is valuable and important to use an "open book" approach. This will work only when a relationship of trust has been established, something that is hard to do. But the developer should always act in a trustworthy manner and attempt to establish trust with the other side. A land purchase contract creates a long-term relationship, because after the purchase and sale agreement (PSA) is signed, there may be a considerable amount of time and issues to be addressed before escrow closes. If issues arise, they are easier to resolve within a relationship of trust.

Time is a major dimension of negotiation. Trying to make a deal quickly is frequently counterproductive. A developer who recognizes the value of persistence over time finds that it is not unusual for deals to evolve over months or years. Patience pays.

PURCHASE STEPS

The generic process leading to a contract for site purchase has these three steps:

■ First, a letter of intent (LOI) or purchase offer is sent by the developer (or representative) to the property owner (or representative), setting forth the proposed purchase price and timing for close of escrow. The LOI is a low-cost vehicle for achieving concurrence on terms before the attorneys draft and wordsmith the purchase contract. A clear, succinct LOI or offer sets forth the major business terms. This stage may last some time while terms are negotiated. It is important to provide a reasonable length of time to execute the full purchase and sale contract.

■ Second, if the parties accept the purchase offer, a PSA is drafted by the parties' legal representatives. It sets forth the business terms of the sale.

■ Third, once the PSA is executed, the due diligence period begins. During this period research is conducted to validate assumptions and verify the site's suitability for the planned development. Usually, there is a deposit into escrow that is refundable if the purchase does not proceed beyond due diligence. If the purchaser is satisfied with the validation and verification from the due diligence period, then the agreement usually requires that the deposit into escrow become nonrefundable.

PURCHASE AND SALE AGREEMENT

Upon execution of the PSA, the property is "tied up"; at this point, spending money on due diligence makes sense. If the buyer uncovers conditions that are at variance with the assumptions made when the purchase contract was signed, then the buyer either attempts to renegotiate the terms of the sale or gets the escrow deposits back and abandons the project.

After the due diligence period, the buyer is typically required to make additional, scheduled, nonrefundable deposits that are credited toward the final purchase price. If the buyer abandons the project for any reason after the due diligence period, the seller keeps these deposits.

The time for depositing the total amount of the purchase price into escrow and closing the purchase is specified in the purchase and sale agreement. The developer should attempt to make close of escrow contingent on receiving the entitlement from the land use authority to proceed with the project. Rarely, if ever, is there a contingency requiring that the project receive a financing commitment from a lender. Frequently, the contract requires close of escrow and payment of the full purchase price within a stipulated time period, even if the entitlement has not been received. The developer should try to minimize the amount of nonrefundable deposits before the close of escrow.

The purchase and sale agreement also details the buyer's conditions for close of escrow, setting forth requirements that the seller must meet in order for the buyer to close. These conditions address a variety of issues:

- Condition of title; essentially, confirmation that the property is owned by the seller and that no exceptions or uncertainties cloud this ownership;
- Clearing of all taxes, loans, or other liabilities that may be liens on the property;
- Environmental condition of the property, as documented in hazardous waste investigations, and assignment of responsibility for site cleanup, if necessary;
- Whether close of escrow is conditioned on receiving entitlement;
- Performance time for seller to cure deficiencies in the condition of the title;
- Performance requirements for purchaser to deposit funds into escrow;
- Conditions for refund of the escrow deposits.

The purchase contract should contain a procedure for notifying the property owner of unacceptable conditions that may be discovered after due diligence and should give the owner a period of time to "cure" those conditions and the developer the option to cancel the purchase if the conditions are not cured.

DUE DILIGENCE

The minimum due diligence period should be no less than 30 days, but the developer should try to negotiate as long a period as the site owner will accept. If information is discovered during due diligence that changes the estimated land value, the developer must attempt to renegotiate the terms of the purchase—or, if not successful, must abandon the purchase. Frequently, adverse information discovered during due diligence causes the parties to extend the due diligence period to allow the information to be addressed within the context of the overall business terms. Typical due diligence issues include environmental and title conditions associated directly with the site, but the buyer's ability to not proceed with the contract is typically not constrained solely to those issues. In any case, at the end of the due diligence period, the good faith deposit becomes nonrefundable; that is, the seller keeps the deposit if the buyer does not close on the property.

Figure 3-4 shows a hypothetical due diligence budget for a small to moderate-sized land acquisition. Costs for major land acquisitions are much higher than the range shown here. In most transactions, the seller has some or all of the title and environmental work done, thus lowering the due diligence cost to the buyer.

Some common issues identified in due diligence that may cause either an abandonment of the deal or an attempt to renegotiate:

- Title to the property is not clear.
- Easements prevent full site utilization.
- A survey finds less land than indicated.
- Soils are not good for construction.
- Environmental hazards exist.
- Zoning or development requirements differ from expectations.
- Development fees will be higher than expected.
- Construction costs will be higher than expected.
- The market is weaker than expected.
- The development will cause more controversy in the community than anticipated.
- Site layout or unit production must differ from plans.

FIGURE 3-4
Typical Due Diligence Budget Range

Item of Investigation	Range of Cost	
	Low	High
Title Investigation and Survey	$2,000	$10,000
Environmental Investigation—Phase I	$5,000	$20,000
Market Analysis	$10,000	$20,000
Community Support Assessment	$5,000	$10,000
Conceptual Architectural Design	$5,000	$10,000
Preconstruction Cost Analysis	$5,000	$10,000
Total Due Diligence Budget	**$32,000**	**$80,000**

Note: Ranges are valid for project development values less than $100 million.

Site Acquisition Dos and Don'ts

DO

- Base a project's value on the market, the expected difficulties of the entitlement process, and validated costs and market prices, not on comps and guesses.

- Understand what the likely predevelopment funding requirements will be and how long it will be before the project can be presented to financing sources.

- Create a relevant list of buyer's conditions to close, as a way of minimizing the risk that the site will not be ready for development.

- Strive to create a relationship of trust during interactions with the owner and public officials.

- Understand the community as much as possible before purchasing a site.

- Be prepared to abandon the site or renegotiate the deal if due diligence discloses information that is inconsistent with the assumptions that determined price.

DON'T

- Close without entitlement unless prepared to live with the consequences of no entitlement.

- Deposit nonrefundable money unnecessarily.

- Make unnecessary commitments to the seller or the entitlement entity.

- Skimp on the cost of researching due diligence issues.

- Proceed beyond due diligence if major issues are unresolved.

- Engage in wishful thinking about resolving due diligence concerns.

As described in chapter 1, the developer constantly updates the project's financial analysis on the basis of new information. If the developer could wait until all the information was gathered to determine the land price, then the risk of buying land at too high a price would be minimal, but that is not how development works. Information costs money, and a developer does not want to spend a lot of money on a site that he or she does not control. Land acquisition, then, is a process of making increasing financial commitments to a development site on the basis of increased confidence that a project built on that site will be economically viable.

Example: Simple Pro Forma for a Mixed-Use Project

Figure 3-5 provides a pro forma model for calculating residual land value based on a cash-on-cash hurdle rate. It presents a simple analytic tool for a mixed-use project. To use this tool, a developer needs to have valid cost, market, and product design information.

As an example, this pro forma presents a 60,000-square-foot site developed with 60 for-sale residential units and 10,000 square feet of commercial space. The project is a podium project of residential for-sale units over a concrete podium deck with parking underneath. A city condition of approval is that 20 percent of the units be built as "affordable" for people with low and moderate incomes. It has hallways and lobbies that add 15 percent to the floor area that will be constructed The commercial space is valued at a cap rate of 6.5 percent. Because this project is located in a state where product liability suits have resulted in legal risk to high-density residential developers, each unit has a "load" of insurance premium to cover this risk.

The model provides a straightforward and accurate way of quickly evaluating residual land value using a return-on-cost hurdle rate. In the case of the example project, the hurdle rate is 20 percent, based on a two-year absorption estimate and 75 percent debt at 6 percent interest.

FIGURE 3-5
Simple Pro Forma for Determining Land Value

Land Area	Acres	Sq. Ft.
Parcel 1	0.92	40,000
Parcel 2	0.46	20,000
Total	**1.38**	**60,000**

DEVELOPMENT PLAN AND PROJECT VALUE					
Residential	**Units**	**Sq. Ft.**	**Cost/Sq. Ft.**	**Total Price**	**Total Value**
Market Rate #1 1BR/1.5 BA	24	1,100	$420	$462,000	$11,088,000
Market Rate #2 2BR/2.5 BA	24	1,280	$400	$512,000	$12,288,000
Affordable Flats	12	1,410	$213	$300,330	$3,603,960
Halls and Lobbies (15%)					
Total Residential	**60**	**85,146**			**$26,979,960**

FIGURE 3-5 (continued)
Simple Pro Forma for Determining Land Value

Commercial	Units	Sq. Ft.	NNN	NOI	Total Value
Ground Floor Retail		10,000	$22	$220,000	$3,384,615
Cap Rate	6.5%				
Total Commercial		**10,000**			**$3,384,615**
Total Project Value		**95,146**			**$30,364,575**

PROJECT COSTS

Construction Costs	Units or Stalls	Sq. Ft.	Cost/Sq. Ft.	Cost/Unit or Stall	Total Value
Residential Building Costs		85,146	$135		$11,494,710
Commercial Building Costs		10,000	$120		$1,200,000
Site Development		60,000	$25		$1,500,000
Parking	140			$15,000	$2,100,000
Total Construction Costs					**$16,294,710**
Per Unit Costs					
Development Fees	60			$10,000	$600,000
Condominium Insurance	60			$10,000	$600,000
Total Per Unit Costs					**$1,200,000**

Soft Costs	Share	Applied to	
Design	4.5%	Construction only	$733,262
Marketing	5.0%	Total project value	$1,518,229
Construction Management	4.0%	Construction only	$651,788
Finance (Based on Construction and Absorption Period)	8.5%	Construction (60%) and per unit	$892,230
Taxes	1.0%	Construction and per unit	$174,947
Contingency	10.0%	Construction and per unit	$1,749,471
Total Soft Costs			**$5,719,927**
Total Project Costs Without Land			**$23,214,637**
Maximum Supported Investment @ Hurdle Rate of 20%			**$25,303,813**
RESIDUAL LAND VALUATION			
Residual Land Value (Maximum Supported Investment less Total Project Costs Without Land)			**$2,089,175**
Cost Per Acre			$1,516,741
Cost Per Sq. Ft.			$34.82
Cost Per Unit			$34,820

CHAPTER 4

Task Management and Budgeting

A fter the completion of due diligence and close of escrow, the developer must focus on managing the ongoing tasks of the development process. Necessarily, these tasks are a continuation of the six areas of focus in site acquisition (described in chapter 1), with an emphasis on community acceptance, market viability, project design, and cost management. To accomplish these tasks, the developer must assemble the development team, form the financing entity, and obtaining financing commitments. As the project proceeds, the developer's tasks broaden to include managing the construction process and gearing up the marketing effort for sale or lease of the project.

As activities proceed from predevelopment to construction, the project needs greater and greater amounts of capital. The source of this capital must be anticipated and the risks of loss monitored to ensure that the project will remain economically viable if built and that sufficient capital is available to get the project to entitlement. Linking each task with its potential and final sources of funding is a significant management challenge during predevelopment.

This chapter discusses the process for successfully managing and funding the tasks in a development project. It describes the scope of tasks and the objective that each accomplishes within the three development phases (predevelopment, development, and close-out) to achieve financial viability. It describes personnel selection and key roles of members on a development team. Finally, it provides an example of how to apply different funding sources tasks as a project proceeds.

Task Management to Achieve Financial Viability

Here are four principles to keep in mind as a project proceeds:
- *Invest in information wisely:* More information can reduce risk, but it comes with a risk of losing the investment needed to obtain it. The developer must avoid committing to expensive tasks until prerequisite tasks are accomplished. As an example, conducting a relatively inexpensive market study to inform product design should occur before incurring large

costs for architectural work on a project. For each task, weigh the potential gain in getting to the point of demonstrating financial viability against the risk of losing the expenditure, and order tasks so that only the most critical tasks are paid for early.

- *Manage time:* The longer the process takes, the more expensive it will be, but delaying the start of expensive tasks to get to a point of assured financial viability makes sense. The entitlement process is the source of the greatest variability in time, so focusing on tasks that can streamline entitlement is a high priority.
- *Manage budgets:* Identify, sequence, and budget all tasks at the start of the project and monitor expenditures carefully. The predevelopment budget should include a source for and application of funds to ensure that adequate resources are available to get the project to the point of demonstrating financial viability to outside capital sources. Until that demonstration is made, the project must rely solely on the developer for financing predevelopment expenses; thereafter, outside capital sources may participate in financing these costs.
- *Anticipate:* Involve the development team in anticipating issues and solving problems early, before they become expensive. Some issues require immediate attention because they affect the ability of the project to proceed, even though they may be relatively inexpensive to address. Early coordination between design and construction is vital to achieving the most cost-effective construction approach. Anticipating issues in entitlement that could cause delay or extra costs enables early action to manage outcomes. As the project proceeds through design, it is also important to recognize the appropriate level of uncertainty in cost estimates and to budget the appropriate contingency.

These four principles guide the order in which tasks are scheduled and completed. Tasks that address project viability have a high priority. It makes sense to invest early in tasks that eliminate a high risk of project failure and to defer other tasks until the risk of failure has been reduced. Also, many tasks create information that is needed for later tasks, so the "critical path" requires expenditures on these tasks in order to meet deadlines later.

The following subsections give an overview of the major tasks, grouped by the six areas of focus, along with some discussion of their timing and contribution to demonstrating financial viability.

SITE

Most site-related tasks must be accomplished very early in the development process. They are described here:

- *Conduct a site survey:* It is critically important to have a valid survey of the site boundaries, easements, and area. If the seller does not provide one, the buyer/developer should complete one as part of due diligence.
- *Resolve title issues:* If title to the property is unclear or if there are easements or liens on the property, effort must go into clearing these exceptions as quickly as possible because they create the risk that the project will not be able to proceed. It is not unusual to proceed on a purchase and sale agreement beyond the due diligence period despite unresolved title issues because those issues have been assessed as straightforward. Usually, it is the seller's responsibility to deliver clear title. Nonetheless, the buyer/developer

must monitor progress to ensure that the seller resolves title exceptions quickly so as to remove the risk of exceptions holding up the close of escrow.

■ *Investigate environmental remediation:* Remediation may be the responsibility of the seller or the buyer, depending on the purchase terms. Usually, the seller anticipates this issue and prepares, at a minimum, a Phase I study—a review of the site history and an assessment of the probability that contaminants exist on site. Depending on the results of the Phase I study, the buyer may require additional investigation, paid for by either the buyer or the seller. This additional investigation may identify a need for a remediation program. Remediation efforts are likely to take a considerable amount of time and expense, requiring on-site activity and interfacing with regulators, which means that the process should start early and be monitored closely. If the outcome is in doubt, then other expenditures should be deferred until the risks have been reduced.

■ *Identify site conditions that affect construction:* The developer must investigate soils, drainage, wetlands, creek restoration needs, and other physical conditions of the site to ensure that they are addressed appropriately in project design. Many of these issues involve regulatory risk, which, again, means that other expenditures should be deferred until the regulatory framework has been clarified and the uncertainty of outcomes reduced.

MARKET

Validating the market is a continuous task throughout the project, even throughout construction. This validation supports the design and implementation of the marketing program that must be fully implemented at close-out. Early market analysis is important first to validate land price and subsequently to present the project to outside capital sources. Here are specific tasks to accomplish:

■ *Conduct a due diligence market review:* With the site tied up, a formal market review should be conducted by an outside consultant to validate the developer's assumptions. Along with the cost verification, this review should validate that the project value is sufficient for project viability.

■ *Profile customers and product types:* After the initial due diligence on the market, further analysis should broaden to develop detailed customer profiles, product types, and marketing considerations. This is the analysis that shapes project design, and it must be completed early so it can inform the work of the design team.

■ *Develop the marketing program:* The customer profile analysis then should be expanded to address marketing strategies. This analysis leads to the planning and staffing of a sale or lease program for the project at close-out. Work on this task should start soon enough to capture opportunities for pre-marketing (marketing before construction is complete). For retail and large office projects, the pre-marketing program begins right away, to secure the commitments of anchor tenants or large users that are necessary to attract financing and also to configure the project to meet the needs of these users.

■ *Conduct periodic reassessments of market conditions:* During the development process, market conditions should be reassessed at least every six months to monitor market trends. A comprehensive reassessment should occur just before the start of construction to evaluate whether market trends signal a high risk of negative change.

- *Plan property management:* All for-lease and many for-sale projects have ongoing management and marketing components. For-lease projects require property management to collect rents, maintain the property, re-lease vacant spaces, and pay maintenance, loan costs, and returns to investors. For-sale projects may entail managing property owners associations, which collect maintenance fees from owners and maintain the property. In recent years, with the increase in mixed-use projects that involve for-sale residential and for-lease retail or office space, such property owners associations have become quite complex.

COMMUNITY

Entitlement has become quite complex, and task management in this realm is as much art as it is science. Building relationships of trust is critical. Monitoring progress and conducting effective communication programs are also key contributors to success. Here are the tasks to accomplish:

- *Map the community entitlement process:* Early identification of community issues is a critical task; it should build on the information already gathered during site acquisition. This ongoing task involves establishing relationships with the professional staff of the land use authority and with the community. It also involves listening carefully to community concerns before responding. Chapter 8 provides detailed suggestions about mapping the process and attempting to reach agreement with the entitling jurisdiction on regulatory steps and conditions of approval. The entitlement process entails inherent risk because of the unpredictability of public involvement, so it is important that the mapping incorporate contingencies.

- *Develop a communication program:* A significant early task is to develop a communication strategy that targets elected officials, professional staff, community groups, and media. This program could involve Web sites, e-mail, one-on-one meetings, group meetings, and media press releases. The goal is to create two-way communication about the project's design. Chapter 8 discusses the dynamics of the communication program in more depth.

- *Make formal submittals:* The entitlement process requires formal submittals of numerous applications and reports. Submittals must be scheduled to coincide with the availability of the information needed to complete the applications.

- *Hold meetings:* Every meeting has costs, so an evaluation must be made of which members of the development team should attend.

- *Oversee plan submission:* One of the regulatory processes that is most taken for granted is the submission of a set of completed construction drawings for a review by the city or county where a project is to be built. This process requires special attention because it typically involves multiple departments, some of which have a very narrow scope. It is important to manage the plan submission process—starting early and leaving enough time. Recognize that routine processes can bite you. (As more than one developer has said, "The fire department will hang you up every time.") Managing the plan submission process continues until the project receives a Certificate of Occupancy.

PRODUCT/PROJECT DESIGN

The design process for a development project is generally thought of in the industry as having five sequential stages: predesign, schematic design, design development, construction documents, and bid documents. Each stage entails certain tasks, along with additional special studies that inform the design process. Coordinating the flow of information that is accumulated lowers the cost of each stage. In addition, new technology can streamline the design process and lower construction costs considerably. Here are the tasks in each stage:

- *Predesign:* During due diligence or shortly thereafter, the developer and architect conceptualize the project through a predesign effort, which serves as the starting point for the development program. Predesign, in effect, creates the baseline development program (often used in evaluating residual land value as part of the land acquisition process described in chapter 3).
- *Schematic project design:* After the due diligence period, the schematic project design is a more in-depth effort to respond to market and community concerns and to site parameters, and to engage in a preliminary analysis of how to construct the project cost-effectively. The developer must evaluate how best to incorporate community concerns into this stage of design. One approach is to use the schematic design as a preliminary proposal to solicit community comment. Another approach is to listen to community concerns before completing the schematic design.
- *Special focused studies:* Tasks in this stage can range from studies that focus on particular aspects of the project—such as traffic, shade, or noise—to full-scale environmental impact studies examining all aspects of the project's impact on the community. These studies should be identified in the site analysis and in the mapping of the entitlement process; they should also be included in the preliminary budget and funding program for the project. These tasks will inform the design, so design work must be managed so it does not get ahead of the information available.
- *Design development:* In this stage, the team creates solutions to issues that were identified in the schematic phase. This stage also provides an opportunity to conduct more detailed cost analysis. Because of the costs that must be incurred to reach this stage, this task is unlikely to occur until some certainty is achieved about the entitlement process.
- *Construction documents:* Detailed construction documents must be submitted to building officials and, typically, to planning officials, to review for compliance with building and planning regulations.
- *Bid documents:* These final plans and specifications incorporate comments from plan checkers. They are the final plans and specs to which the project will be bid and built. The project may not necessarily go to a competitive bid, depending on the construction management approach taken by the developer.

COST AND CONSTRUCTION MANAGEMENT

The specific tasks that occur in cost and construction management depend on the way in which the developer engages the construction contractor to build the project. There are four models:

- Design-bid-build;
- Negotiated;
- Design-build; and
- Integrated project delivery.

DESIGN-BID-BUILD

Design-bid-build is the conventional model, dividing the project into separate contracts for design (architect) and construction (contractor). The developer retains the architect, and the architect prepares the bid documents. The architect then assists the developer in evaluating bids and proposals and awarding a contract or contracts for construction. The contractor or contractors then build the project, meeting the specifications in the plans. If there are design changes during construction, a "change order" is executed to reflect the cost of the changes.

The theoretical benefits of this approach are that the arm's-length relationship between the architect and contractor safeguards the developer's interests through the competitive pricing process and that this process maximizes the potential for discovering errors and omissions in the drawings. However, this process frequently results in problems. There is a potential for adversarial relationships between the developer, architect, and contractor. Cost estimates are frequently incorrect because they are not prepared by the party responsible for the work. There is less control over the contractor. And—an area of significant shortcoming in modern buildings—there is limited potential for the integrated design of mechanical, electrical, and plumbing (MEP) systems because the architect is unable to work directly with the contractor until after the bid award.

NEGOTIATED

In the negotiated model, the developer again retains the architect, who then prepares the drawings and specifications. But the developer also retains the contractor early, as a fully integrated member in the decision-making process. When the project is completely designed, the developer and contractor negotiate a price. At some point, the contractor may commit to a guaranteed maximum contract, assuming the risk of completing the contract at that price.

This model has several advantages over the conventional design-bid-build model. It fully integrates cost oversight into the design because the pricing is prepared by the party responsible for execution. It also builds into the design process "constructability" reviews, which help ensure that complicated components of the project are designed for the most cost-effective construction. Constructability reviews are particularly beneficial for complicated MEP systems. The negotiated model enables early ordering of materials that may have long delivery times or that are experiencing cost inflation (steel or glass, for instance). And it allows full disclosure of the cost parameters for subcontractors, with a focus on two categories of contractor's costs: general requirements, and overhead and profit. For these reasons, this is the most commonly used model.

DESIGN-BUILD

In the design-build model, the developer contracts with a single entity as the design-builder. This entity may have design and construction capacity in house, or it may be an architect-led organization, or—the most common case—it may be a contractor-led organization. The entity subcontracts for whatever skill set it does not already have in house. In this model, the developer contracts with the design-builder, who then is responsible for designing and building the project.

The benefits of this model are that it creates a single point of responsibility for cost and quality, and an early focus on meeting a budget by a fully integrated team. It has shortcomings, however: it limits competitive pricing through bidding, and it sometimes suffers from not meeting design objectives within budget limitations, because the budget may not have taken into account all design issues. This model is often used for developing corporate or public sector facilities within a specified budget.

INTEGRATED PROJECT DELIVERY

The collaborative model of integrated project delivery utilizes the talents and insights of all project participants through all phases of design and construction. The developer, architect, and contractor are one team and share the risks and rewards of project success. This model, in effect, creates incentives for the architect and contractor—whose services are normally fee-based—to participate in project success. It focuses on minimizing cost and schedule overruns through collaboration, information sharing, and new building design technology. It has evolved since a 2004 report by the Construction Users Roundtable, which is composed of large facility users such as Boeing, Cisco, IBM, Intel, and the General Services Administration. This model is documented in several publications by the American Institute of Architects (AIA), including the November 2007 "Integrated Project Delivery: A Guide." The latest version of this guide is available at the Web site of the AIA.

Regardless of the model used to construct the project, several realities associated with construction should drive the task planning. First, the ability to affect the cost and functionality of the project declines as the project proceeds through the design phases to construction. Second, the cost of design changes increases as the project proceeds. Both of these realities argue strongly for engaging the contractor early and involving the contractor in the design of the project. Although bringing in the contractor early in the process may involve early out-of-pocket costs for the developer, such participation is critical to ensuring cost-effective construction that is on budget and on schedule.

In addition to early involvement of the contractor, the developer must ensure that communication between the design team and the contractor focuses on cost and quality control. The key to success here is to avoid adversarial relationships and to foster collaborative, timely problem solving.

Success in the construction phase is grounded in having a complete list of tasks and good communications between the architect, contractor, and developer. The typical communications process includes regular project meetings at which issues are resolved. Issues are usually tracked by sending a memorandum called a "request for information" or RFI. With project management software, these RFIs are automatically logged, distributed, and managed so they are dealt with in a timely way.

Because so much specialty work (MEP, concrete, etc.) is done by subcontractors, a key contributor to success is for the contractor to select only subcontractors with good track records and references. It is also important that the developer be on the site every day and be disciplined about how the project proceeds. Timely payment of construction invoices is critical, as is timely resolution of construction issues. If the developer is not disciplined, the team will not be disciplined.

Timely close-out is critical, to avoid costly compounding of interest on loans and deliver preferred returns on investment. This requires the contractor to close out punch list items quickly and to receive the certificate of occupancy without delays.

Another effort that contributes to success is to recognize the inherent uncertainty of estimates by ensuring that budgets, schedules, and cost contingencies are adequate. To avoid surprises, cost contingencies should be adjusted as the project proceeds through design, using the following percentages as rules of thumb:

■ Predesign, 15 to 18 percent
■ Schematic design, 12 to 15 percent
■ Design development, 10 to 12 percent
■ Construction documents, 5 to 7 percent.

FINANCE

Financing tasks involve conducting analysis, demonstrating financial viability, and organizing the development entity. Here are more detailed descriptions:

■ *Update financial analysis:* As the project evolves, the developer must update the financial analysis regularly to ensure that the project economics reflect the reality discovered during the design, entitlement, and cost management tasks.

■ *Obtain financing commitments:* When it is clear that the project has a high likelihood of approval from the land use authority and when the project's economic viability has been established through verified market and cost analysis, the developer should begin discussions with financing sources. This is not to say that a developer should not have ongoing discussions with multiple financiers at earlier points. It is important to maintain relationships with multiple lenders and financiers, to ensure competitive pricing and terms for financing.

■ *Form development/financing entity:* This task may take place in stages. In the early phases of predevelopment, separate entities working together on the project may form a joint venture. Subsequently, when investment partners have made financing commitments, another development entity involving those partners is formed. Chapter 7 discusses forming the development/financing entity in more detail.

PERSONNEL SELECTION

The key to success in most of these tasks is to foster teamwork among the many professionals who work on the project and to create an effective team of players from many disciplines:

■ Architects
■ Contractors
■ Engineers (soils, traffic, structural, etc.)
■ Attorneys
■ Public relations consultants
■ Environmental consultants
■ Marketing firm or broker
■ Property manager
■ Finance expert, if the developer needs that expertise.

It is especially important to focus on the relationship between the architect and contractor. As much as 80 to 85 percent of project costs are spent through the contractor, and another 5 to 7 percent through the architect. These two disciplines must work together. The following discussion addresses how key professionals are selected and paid and how important the selection of individual personnel is to the success of a project.

ARCHITECT AND CONTRACTOR SELECTION

Bringing both the architect and the contractor to the project early ensures that their relationship is collaborative and not confrontational. Sometimes this is a challenge, because each discipline has a different role: for the architect, to design a project that is distinctive and for the contractor, to build a project on time and on budget. Success requires creating a team in which the contribution of each discipline is valued and conflicts are resolved early.

Developers should select the architect and contractor on the basis of professional qualifications, not bids. Even though these two disciplines represent 85 to 90 percent of total project costs, selecting these services on the basis of cost is a false economy. Because development is a relationship-based business, successful developers rely on business relationships founded on a track record of successful projects as the key criterion for selecting services.

For architects, fees can be hourly, depending on the type of project. They also can be set in a fee schedule, based on project cost. All fees are negotiable, so a developer should spend time early in the relationship establishing how the fee arrangement will work, including incentives and communication protocols for limiting fees. Architects usually start billing to a project early in the predevelopment process, though, depending on the business relationship, the architect may provide a substantial amount of preliminary design work on a project for no fee. This is especially true if the developer is working with the architect on multiple projects. Regardless of the billing approach, the developer must make sure that it is negotiated and understood early in the process.

Contractors earn fees from several sources: they can charge for services they provide to the project just as any subcontractor would. "General requirements" is a category of on-site management and activity that the contractor provides to the project; it involves coordination, on-site services, and subcontractor coordination. The contractor also may provide such services as rough carpentry, finish carpentry, or concrete work. Depending on the capabilities of the contractor, much of the work on a project is contracted out to specialized subcontractors. The contractor also charges for overhead (administrative cost) and profit. Profit fees for the volume of work associated with a large project are in the range of 3 to 5 percent of the total construction contract, depending on the level of complexity and the degree of guarantees on costs. Overhead and profit fees are negotiable.

Contractors also may provide a substantial amount of preconstruction services at no fee based on the business relationship, especially if the developer and architect are working on multiple projects. Contractors recover the costs of these services by getting the job of constructing the project—so if the project fails to proceed, they may end up billing for those services.

In general, architectural skills are portable, so it is not unusual to see architects practicing in many different locations. Contractors have less flexibility, though many firms have a regional or national presence. For contractors, knowledge of the local subcontractor

Source of Funds and Their Application to Development Tasks

This example shows project tasks, budgets, schedules, and funding sources for a hypothetical moderate-sized, mixed-use project of 100 units of condominiums built over 20,000 square feet of retail. It illustrates a preliminary budget that matches funding sources to tasks through the development process. The budget, along with schedules and sequencing, would be updated regularly throughout the development process. The project value is estimated at $49,655,615, with costs of $40,253,450. Figure 4-1 shows the project scope, costs, and value.

The land cost is $4 million. The contract for purchase provides for an initial refundable deposit of $50,000 for a 60-day due diligence period. If the developer decides to proceed at the end of the due diligence period, another $100,000 deposit is due and the entire $150,000 becomes nonrefundable. At 180 days, an additional $200,000 deposit is due, and at 360 days, another $200,000 deposit. The remaining land price is due 30 days after entitlement. Figure 4-2 shows the anticipated project financing, with a 70 percent LTC ratio and a 10 percent co-investment requirement for the developer.

Figure 4-3 shows 35 tasks to complete over 900 days, from the beginning of the due diligence period to close-out. For tasks 1 through 26, the development entity is the sole funding source. At day 390 (approximately 13 months into the project), with the take-down of the land, the equity investors begin funding.

Note that updates of the market study occur at approximately six-month intervals. Also, the marketing program begins implementation at day 360, approximately five months before the end of construction.

Note also the point at which funding sources are approached. This occurs at day 105, after the schematic design is complete and the entitlement process has progressed to the point of some certainty. Shortly after the funding commitments are secured, the development entity is formed.

Finally, note when the lender funds: that is, after all the developer and equity investor funds have funded and at the start of construction. This funding does not occur all at once but is provided as payments that draw down the loan amount over the construction period as construction payments are due, so the amount outstanding on the loan starts at zero when construction begins and increases with construction draws so that the entire committed loan amount is outstanding at the end of construction.

FIGURE 4-1
Example Project: Scope, Costs, and Initial Value Estimates

Land Area	Acres	Sq. Ft.
Parcel 1	4.00	174,240

DEVELOPMENT PLAN

Residential	Number	Sq. Ft.	$/Sq. Ft.	Average Price	Total Value
Model 1, Market Rate	40	1,247	$350	$436,450	$17,458,000
Model 2, Market Rate	40	1,581	$325	$513,825	$20,553,000
Affordable	20	1,581	$135	$213,000	$4,260,000
Total Residential	100	144,740			**$42,271,000**
Commercial			Rent ($/Sq. Ft.)	Cap Rate	
Retail	20,000		$24	6.5%	$7,384,615
Total Value					**$49,655,615**

FIGURE 4-1 (continued)
Example Project: Scope, Costs, and Initial Value Estimates

PROJECT COSTS

Construction Costs		Sq. Ft./Unit	$/Sq. Ft.		Total Costs
Building Costs					
Residential		144,740	$120		$17,368,800
Commercial		20,000	$120		$2,400,000
Additional Parking		110	$3,000		$330,000
Site Development		174,240	$25		$4,356,000
Total Construction Costs					**$24,454,800**

	Units			$/Unit	
Development Fees	100			$20,000	**$2,000,000**
Land					**$4,000,000**

Soft Costs	%	Applied to:			
Design	5.0	construction costs			$1,222,740
Management	4.5	construction costs			$1,100,466
Marketing	4.0	sales value			$1,690,840
Financing	8.0	construction costs and development fees			$2,116,384
Contingency	15.0	construction costs			$3,668,220
Total Soft Costs					**$9,798,650**
Total Project Costs					**$40,253,450**
Maximum Supported Investment @ Hurdle Rate 20%					**$41,379,679**

FIGURE 4-2
Example Project: Financing

COSTS	
Construction, Development Fees	$26,454,800
Soft Costs	$9,798,650
Land	$4,000,000
Total Costs	**$40,253,450**
Less Marketing[a]	$1,690,840
Net Costs Financed from Debt and Equity	**$38,562,610**
FINANCING PACKAGE	
Bank Loan at 70%	$26,993,827
Equity Investment	$11,568,783
Total Financing	**$38,562,610**
Source of Equity	
Outside Investors at 90%	$10,411,905
Developer at 10%	$1,156,878
Total Equity Investment	**$11,568,783**

a. Marketing costs are funded out of sales and not included in financing.

FIGURE 4-3
Example Project: Source and Application of Funds to Tasks

	Task	Start Day	Complete Day	
1	Review all legal, regulatory, and environmental issues with legal counsel and city. Identify key issues -to resolve in predevelopment.	1	30	
2	Make initial land deposit.	1	1	
3	Conduct market study.	1	30	
4	Carry out pre-design.	1	30	
5	Conduct survey.	1	30	
6	Conduct environmental due diligence.	1	30	
7	Conduct contractor analysis of pre-design.	30	45	
End of Due Diligence				
8	Increase land deposit.	60	60	
9	Conduct preliminary traffic study.	45	75	
10	Develop schematic design.	75	90	
11	Conduct contractor analysis of schematic design.	90	105	
12	Review schematic design with city.	105	120	
13	Conduct final traffic analysis.	90	120	
14	Visit financing sources and get preliminary commitments.	105	120	
15	Prepare zoning, tentative map, and design review applications.	120	180	
16	Pay zoning and map application fees.	180	180	
17	Form development entity with investor group.	120	180	
18	Update market study.	150	180	
19	Make additional land deposit (six months).	180	180	
20	Processing of applications by local officials (planning commission, design review, city council).	180	360	
21	Conduct design development.	300	360	
22	Conduct contractor review of design development.	360	375	
23	Update market study.	340	360	
24	Implement marketing program.	360	390	
25	Make additional land deposit (one year).	360	360	
26	Obtain development approval from city.	360	360	
27	Prepare construction documents.	375	465	
28	Take down land.	390	390	
29	Update market study.	480	495	
30	Submit to city for plan check.	480	480	
31	Plan check is complete.	540	540	
32	Revise construction documents.	540	555	
33	Negotiate final price from contractor.	555	570	
34	Begin construction.	570	570	
35	Begin marketing.	750	900	

Notes	Payment	Total Cost	Developer	Equity Investor	Lender
				Funding Sources	
Discuss all issues with legal counsel before discussion with city. Costs are for legal counsel only.	$5,000	Total, tasks 1–7: $90,000 ($40,000 for due diligence tasks $50,000 for initial land deposit)	$90,000	$0	$0
Make initial refundable deposit.	$50,000				
Verify acquisition assumptions.	$5,000				
Develop conceptual design.	$7,500				
Confirm site size and boundaries.	$7,500				
Conduct Phase I environmental study.	$7,500				
Get the costs right.	$7,500				
All deposits are nonrefundable.	$100,000	Total, tasks 8–15: $240,000	$240,000	$0	$0
Involve traffic analysis in preliminary site layout.	$10,000				
Build in market analysis and result of traffic study.	$20,000				
All deposits are nonrefundable	$10,000				
Review will determine issues to address in final submittal.	$5,000				
Analysis is needed for final submittal.	$15,000				
Include discussion of schematic design, market, and cost analyses.	$5,000				
Allow two months for work by architect and engineer.	$75,000				
These are city fees.	$40,000	Total, tasks 16–26: $685,000	$685,000	$0	$0
This entails legal costs.	$20,000				
Monitor market.	$2,500				
Make third deposit, for a total of $350,000.	$200,000				
Estimate six months.	$100,000				
Begin two months before estimated completion of entitlement.	$100,000				
This is the final review before preparation of construction documents.	$20,000				
Monitor the market.	$2,500				
Engage brokers.					
Make fourth deposit, for a total of $550,000.	$200,000				
This event starts the 30-day period to close escrow.					
This marks 90 days to completion of tasks.	$300,000	Total, tasks 27–33: $5,872,500	$141,878	$5,730,622	$0
Thirty days after entitlement, pay balance remaining after deposits.	$3,450,000				
Monitor the market.	$2,500				
Pay plan check and development impact fees.	$2,100,000				
Respond to plan check.	$20,000				
Sign final contract.					
Receive project funds.	$31,675,110	$31,675,110		$4,681,283	$26,993,827
Broker starts work on marketing.	$1,690,840	$1,690,840	Funded from sales and leases		
Total Funds	$40,253,450	$40,253,450	$1,156,878	$10,411,905	$26,993,827

market is critical to success. If a developer uses a contractor that has limited experience in a region, it is important to get that contractor involved early enough to achieve familiarity with local subcontractors.

Another criterion for selecting the architect and contractor relates to their familiarity with the product type. Some architects and contractors specialize in only one or two product types. In addition, the particular market segment is a factor, so the selection of the architect and contractor may require consideration of whether they can design and build a product to appeal to the particular market.

In addition to hiring competent firms to do the work, a developer must take a special interest in the personnel assigned by the firms. For the architect, the key personnel are the project manager and the project principal. These two people must have extensive experience with the product type. They are also the key people who will liaise with the contractor. For the contractor, the developer should interview two key people:

- The construction project manager, who
  - Provides the conceptual budget and schedule;
  - Creates the bidders list;
  - Builds the production schedule and delivery sequence;
  - Qualifies bids;
  - Defines the scope of work and negotiates with subcontractors;
  - Manages administrative controls; and
  - Acts as the liaison between the architect or developer, and production personnel on specifications and change orders.
- The job superintendent, who
  - Coordinates and inspects the work of subcontractors;
  - Manages the schedule;
  - Expedites the delivery and storage of material;
  - Processes project paperwork; and
  - Ensures the site is clean and orderly.

OTHER SERVICES

The remaining services involve legal, engineering, market analysis, marketing, and specialized consultants, such as for traffic, noise, environmental issues, or wetlands. These services are usually provided on an hourly basis, but they may be charged at a fixed price based on a scope of work.

One of the early services involves a market study. The developer should contract with a firm that specializes in these studies. Some developers use brokers to assist with the market analysis, and some brokerage firms do have the capacity to perform this function. However, a broker's opinion is probably not sufficient to convince financing sources of the validity of the market analysis, so hiring a firm that specializes in these studies makes sense, especially in tumultuous market conditions.

Legal services are usually provided by a law firm that contracts directly with the developer, working on retainer or on an hourly basis. Some specialized services are contracted for by the architect or contractor, some by the developer. For instance, the architect may hire the noise or traffic consultant. Non-design-related services, such as environmental or market analyses, are contracted for by the developer. In general, engineering services are provided by local firms familiar with local conditions that are almost always retained by the architect. Marketing services are most often provided through a brokerage service, which gets paid from sale or lease commissions.

Task Funding

As the developer maps out and budgets the tasks for a development project, it is important to match the funding sources to the task. The developer must estimate how much developer capital is needed in order to demonstrate to outside capital sources that the project is financially viable, so that these sources will start participating in funding tasks. The expenditures necessary to reach that level of certainty about financial viability can be significant, and they should be planned.

In today's capital markets, the developer usually has a coinvestment requirement of 10 percent of the equity component of the project. This means that the developer usually funds project costs up to the level of the coinvestment before the equity investors put their funds into the project.

CHAPTER 5

Capital Markets for Real Estate

R eal estate prices, values, and investment activity depend significantly on circumstances in the broader capital markets. This chapter begins with a brief discussion of the relationship of commercial real estate to conditions in the capital markets. It then describes the major categories of capital sources and profiles their activity. Because many capital sources invest money they receive from others, this chapter discusses how fiduciary principles create accountability, transparency, and shared control of a project. Finally, it outlines categories of investment types and describes how project characteristics affect project financing.

Private nonresidential real estate investment (excluding corporate, nonprofit, and government equity holdings) in 2008 totaled $4.76 trillion, with 75.6 percent funded from debt and 24.4 percent funded from equity, according to Roulac Global Places (as cited in *Emerging Trends in Real Estate 2009*). Figure 5-1 shows the distribution of this investment among broad categories of capital sources.

The crash of 2008 had a significant effect on these sources, dramatically reducing real estate values and causing changes in capital availability and investment criteria. Because this extreme turmoil will significantly influence how lending and investing occur over the next decade, this chapter includes a brief discussion of the underlying dynamics of the crisis.

Capital Market Conditions

Over the past 25 years, commercial real estate investment has been tremendously affected by innovation, capital flows, and the velocity of transactions in the broader capital markets, with glaring evidence of this in the turmoil of the period from 2007 to 2010. New players—equity real estate investment trusts (REITs), unlisted public REITs, commercial mortgage–backed security (CMBS) issuers, private equity funds, opportunity funds, and hedge funds—have entered the real estate space looking for value and creating new investment and transaction structures. These new players created new avenues for small investors, institutional investors, and high–net worth investors to invest in real estate, including high-risk/high-return approaches often focused on quick transactions, development, or "turnaround" properties.

FIGURE 5-1
Capital Sources for Nonresidential U.S. Real Estate, 2008

Total: $4.758 trillion

Debt: $3.60 trillion (75.6%)

Equity: $1.16 trillion (24.4%)

Life Insurance Companies: 9%
REIT Debt: 4.5%
Government Credit Agencies: 5%
Pension Funds: 1%
Banks, S&Ls, Mutual Savings Banks: 55%
Public Untraded Funds: >0%
Commercial Mortgage–Backed Securities: 26%

Foreign Investors: 5%
Life Insurance Companies: 3%
Private Financial Institutions: 2%
Public Untraded Funds: 3%
Equity REITs: 26%
Pension Funds: 13%
Private Investors: 48%

Note: Excludes corporate, nonprofit, and government equity real estate holdings, and single-family and owner-occupied residences.
Sources: Roulac Global Places, American Council of Life Insurers, Commercial Mortgage Alert, Federal Reserve Board, FannieMae.com, IREI, NAREIT, PricewaterhouseCoopers, and Real Capital Analytics.

Niall Ferguson, in *The Ascent of Money*, describes the backdrop of the frenetic change in capital markets that led to the crash of 2008:

> *At times the ascent of money has seemed inexorable. In 2006 the measured economic output of the entire world was around $47 trillion. The total market capitalization of the word's stock markets was $51 trillion, 10 percent larger. The total value of domestic and international bonds was $68 trillion, 50 percent larger. The amount of derivatives outstanding was $473 trillion, more than ten times larger. Planet Finance is beginning to dwarf Planet Earth. And Planet Finance seems to spin faster too. Every day $2 trillion change hands on foreign exchange markets. Every month $7 trillion change hands on global stock markets. Every minute of every hour of every day of every week, someone, somewhere, is trading. And all the time new financial forms are evolving. … An explosion of "securitization," whereby individual debts like mortgages are "tranched," then bundled together and repackaged for sale, pushed the total annual issuance of mortgage-backed securities, asset-backed securites, and collateralized debt obligations above $3 trillion. … Before the 1980s such things were virtually unknown. … If the last four millennia witnessed the ascent of man the thinker, we now seem to be living through the ascent of man the banker.*

Real estate investment, as discussed in chapter 2, uses leverage to enhance returns on equity, a practice that was pushed to its breaking point with the 2008 crash. As Ferguson continues,

The first hedge fund was set up in the 1940s and, as recently as 1990, there were just 610 of them, with $38 billion under management. There are now [in 2008] over 7,000, with $1.9 trillion under management. Private equity partnerships have also multiplied, as well as a veritable shadow banking system of "conduits" and "structured investment vehicles" (SIVs) designed to keep risky assets off bank balance sheets.[1]

As changes have occurred in the pace and form of capital markets generally, real estate investment has become more entwined with market conditions in other sectors and has experienced substanstial swings in valuations and viability as a result. At the beginning of 2008, the valuation of commercial real estate had increased by almost 37 percent since 2005—not as a result of commensurate growth in net operating income but, many would argue, because of the growing "weight of capital" seeking real estate investments and the increased use of leverage enhanced with low-cost or interest-only debt. Other investment sectors saw similar gains, fueled by the weight of capital and the run-up in leverage. The U.S. stock market valuation in early 2008 was about $15 trillion—an increase of about 21 percent since 2005. The valuation of the world's stock markets in 2008 was $51 trillion, an increase of more than 37 percent since 2005.

But these gains came crashing down in concert with the collapse of the residential mortgage–backed security market. By the end of 2008, stock market values had dropped precipitously, with U.S. stocks losing 36 percent and stocks worldwide almost 44 percent. Commercial real estate values—as measured by the Massachusetts Institute of Technology Center for Real Estate (MIT CRE) index—dropped 23 percent; they dropped another 13 percent through November 2009. REIT share prices also dropped, with a loss of 47 percent in the price of the i-Shares Dow Jones U.S. Real Estate exchange-traded fund (ETF), which measures a basket of U.S. REITs, and a loss of 37 percent in the National Association of Real Estate Investment Trust All REIT Index. Housing prices experienced an 18.3 percent drop in the Standard & Poor's Case-Shiller residential property value index.

The entwining of real estate and other sectors is particularly striking when looking at the U.S. bond market, which includes both public and private debt issues. According to the Financial Industry Regulatory Authority, in 2007, the total amount of debt outstanding in the U.S. bond market was $29 trillion. Much of this debt was tied to real estate; approximately 25 percent ($7.2 trillion) consisted of securities backed primarily by private residential mortgages and secured by residential real estate value. Another 10 percent of these securities were backed by commercial mortgages. And another 10 percent ($2.9 trillion) were Federal agency bonds, also mortgage-related because they involve the activities of the Federal National Mortgage Association (Fannie Mae) and the Federal Home Loan Mortgage Corporation (Freddie Mac), the two principal public purchasers of residential mortgages. In other words, 45 percent of the debt outstanding in the U.S. bond market was related to real estate.

Most experts attribute the crash of 2008 to the collapse in value of residential mortgage–backed securities resulting from declines in home prices and the sudden change in perception of the underlying residential real estate values—namely, that they were insufficient to secure the bonds.[2] With the implosion of bond values in this sector, a cascade of insolvencies occurred among both holders and insurers of the securities, with a consequent freezing of credit in all sectors. The result was a black hole of downwardly spiraling values generally in real estate and all other equity sectors.

Commercial real estate investment is, of course, a different industry than residential mortgages, despite some similarities in terminology and financial structure. Unlike most residential borrowers, commercial borrowers tend to be real estate professionals and their project financing rests on an assessment of property income rather than on personal income. Consequently, loans in commercial real estate have more consistent underwriting criteria than existed in the residential arena.

Nevertheless, valuations in commercial real estate did decline significantly as a result of the crash of 2008, creating significant losses for investors and lenders. Many of these losses were unrealized and deferred because many lenders kept marginally performing loans on their books in hopes that economic conditions and valuations would recover (the so-called "extend and pretend" practice). This strategy did succeed in avoiding precipitous losses but also shifted problems into the future.

Part of the fallout and a hallmark of this crisis is the so-called "maturity wall" of commercial real estate loans expiring through 2014 that will have to be refinanced in the face of lower market values and lower leverage criteria. The effect of this refinancing challenge on capital markets was uncertain at the time of this writing, but as the Congressional Oversight Panel established under the Emergency Economic Stabilization Act of 2008 noted in a February 2010 report, it could significantly affect real estate lenders:

> Between 2010 and 2014, about $1.4 trillion in commercial real estate loans will reach the end of their terms. Nearly half are at present "underwater"—that is, the borrower owes more than the underlying property is currently worth. Commercial property values have fallen more than 40 percent since the beginning of 2007. Increased vacancy rates, which now range from 8 percent for multifamily housing to 18 percent for office buildings, and falling rents, which have declined 40 percent for office space and 33 percent for retail space, have exerted a powerful downward pressure on the value of commercial properties. The largest commercial real estate loan losses are projected for 2011 and beyond; losses at banks alone could range as high as $200 to $300 billion.

On the upside, though, these declines have created significant buying opportunities for those able to capitalize on distressed and low property values. Numerous pools of capital have been formed for this purpose, and it is likely that once losses are realized, an orderly flow of capital will be restored.

Some characterize the crash of 2008 as a return to normal, and perhaps the lower leverage and tighter underwriting standards post-crash will persist, at least until complacency sets in and the next bubble occurs. Until recovery occurs, however, developers are likely to see replacement costs (the cost of new development) remain at substantially higher levels than market values and, as a consequence, are likely to experience difficulty in obtaining capital for new development in most markets.

Capital Sources

Depending on their risk-return profile, capital sources tend to specialize in different financing components of a real estate project. The low-cost debt layers, secured by the ability to foreclose on the property if the debt is not paid, fund the lowest-risk component. After

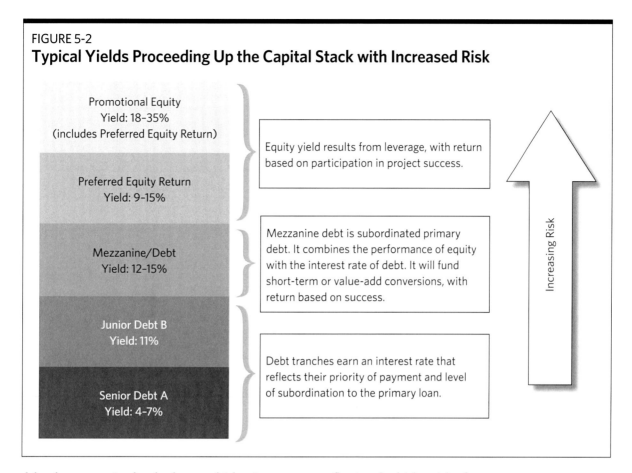

FIGURE 5-2
Typical Yields Proceeding Up the Capital Stack with Increased Risk

Promotional Equity
Yield: 18–35%
(includes Preferred Equity Return)

Preferred Equity Return
Yield: 9–15%

Mezzanine/Debt
Yield: 12–15%

Junior Debt B
Yield: 11%

Senior Debt A
Yield: 4–7%

Equity yield results from leverage, with return based on participation in project success.

Mezzanine debt is subordinated primary debt. It combines the performance of equity with the interest rate of debt. It will fund short-term or value-add conversions, with return based on success.

Debt tranches earn an interest rate that reflects their priority of payment and level of subordination to the primary loan.

Increasing Risk

debt, the mezzanine levels charge a higher interest rate, reflecting the higher risk of a lower priority of payment subordinated to senior and junior debt. The equity layers have the highest risk because payment comes solely from project performance after paying the senior, junior, and mezzanine debt. Figure 5-2 illustrates how the return needed to attract capital to each layer of funding increases with risk, from debt to equity.

The sources of real estate capital are diverse, ranging from individuals to large organizations and institutions. Individuals can include a project operating partner who recruits friends, family members, and business associates to invest on the basis of personal relationships. Organizations and institutions can include commingled funds of high–net worth individuals and organizations, pension funds, endowments, life insurance companies, banks, corporations, and many more types.

Most projects have multiple capital sources participating, which requires that a development entity be legally structured to protect the interests of all sources. With multiple lenders, there will be inter-creditor agreements to stipulate the priority of recovery in the event of default. In addition to priority of participation in profits, there will be other issues such as governance, assignment of liability, and approval rights. Chapter 7 describes how a development entity is organized and how these issues are addressed. Figure 5-3 summarizes the major categories of capital for commercial real estate and the primary focus of their funding activity.

FIGURE 5-3
Sources of Capital for Real Estate

DEBT SOURCES	DESCRIPTION
Banks	U.S. banks are the largest source of capital for real estate investment; they have almost $2 trillion in construction and permanent loans. Smaller banks hold a disproportionate share of loans; they have only about 20% of total bank assets but hold 47% of loans.
Commercial Mortgage–Backed Securities	CMBS are securities issued on a pool of commercial loans. The total dollar value outstanding in 2008 was 26% of debt. Issuance declined precipitously in 2008 and 2009 and resumed on a limited scale in 2010.
Insurance Companies	Life insurance companies provide 9% of total debt. They have historically been commercial real estate lenders, putting to work cash from policy sales.
Mortgage REITs	Publicly traded mortgage REITs provide 4% of debt, raising capital through public sale of stock.
Government Credit Agencies	About 5% of debt is provided through bonds issued by agencies such as Fannie Mae and Freddie Mac.
Pension Funds and Private, Nonbank, Untraded Funds	Providing about 1% of debt, this diverse group of lending sources operates through syndicates or firms, such as GE Capital, providing primary and mezzanine loans.
EQUITY SOURCES	
Private Investors (including private equity and private untraded funds)	This diverse category includes individuals, syndicates, private equity funds, private financial institutions, and private untraded funds. These sources represent 53% of total equity. These investors include nine types: • Developer assets and equity • High–net worth local investors and "country club" sources • Land owners • High–net worth national investors • 1031 Tenant in Common investors • Opportunity funds • Hedge funds • Private untraded funds • Private financial institutions.
Equity REITs	Providing 26% of equity, these REITs raise capital through public offerings and engage directly in development.
Pension Funds	Providing 13% of equity, pension funds typically place allocations of assets into real estate through an investment manager.
Foreign Investors	Providing 5% of equity, investors from Europe, Australia, and the Middle East place their investments primarily through investment managers.

Note: Percentages are from 2008 data provided by Roulac Global Places, as cited in *Emerging Trends in Real Estate 2009.*

The following sections provide short profiles of each major capital source discussing its source of funding and investment criteria, starting with the major debt and equity sources.

BANKS, SAVINGS AND LOANS, AND MUTUAL SAVINGS BANKS

Banks are the largest investor in commercial real estate at approximately $2 trillion, more than 40 percent of the total capitalization in the industry. Most loans are "relationship based"; that is, made in the context of a business relationship that involves multiple projects and broader services. Most banks are also "whole loan" lenders that keep all or significant percentages of loans, often construction loans, on their books—though banks also syndicate loans to diversify risk.

As highlighted in figure 5-3, small banks keep more of the loans they originate on their books than large banks. Commercial real estate loans make up less than 15 percent of assets for all banks. But banks with assets greater than $10 billion—that is, with almost 80 percent of assets—have only 53 percent of these loans (constituting less than 9 percent of their total assets). Smaller banks with assets lower than $10 billion have 20 percent of total assets and hold 47 percent of the loans (constituting about 31 percent of their assets). Figure 5-4 summarizes the distribution of commercial real estate debt (including whole loans and holdings of CMBS) held by the approximately 6,900 banks insured by the Federal Deposit Insurance Corporation in October 2009.

Because of competitive pressures, smaller banks specialize in a portion of the commercial real estate capital market. The Congressional Oversight Panel, in February 2010, described how this competition resulted in smaller banks specializing in lending for all but the larger commercial projects:

FIGURE 5-4

Commercial Real Estate Exposure of Commercial Banks, as a Share of Assets, 2010

Commercial Banks (by Asset Size)	Number of Banks	Share of Total (%)	Assets ($ Trillions)	Share of Total (%)	Total CRE Whole Loan Exposure ($ Billions)	Share of Total (%)	Proportion of CRE Loan Exposure to Total Assets (%)
More than $10 billion	85	1.2	9.5	79.7	84.3	53.1	8.9
$1 billion–$10 billion	440	6.4	1.2	9.8	364.5	23.0	31.5
$100 million–$1 billion	3,798	55.0	1.1	9.3	353.7	22.3	32.0
Less than $100 million	2,588	37.4	0.1	1.2	27.0	1.7	18.9
Total	6,911		11.9		1,587.9		

Note: CRE = commercial real estate.
Source: FDIC.

During the boom in residential real estate in the early to mid-2000s, larger institutions and less regulated players came to dominate most credit offerings to individual consumers, such as home mortgages and credit cards. In response to this increased competition in other areas, smaller and community banks increased their focus on commercial real estate lending. Commercial real estate lending, which typically requires greater investigation into individual loans and borrowers, also caters to the strengths of smaller and community financial institutions.

As a result, these smaller institutions could generate superior returns in commercial real estate, and many institutions grew to have high commercial real estate concentrations on their balance sheets.

At the same time, commercial real estate secured by large properties with steady income streams, the highest-quality borrowers in the space, gravitated towards origination by larger institutions with subsequent distribution to the CMBS market. These properties typically require larger loans than smaller and community banks can provide, and the greater resources of larger institutions and the secondary market can better satisfy these needs. The CMBS market therefore captured many of the most secure commercial real estate investments.

Smaller banks, holding the bulk of loans for smaller projects in secondary markets, have focused in the past and are likely to focus in the future on "relationship-based lending." As long as an existing loan is performing, such banks have been able in the aftermath of the 2008 crash to avoid looking too closely at the drop in loan-to-value (LTV) ratios, which has inevitably occurred as a result of the drop in real estate values. For non-performing loans, banks pick and choose whether to work with the borrower and wait out the downturn by forbearing on foreclosure and renegotiating the loan terms to see what happens. This alternative is more likely to occur with a customer that has a long-term relationship with the bank and a solid business plan.

The banks must also deal with loans for which forbearance has no likely upside. For these loans, foreclosures wipe out equity, including any mezzanine debt, likely leaving banks with an inventory of REO (real estate owned) properties that they must sell. Frequently, the buyers of these properties ask banks to provide seller financing (that is, financing by the banks who own the properties), which has the effect of keeping the loans on the banks' balance sheets, albeit at a lower value. The new loans are then categorized as "performing" and therefore add to the banks' balance sheets.

For some time, banks will be in a much stronger position to set loan terms and select which projects to finance. Lending is likely to be limited to customers that have other banking relationships and strong reputations for reliability and competence. Loan terms are likely to have lower leverage, high debt coverage ratios, and conventional amortization structures. Along with the other "whole loan" lenders (life insurance companies and REITs), banks will have a very strong ability to enforce terms favorable to the lender (themselves) on most loans over at least the next five years. In mid-2010, however, there was already evidence that lending standards are loosening for prime properties in prime markets.

These observations lead to two conclusions:

- The large money center banks will continue to originate the majority of commercial real estate loans for larger projects in primary markets. As the CMBS market recovers, many of these loans will increasingly be securitized through that market.
- Smaller institutions will continue to be players in commercial real estate for smaller projects and in secondary markets.

COMMERCIAL MORTGAGE–BACKED SECURITIES

As ULI's 2006 publication, *Emerging Trends in Real Estate*, said, "Nothing short of revolutionary, the CMBS impact on U.S. real estate markets has been mostly responsible for providing a strong, consistent source of liquidity to property owners." Until 2008, that is.

The CMBS market was created as an outgrowth of the liquidation of assets from the Resolution Trust Corporation, the entity formed in the late 1980s and early 1990s to take over and sell foreclosed assets from the savings and loan crisis. This market securitized loans on commercial real estate similarly to the way residential mortgages are securitized in the residential market. Banks, life insurance companies, and loan originators would write the loan and then sell it to a pool of loans classified into rated tiers, which were securitized and sold as bonds. Figure 5-5 illustrates the process of pooling mortgages and selling the resulting securities in rated tiers (or tranches).

FIGURE 5-5
Process for Securitizing Mortgages into Rated Tranches

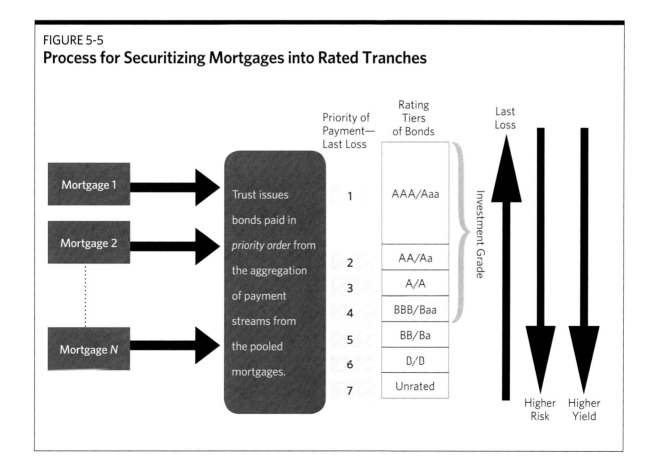

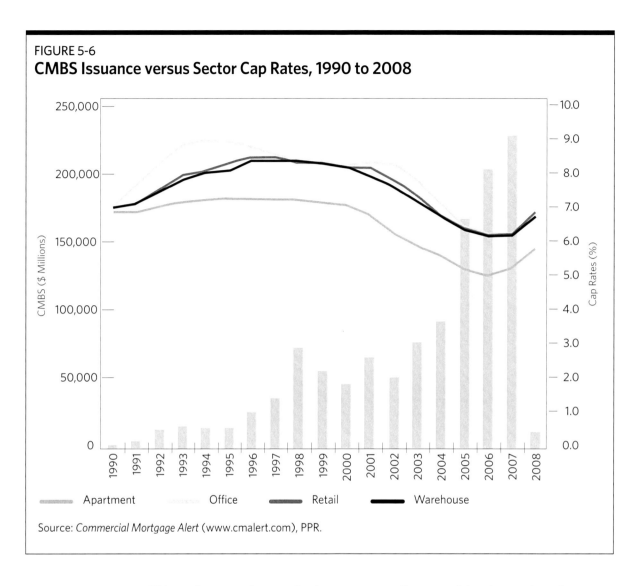

FIGURE 5-6

CMBS Issuance versus Sector Cap Rates, 1990 to 2008

Source: *Commercial Mortgage Alert* (www.cmalert.com), PPR.

This market created a completely new source of commercial real estate loan financing. Because it enhanced leverage opportunities, the effect of the greater liquidity in debt markets that CMBS created was to lower cap rates and increase property values. Figure 5-6 shows the progression of this financing source from 1990 to 2008. CMBS issuance peaked in 2007 with $200 billion. As the market collapsed in 2008, cap rates turned up, property values turned down, and CMBS issuance essentially stopped.

At the beginning of 2010, several large institutions (Bank of America, Citigroup, Goldman Sachs, JP Morgan, Bridger) re-entered the CMBS market looking for projects to underwrite on remarkably favorable terms: typically 60 to 75 percent of LTV, and five-year to ten-year terms with 30-year amortization at 6.75 to 7.5 percent interest. Underwriting was confined to stabilized properties in primary markets with some sectors, such as retail or hospitality, disqualified from some of the programs because of concerns about sector risk. Financing for new development projects through CMBS may follow eventually, but the valuations of existing properties will need to climb above replacement costs for this to occur.

As the Congressional Oversight Panel noted in its February 2010 report,

Unlike the residential real estate market, where banks generally kept the best residential mortgages and securitized the riskier loans into [residential mortgage–backed securities], CMBS loans were generally made to higher-quality, stable properties with more reliable cash flow streams (e.g., a fully leased office building).

The CMBS market was able to siphon off the highest-quality commercial properties through lower interest rates and more allowable leverage. Banks, particularly mid-size and small banks, were left lending to transitional properties or construction projects with more uncertain cash flows or to less sought-after properties in secondary or tertiary markets.

Even with the focus on higher-quality properties, many of the same lax loan practices that started in the residential market made their way into the CMBS market before the collapse. As noted in the Congressional Oversight Panel report, many loans from 2006 onward were underwritten based on pro forma analyses, not actual net operating income; debt calculated as "interest only" for the first few years of the loan to meet debt-coverage ratios; and financing of an interest reserve in the loan, which allowed a project to buy time to generate cash flow. The CMBS sector will be working out a significant number of these problem loans before it completely recovers.

Fixing problem loans has long been understood as a weakness in the CMBS sector; the post-crash difficulties have simply magnified it. Since its inception, the reputation of the CMBS sector has been that "there is no one to work with if you have a problem." The trustee (also a master servicer or special servicer) of a CMBS pool has limited options in working with the owner of a distressed CMBS-funded property that experiences difficulties, such as the bankruptcy of a major tenant or a drop in appraised value below the LTV covenant. Problems such as these, whether real or technical default, often require the trustee to foreclose. Of course, the borrower can attempt to find other capital sources to stanch the funding gap, but at the lower property values, these other sources will have the effect of diluting existing equity or creating additional lien holders subordinated to the primary mortgage. Until 2008, the primary solution for CMBS borrowers was to replace the original CMBS loan with another short-term CMBS loan set to expire after the temporary difficulty was expected to be resolved. As more and more CMBS properties face foreclosure, property value reductions generally in the commercial market mean that a number of loans will be written down significantly.

Going forward, the CMBS sector will experience losses and it will tighten underwriting standards, to fund only the best properties and to attract buyers of the securities. There will also likely be greater government oversight and regulation as a prerequisite to any return of this important form of conduit financing.

PRIVATE EQUITY CAPITAL

Private equity is an extremely diverse category of capital. It ranges from private local investors that purchase for their own account or partner with a developer to large private equity funds of "institutional" money managed by private equity firms.

HIGH–NET WORTH INDIVIDUALS, SYNDICATES, AND 1031 TIC INVESTORS

Some high–net worth individuals invest directly through a direct purchase or equity investment. These investors tend to be low-leverage, long-term holders of property. They are also a principal source of tax-deferred exchange transactions involving trading up to a higher-priced property to avoid capital gains tax under IRS Code Section 1031. Because properties worth less than $5 million are a target of such investors, transactions in this category are frequently more numerous than in other categories and cap rates for properties in this price range compete with those of the trophy properties in primary markets. Figure 5-7 shows this distribution of transaction volume for retail projects in the United States in 2008.

Other high–net worth individuals invest indirectly by participating in a syndication, sometimes called a commingled fund. This frequently takes the form of a limited partnership or, less frequently, a corporation or private REIT. These syndications typically have a syndication manager, often the general manager of a limited partnership, who manages the pool of assets with a focus on specific investment objectives for which the investment pool was raised. The syndicator usually does not invest much of its own capital, instead earning a management fee.

Some of these syndications are closed-end funds that accumulate and deploy a pool of capital over a planned time period with a planned liquidation date at which the investors receive a final pro-rated distribution. Frequently, a closed-end fund trades among sophisticated investors, usually at some discount compared with asset value. Open-end funds allow investors to sell and redeem shares directly, on the basis of the current asset value, which is usually based on an appraisal.

Aside from limited partnerships, real estate investors use numerous other types of syndication structures. They include "blind pools," in which the syndicator has great discretion over the properties or types of investments to be funded, and public syndicates, which are structured to allow the interests to be sold to investors in different states. One form of these pools is the 1031 Tenant In Common (TIC) structure. It allows individuals to aggregate properties into a pool that is professionally managed, with each participant owning a share and receiving income and an allocation of tax losses. The shares can be traded for shares in other TIC pools to enable the deferral of capital gains taxes or they can be sold.

Syndications are formed around particular investment objectives. Objectives, which vary widely, are articulated in the offering circular for the pool. Examples of objectives include the following:

■ Focus on acquisition of distressed or underperforming properties at a favorable price with the intention of repositioning the property through renovation or retenanting;

■ Purchase of property to obtain development entitlements after which the property is sold at a higher price reflecting the new use; and

■ Purchase of "opportunity" properties from financial institutions that have foreclosed and wish to move the asset off their balance sheets and take the writedown for loss in value.

These investment vehicles are sometimes traded, but more often not. In general, these investment options require that a private investor be an "accredited" or "sophisti-

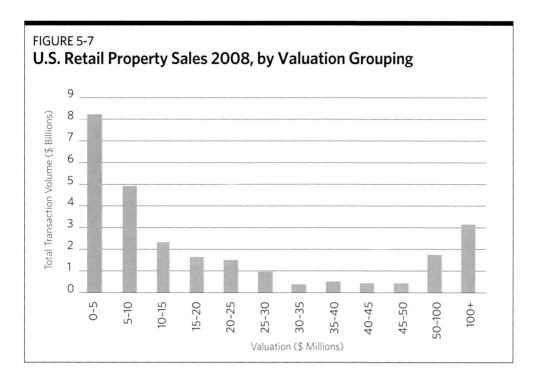

FIGURE 5-7
U.S. Retail Property Sales 2008, by Valuation Grouping

Total Transaction Volume ($ Billions) / Valuation ($ Millions)

cated" investor. An accredited investor is defined in Regulation D of the Securities Act of 1933, as well as in state regulations. In general, such an investor is either an individual with a net worth of at least $1 million or a regular annual income of at least $200,000 ($300,000 when combined with spouse), a business organization with total assets of at least $5 million, or some other category defined in the regulation.

PRIVATE EQUITY FUNDS SPONSORED BY PRIVATE EQUITY FIRMS

Moving up the spectrum from local real estate syndications, there are the larger private equity funds sponsored by private equity firms. These funds aggregate capital from institutional investors primarily and sometimes, if minimum investment requirements are low enough, from accredited investors. Institutional investors include pension funds, endowments, foundations, hedge funds, mutual funds, banks, and insurance companies.

A private equity firm manages the pool of resources in a fund according to a strategy articulated at the fund's formation. Participants in the pool commit their contribution at the outset of the fund and pay it into the fund during the first few years of operation as capital is deployed into investments. Usually, the fund liquidates within a ten-year period.

The private equity firms, which include the Blackstone Group, the Carlyle Group, Apollo Management, and Kohlberg, Kravis, and Roberts, often engage in a wide spectrum of investments beyond real estate investment, including leveraged buyouts, venture capital, growth capital, distressed investments, and mezzanine capital. Private equity real estate funds emerged in the early 1990s to invest in high-risk/high-return opportunities, often focusing on opportunistic investments and short-term turnaround properties.

Perhaps the most iconic example of investment by these private equity real estate funds was the February 2007 purchase, by a fund managed by the Blackstone Group, of Sam Zell's Equity Office Properties REIT portfolio for $23 billion plus $16 billion in assumed debt. The portfolio of 573 properties was then the largest private equity deal in history (it was surpassed in October 2007 by the KKR purchase of the Texas utility company, TXU). Blackstone immediately resold 70 percent of the portfolio for $27 billion to 16 other companies, retaining only 105 of the properties.

Within months, however, this deal turned sour as property values dropped and many of the purchasers faced foreclosure on debt that they had incurred to make their purchases. A *New York Times* article of February 6, 2009, characterized this transaction as follows:

> *Buyers purchased buildings at what, in retrospect, were vastly inflated prices. Lenders provided lavish, even excessive, financing based on unrealistic expectations of rising rents. And now that values are tumbling, vacancy rates are rising, and credit has become impossibly tight, many on both sides are struggling against default, foreclosure, or bankruptcy.*

Quoted in the same article, Michael Knott, a real estate analyst at Green Street Advisors, said, "Those who bought from Blackstone have not fared well at all. Blackstone was a huge winner at the time, although the value of what they still hold has fallen probably 20 percent." Like most private equity firms, Blackstone Group is a limited partnership. In June 2007, however, Blackstone completed a $4 billion initial public offering to become one of the first major private equity firms to list shares in its management company on a public exchange.

Compensation to the private equity firms for their fund management is in two forms: first, they receive an annual fee of 1 to 2 percent of assets under management; second, they receive a percentage (usually 20 percent) of earnings after returning investors' principal. This "carried interest" is a share of earnings from the investments.

The tax treatment of earnings from private equity funds has generated some controversy. Because the private equity firms are organized as limited partnerships, the earnings paid to fund participants are paid out without an entity tax as investment earnings, not ordinary income. Carried interest income to the fund manager has also been treated as investment income taxed at capital gains rates instead of ordinary income rates.

Other terms of private equity funds include the following:

■ At fund formation, the manager typically commits to paying investors a preferred return of 8 to 12 percent before carried interest is paid.

■ Investment in a private equity fund is typically not transferrable or if allowed, is transferrable only with the consent of the fund manager.

■ The manager of the fund usually has broad discretion to make investment decisions with only general controls from the limited partners (the investors) on the type, size, geographic focus, or duration of investments.

Even as their legacy investments struggle after property price declines, private equity firms continue to be major players in real estate capital markets, forming new opportunity funds to take advantage of buying opportunities.

HEDGE FUNDS

Hedge funds are a type of private equity fund that tends to attract high-leverage, high-risk players focused on transactional shorter-term opportunities. They are recent players in real estate investment, often entering the space as an offshoot of a transaction involving the real estate of a target investment. For instance, a typical transaction of a hedge fund involves stripping the real estate assets from a company that is the target of investment. So, for instance, the sites of a retailer that owns its stores could be sold and then leased back from the purchaser.

Hedge funds share many of the characteristics of private equity funds in terms of investors, fees, and management, but their investment strategy tends to focus on shorter-term investments. As high-leverage players with limited experience and a focus on opportunistic, high-yield/high-risk transactions, their participation in real estate in the future is uncertain.

REAL ESTATE INVESTMENT TRUSTS

According to the National Association of Real Estate Investment Trusts, a REIT is a company that has

> *most of its assets and income tied to real estate investment and must distribute at least 90 percent of its taxable income to shareholders annually in the form of dividends. A company that qualifies as a REIT is permitted to deduct dividends paid to its shareholders from its corporate taxable income. As a result, most REITs historically remit at least 100 percent of their taxable income to their shareholders and therefore owe no corporate tax. Taxes are paid by shareholders on the dividends received and any capital gains.*

Created by federal law in 1960, REITs capture some of the tax advantages of a limited partnership, because income is not subject to an entity tax as long as at least 90 percent of income is distributed to shareholders. This ownership structure eliminates the "double taxation" of corporate profits that U.S. corporations experience when they pay corporate income tax on overall profits and their stockholders pay tax on any distribution of a portion of these profits as dividends. A disadvantage is that tax losses are trapped inside REITs and not permitted to be passed directly to investors as they are with partnerships, limited liability corporations, and S corporations.

Changes in the federal tax law in 1986 permitted the consolidated ownership and management of real estate by REITs, broadening their role from that of merely real estate lenders and investors (mortgage REITs). This change resulted in a dramatic expansion of the role REITs play in real estate investment. Growth accelerated in the early 1990s, with market capitalization peaking in 2006, followed by dramatic losses through 2008 and the start of recovery in 2009. Figure 5-8 depicts the growth of REITs from 1971 through 2009.

The most widely known REITs, making up the bulk of the industry, are publicly traded equity REITs that own, buy, sell, operate, and often develop income-producing real estate. Mortgage REITs are also publicly traded, but own mortgages rather than properties. Hybrid REITs own both property and mortgages. There are also private REITs and unlisted REITs that are not publicly traded but still benefit from the preferred tax status that REITs enjoy. The REIT universe contains some well-known names, including Simon Property Group, AvalonBay Communities, ProLogis, Regency Centers Corporation, and Vornado Realty Trust.

Because shares in a REIT are stock in an enterprise that invests in real estate, offering substantially enhanced liquidity for real estate investment, REITs provide investors

FIGURE 5-8
REIT Growth, 1971 through 2009

End of Year	Composite REITs		Equity REITs		Mortgage REITs		Hybrid REITs	
	Number	Market Capitalization ($ Billions)	Number	Market Capitalization ($ Billions)	Number	Market Capitalization ($ Billions)	Number	Market Capitalization ($ Billions)
1971	34	1.49	12	0.33	12	0.57	10	0.59
1980	75	2.30	35	0.94	21	0.51	19	0.85
1985	82	7.67	37	3.27	32	3.16	13	1.24
1990	119	8.74	58	5.55	43	2.55	18	0.64
1995	219	57.54	178	49.91	24	3.40	17	4.23
2000	189	138.72	158	134.43	22	1.63	9	2.65
2005	197	330.69	152	301.49	37	23.39	8	5.81
2006	183	438.07	138	400.74	38	29.20	7	8.13
2007	152	312.01	118	288.69	29	19.05	5	4.26
2008	136	191.65	113	176.24	20	14.28	3	1.13
2009	142	271.20	115	248.36	23	22.10	4	0.74

with an opportunity to invest in managed real estate holdings, to spread risk through diversified holdings, and to acquire interests in assets that would ordinarily be beyond their means. However, because REITs are publicly traded companies, the prices of these securities can be volatile, with steep declines or increases over short periods.

The access that REITs have to capital has placed them in a particuarly strong position to succeed post-crash. Through the sale of additional shares or unsecured debt offerings, REITs were able to raise signficant capital in 2009 when capital markets were generally highly constrained; this gave them access to low-cost capital to repair balance sheets damaged by the drop in property values. This success has caused many private capital operators to consider converting to a publicly traded REIT.

In recent years, some REITs have used forms of partnership structures to acquire properties and to combine the capital-raising ability of a REIT with the tax and ownership advantages of a partnership. Umbrella partnership REITs (UPREITs) and downREITs use REIT capital to make limited partnership investments in property owned by a separate or subsidiary partnership. In the typical UPREIT, the partners in an existing partnership form a new operating partnership with a newly formed REIT. The REIT raises cash through the public offering of shares and the old existing partnership contributes its properties. The REIT typically is the general partner and the majority owner of the new operating partnership. Over time, the partners trade their properties for shares in the REIT, resulting in a tax deferred gain to them. A downREIT is like an UPREIT, except the REIT owns and operates properties instead of being the general partner in the operating partnership. These variations on the structure have increased the flexibility with which capital enters the real estate market and created more tax-efficient structures for real estate ownership.

LIFE INSURANCE COMPANIES

Primarily lenders but also investors in real estate, life insurance companies look for asset diversification and reliable income to put premium funds to work while maintaining sufficient liquidity to pay claims. Real estate is an ideal investment for a life insurance company because the duration match between asset and liability is parallel; that is, the long-term holding period for real estate matches the long-term liabilities of insurance companies.

In addition, life insurance companies are significant equity investors in commercial real estate. The tax losses associated with depreciation of equity real estate investment can shelter income and thus enhance net return. Life insurance companies have also become large purchasers of tax credits (described in chapter 9) that provide equity to real estate projects. These credits shelter income from other assets and enhance the return on the entire company portfolio.

Life insurance companies have had extensive experience in real estate over many years and have been associated with some of the iconic real estate developments of the 20th century (three Metropolitan Life projects are described in the following profile of pension funds). Their role as direct lenders declined with the growth of CMBS, but their prominence as lenders has increased more recently with the decline of CMBS. As significant investors in CMBS, they were able to have a large real estate–related portfolio without a large staff to oversee the mortgage pool.

Life insurance companies, like banks, have become more active in real estate as "relationship" lenders, taking up some of the market share created by tighter underwriting standards in the CMBS sector. They tend to focus on large, high-quality assets.

PENSION FUNDS

Pension funds got into real estate investment beginning in the 1970s, seeking diversification, stability, and an inflation hedge for their investment portfolios. At the same time, they became big investors through real estate investment managers, private equity, and hedge funds, seeking the double-digit yield that these investment vehicles seemed to promise. Gradually, real estate emerged as a legitimate part of the asset allocation model typically used by pension funds, with many pension funds targeting 5 to 15 percent of their portfolios toward real estate.

Although yield has been the motivating factor for pension funds, most have invested at low leverage, indicating an aversion to the risk of loss of principal through changes in market value. The majority of pension fund investments in commercial real estate are typically low leverage with a strong income focus.

Existing core-asset real estate portfolios provide the mainstream investment option for pension funds, usually under the direction of a third-party investment manager. A typical portfolio investment consists of ten or more properties, in various property sectors, located in different geographic markets. Investing in multiple properties in multiple locations diversifies the risk while making it possible to capture economies of scale in property management and increases in the value of individual properties through repositioning or retenanting.

Pension funds are similar to life insurance companies in their need to match real estate asset income to their liability for retirement benefits. With the rest of the investment portfolio governed by an asset allocation model, a fund sometimes experiences significant liquidity challenges as all classes drop in value. To liquidate any asset class in down markets locks in losses. In 2008 and 2009, many pension funds' real estate investments became completely frozen and could not be liquidated. As a result, pension funds sold other asset classes to meet their liquidity needs for paying benefits—an out-of-balance allocation of resources compared with the investment model. Such "misallocation" may result in changes to the percentage of investments that pension funds devote to real estate in the future.

Pension fund investments sometimes cause political unrest when losses become public. For this reason, pension funds usually avoid investments in large development projects. A highly publicized exception to this aversion to development risk was the joint venture deal on LandSource Communities Development made by the California Public Employees Retirement System (CalPERS) with Lennar Corporation through MacFarlane Partners in February 2007. In mid-2008, CalPERS lost its entire equity investment when the joint venture went bankrupt because it was unable to service the $1.2 billion in debt.

Pension funds also try to avoid investing where there is political controversy. Three bellwether investments by CalPERS just before the crash illuminate some of the pension fund's difficulties with controversy that is associated with value-added investment. Riverton Houses in Harlem, Stuyvesant Town and Peter Cooper Village on Manhattan's East Side, and Parkmerced in San Francisco are apartment projects built in the 1940s by Metropolitan Life Insurance Co. in response to a national housing crisis and special tax breaks for keeping rents and profits low. In 2005 and 2006, CalPERS participated as a mezzanine lender in the acquisition of all three properties: with Steller Management and Rockpoint Group for Riverton Houses (acquired and refinanced for $250 million); with Tishman Speyer Properties for Stuyvesant Town and Peter Cooper Village (acquired for $5.4 billion), and with Steller Management and Rockpoint Group for Parkmerced (acquired for more than $600 million). Debt on all three properties was sized to be repaid from increased rents as the new owners invested in upgrades to the properties and raised the regulated rents to market rates. By early 2010, however, all three projects were forced to default on their original loans and were in various stages of foreclosure. The increase in rents in the projects did not occur because of tenant resistance and a decline in rents generally. CalPERS lost $750 million in mezzanine loans as a result of the foreclosures; in addition, it was being asked why it had invested in programs designed to systematically raise rents for middle- and low-income tenants.

Many pension funds experienced dramatic drops in valuation in both their stock and real estate portfolios in 2008. As one example, CalPERS recorded a 23 percent decline in assets (including real estate), for the year ending June 30, 2009—a $55 billion loss in asset value. This decline reduced CalPERS' ratio of funding of its liabilities for pension payments to less than 70 percent, resulting in the need to increase contribution levels for participating employers and in political pressure to raise retirement ages for program participants.

Going forward, pension funds will continue to seek yields, and real estate may offer attractive opportunities for buying at reduced prices. As pension funds look at their asset allocation, they may also reflect on some of the negative experiences before the crash and implement policies to avoid some of what turned out to be high-risk investments.

GOVERNMENT CREDIT AGENCIES

For many multifamily residential projects after the crash, government-issued mortgages through Fannie Mae and Freddie Mac represented one of the most available and lowest-cost debt financing sources available. These mortgages are funded by bonds issued by the two entities, which were privately owned and operated agencies with an implicit or actual federal government guarantee. The bond proceeds are used to purchase qualifying mortgages and securitize them as debt of the agencies.

In 2008, these agencies were hit hard by all the problems afflicting the residential mortgage-backed securities sector following the subprime market collapse and the residential market collapse. A U.S. government rescue restored these agencies to a functioning state, and it appears that their role in providing liquidity will continue, albeit under stricter underwriting standards. These agencies have been critical players in providing debt capital and liquidity to both the residential mortgage market and the multifamily mortgage business for many years. Their future is being evaluated and considered by Congress as this book is being written, and the outcome of congressional decisions will significantly affect residential mortgage finance in the future.

FOREIGN INVESTORS

Foreign investors in U.S. real estate include high–net worth investors (individuals and networks), foreign pension funds, foreign banks, sovereign wealth funds, corporations, and finance companies. Capital flows in recent years have come from Australia, Canada, Europe, the Middle East, and increasingly China. Australian development companies, stimulated by pension fund regulations that require international diversification of assets, have made a particularly significant investment in U.S. real estate and were particularly hard hit as a result of the 2008 drop in valuations.

Foreign investors tend to focus on first-tier U.S. cities, looking for class A properties. Obviously, U.S. dollar reserves accumulated by foreign investors as a result of massive trade deficits create the potential for more foreign investment at the point that valuations become attractive. The Foreign Investment in Real Property Tax Act of 1981 has been an impediment for some foreign investors, and efforts are being considered to modify this law to attract more foreign capital to real estate.

Fiduciary Principles

As the discussion of capital sources illustrates, most capital for real estate development and investment beyond a developer's own capital comes primarily from sources that are accountable to third parties, either clients for whom the funding entity is managing capital or depositers, shareholders, or investors. Except for those high-wealth individuals who invest directly on their own behalf, capital sources thus tend to follow fiduciary principles that ensure transparency, accountability, and joint control on behalf of third-party stakeholders.

Because of this need to protect stakeholders' interests, investment in real estate usually occurs through some form of joint venture (described in chapter 7) that creates shared information, responsibilities, and control. Lenders also require validated information, along with performance guarantees for construction loans and the pledge of recourse assets to back up the guarantees.

Here are the parameters that capital sources bring to a typical real estate investment, applying fiduciary principles common to most deals:

■ *Financings are about relationships, not transactions*. The trustworthiness and reliability of the developer is just as important as the merits of the particular project. A developer's track record of performance is the primary metric that capital sources use in evaluating trustworthiness and reliability. The track records of key team members, especially the architect and contractor, are also critical—particularly if the developer is new to the business and does not have extensive project experience. New developers have difficulty establishing credibility unless they have a reputation in a closely related discipline such as construction, design, legal, or finance. Increasingly, financing sources also look to a real estate professional's training—a reflection of the increasing professionalization of the field—with a greater emphasis on advanced academic degrees and professional certification programs.

■ *Validate all the assumptions*, but especially the market and the costs. While a developer must be familiar with the market and costs to conceive a project and to tie up the land, capital sources require third-party verification of the market support for the project value and of the costs of building the project. Market verification usually requires analysis by a market consultant that provides detailed information on customer profiles as well as pricing and marketing plans. Cost verification usually requires an independent analysis and verification of the cost estimates. The capital sources also review the adequacy of the construction management and may require changes to correct perceived deficiencies.

■ *Require performance guarantees and adequate project value*. During construction, the developer frequently is required to guarantee the completion of construction by giving the lender recourse to nonproject assets. This recourse may be waived if the developer is viewed as particularly reliable. In sizing the permanent loan on the completed project, the lender focuses on the reliability of the estimate of market value and lowers the permanent loan as a percentage of market value if there is a perceived risk of the market weakening after the project funds and construction starts. In situations when the risk of market deterioration during construction is perceived as high, lenders provide less leverage and equity investors must evaluate whether they are willing to risk the loss of all or a portion of their investment through a drop in market value.

■ *Require the developer to co-invest*. Most capital sources require that the developer have some skin in the game to ensure that the financial interests of the developer and equity investors are aligned. This normally means that the developer is required to invest at least 10 percent of the equity requirement into the project. During the real estate run-up of the late 1990s through 2007, this requirement was sometimes waived, but it returned with the weakening of the market in 2008.

■ *Confirm that the developer's financial transactions are open and transparent to the outside investors.* Lenders and equity investors insist that the developer keep them completely and accurately informed about the status of the project, including the project's financial operations and any significant events.

■ *You will spend 95 percent of the time negotiating 5 percent of the issues that never occur.* A joint venture contract can take many different forms and cover a lot of potential circumstances that will probably never occur. They include the consequences of an investor not making a required capital contribution on schedule, the project costs exceeding the estimates, or the entitlement for the project being delayed and requiring the close of escrow on the land. Although the chances may be remote that some of these events will occur, negotiating their solution in advance avoids possible chaos if they do occur.

■ *Ensure that major decisions are made jointly.* Projects do not always go as planned, so major decisions need to be made about how to respond to change. If a major tenant drops out, or construction is delayed and there is a need for more capital, the developer and investors must decide jointly what to do. Other major decisions include the timing of a capital event (refinancing or sale), especially if one party believes that it needs to occur at a different time than originally planned.

■ *Include a "buy/sell" provision, but never rely on it as the rationalization for not ensuring a complete alignment of interests.* A "buy/sell" provision is exercisable if the developer and equity investors reach such a complete impasse that one party decides that the partnership must be liquidated. Such a provision allows one party to appraise the value of the project and the other party to opt to either purchase or sell (put) at that price. It provides a default escape clause but is rarely exercised unless the relationship between the investors and the developer ruptures so thoroughly that it cannot be restored.

■ *Include provisions in the joint venture agreement allowing removal of the developer for cause.* Reasons for removal for cause can include malfeasance or misfeasance. Obviously, enforcement of such a provision requires some form of due process. However, the existence of a provision allows relief to the equity investors in egregious circumstances. Provisions in loan documents allowing for removal are called "bad boy" clauses.

■ *Provide for success fees to the developer and investor group upon a sale or refinance after meeting the required IRR hurdle rate.* As described in chapter 2, the profit distribution percentages between the developer and equity investors from the annual income waterfall will probably differ from the distribution of the profit obtained from a sale or refinance. Because a sale or refinance is based on the value achieved by the project, which takes into account market conditions as well as annual performance, the timing of a sale or refinance can provide quite a windfall compared with the annual profit distribution. With success in these transactions should come rewards that provide incentives to the developer to look for these opportunities

■ *Provide for a three- to seven-year holding period.* Sell when the business plan is completed—win, lose, or draw, it rarely gets better. Most real estate investors do not plan to have their investment tied up indefinitely. The standard time period for liquidating and returning investors' principal and any profits is usually three to seven years. Obviously, market conditions may warrant change, but a decision to hold beyond the planned period must be made jointly.

- *Take profits when they are available.* Although there is likely to be a planned holding period, there will also be opportunistic provisions for selling or refinancing when circumstances are particularly favorable.

- *Allow the developer to take market rate fees for services (property management, construction, etc.).* In addition to providing the vision and management to turn the project from an idea to reality, the developer may be able to provide services to the project that would otherwise need to be purchased from an outside party. To avoid overburdening the project with costs in excess of what these services would otherwise cost, the joint venture agreement usually provides that they be provided at a cost that is comparable to what these services cost in the market. Investors and lenders closely monitor these fees to ensure that the developer is not realizing profit early and undermining the alignment of interests.

Investment Strategies

This discussion has highlighted the diverse range of capital sources, each reflecting a different risk appetite and return requirement in its investment strategy. Understanding these different investment strategies helps a developer choose the capital source that is best suited for a project and communicate effectively how the project fits into the strategy. This section discusses how sources evaluate a project's characteristics to determine whether a project fits into their investment strategy.

Figure 5-9 summarizes the generally accepted categories of investment strategies, showing their income-valuation blends, risk levels, and leverage. As expected, the returns that investors in each category seek increase with the risk associated with that category.

Equity investors have much greater diversity in their investment strategies than lenders. Some equity investors seek reliable income with stability in property value. Their investment objective focuses more on preservation of value and income and less on opportunistic value creation. These investors accept lower returns to achieve the lower risk and higher stability. At the other end of the risk spectrum are investors who focus on value creation. For these investors, the reliability of current income is of less interest than the opportunity to invest in a strategy that adds value through repositioning, retenanting or development. These strategies carry much higher risk but they also have the potential for much higher returns.

Core asset investors seek a reliable income that is based on a diversified portfolio of good-quality, well-leased properties that are well maintained, in strong markets, and in traditional asset classes. These investors may be pension funds, life insurance companies, and publicly traded REITs that have either predictable liabilities to meet or shareholders with a low risk appetite.

In the higher-risk investment strategies, current income as a contributor to return declines and value creation becomes the dominant contributor. The value creation opportunities range over a growing number of property types and circumstances. For instance,

FIGURE 5-9
Equity Investment Strategies Compared

Investment Strategy	Typical Net IRR, 2010 (%)	Source of Return	Asset Types	Market Focus	Portfolio	Debt
Core	7–9	Focus on income	Class A and premium multitenant	Primary markets	Well diversified, low risk	Low: <30%
Core-Plus	9–12	Income and some value creation	Core-type assets with vacancies or repositioning potential	Primary or secondary locations	Diversified, moderate risk	Moderate: <55%
Value-Add	12–16	Value creation with some income	Class A and B with high vacancies Rents below market Obsolete properties with repositioning potential	Recovering primary or secondary and tertiary markets	Moderate to high risk	High: up to 70%
Opportunistic	>16	Value creation	Development Conversion Repositioning Obsolete Redevelopment	New development or secondary and tertiary markets	High risk Vacant land Distressed companies and properties	High: over 70%
Mezzanine/ Debt	9–12	Value creation	Distressed loans Gap financing Value-add play Repositioning	All markets	Moderate risk Position subordinate to primary lender	High: over 70%

Source: Steven Ott, University of North Carolina, Charlotte.

investors in the core-plus categories expect to get higher returns by buying core assets at the right price and making minor investments in retenanting.

For the higher-risk investment strategies, timing and skill become more important to achieving return. Repositioning and retenanting an old shopping mall, for instance, calls for a much different set of skills than competently managing a Class A office building. Opportunistically investing in and redeveloping obsolete and distressed properties requires vision, patient capital, buying at the right price, and problem-solving skills. Such investments also often involve higher levels of debt to leverage returns. Investors in these higher-risk categories, consequently, vet the performance and reputation of the managing partner in the project much more closely, because returns in such deals depend so much on skill.

Property Characteristics

To determine where a project fits in a capital source's investment strategy, its characteristics are evaluated in terms of its sector, its regional market, its vacancy rate and rent levels, its tenants, its potential for value-added repositioning, and how it fits into the source's risk-reward profile.

SECTOR RISK

Different sectors enjoy better financing, depending on how capital sources perceive their ability to provide returns and hold value, on the basis of what direction the property and capital markets are expected to move. These perceptions change as market conditions change. For instance, until 2007, retail and multifamily residential cap rates were significantly below those of other sectors (see figure 5-6). After the 2008 crash, retail fundamentals declined and retail saw dramatic increases in cap rates (and much more expensive financing terms) because of a dramatic contraction in retail demand and dramatic reductions in occupied retail space owing to bankruptcy or retrenchment of large retail chains in most areas. However, as retail spaces were vacated and rents renegotiated to lower levels in 2010, the lower market values of retail properties presented attractive buying opportunities and the retail sector began to recover. Figure 5-10 provides a snapshot of typical loan rates applicable to different sectors in mid-2009, reflecting the perceived strength of the market for each sector. These data reflect the perceived market strength for multifamily residential and perceived weakness for regional shopping malls, with other sectors perceived similarly.

One sector that capital sources are still trying to understand is mixed-use development. This emerging sector has difficulty attracting favorable financing because of its physical and operational complexity. Developers and communities are gaining expertise on how to address these issues, but financing sources still charge premiums because of the perceived higher risk and complexity. Frequently, a public/private partnership is needed to address this risk and complexity. Chapter 9 discusses the crafting of such partnerships.

FIGURE 5-10

Loan Rate Spread for Real Estate Sectors Compared with Ten-Year Treasury Notes, Mid-2009

Market Sector	Basis Point Spread Over Ten-Year Treasury Note
Multifamily Residential	280
Regional Mall	515
Strip Mall or Power Center	463
Multitenant Industrial	460
Central Business District Office	455
Suburban Office	460

Source: David Blitz, Nebo Capital.

REGIONAL STRENGTH

As national and international investors and lenders have grown in importance in real estate markets in recent decades, real estate investors have increasingly sought to evaluate regional strength and investment prospects as key variables for investing and for diversifying a portfolio. Investors seek returns in whichever regional market seems to present the lowest risk and highest return. The result is lower financing costs in favored "primary" markets and higher financing costs in out-of-favor ("secondary or tertiary") markets.

The U.S. cities with the highest investment prospects in 2011, according to *Emerging Trends in Real Estate 2011*, are Washington, New York, San Francisco, Austin, Boston, Seattle, San Jose, Houston, Los Angeles, and San Diego. These cities have received high ratings in this survey for several years. However, perceptions change and the 2008 crash has significantly altered investor attitudes toward some markets. For instance, during the early part of the 2000s, the Phoenix, Orlando, and Las Vegas markets were viewed as growth-oriented primary markets with good prospects. All three regions had grown through unconstrained land use policies, with construction employment constituting a significant percentage of overall employment. After the crash of 2008, these markets experienced a precipitous decline in property values and jobs.

Richard Florida coined the phrase, "Place will be the organizing economic and social unit." In an article in the March 2009 issue of the *Atlantic Monthly*, he described the effect of the crash in a way that captures the essence of why some regions are favored and others are not:

> *Big, talent-attracting places benefit from accelerated rates of "urban metabolism,"...
> [S]uccessful cities, unlike biological organisms, actually get faster as they grow. ...
> "[T]he larger a city's population, the greater the innovation and wealth creation per
> person." Places like New York with finance and media, Los Angeles with film and
> music, and Silicon Valley with high-tech are all examples of high-metabolism places.*
>
> *Metabolism and talent-clustering are important to the fortunes of U.S. city-regions
> in good times, but they're even more so when times get tough. In the heady days
> of the housing bubble, some Sun Belt cities—Phoenix and Las Vegas are the best
> examples—developed economies centered largely on real estate and construction.
> With sunny weather and plenty of flat, empty land, they got caught in a classic boom
> cycle. Although these places drew tourists, retirees, and some industry—firms seek-
> ing bigger footprints at lower costs—much of the cities' development came from, well,
> development itself. The boom itself neither followed nor resulted in the development
> of sustainable, scalable, highly productive industries or services. It was fueled and
> funded by housing, and housing was its primary product. Whole cities and metro
> regions became giant Ponzi schemes.*

Real estate investment flows to the regions perceived to have strong and stable economies. Las Vegas, Phoenix, and Orlando all have had strong economies and likely will be strong again, but they are also susceptible to boom and bust cycles that present concerns for investors. The Great Recession revealed the fragility of economies that are over-concentrated in one segment (in the case of all three of these markets, the over-concentration was in construction). As a counterexample, the San Francisco Bay Area is now viewed (despite the state's fiscal woes) as an attractive real estate investment market because of its significant constraints on development, because of its growth potential, and because of its residents' capacity for innovation.

Obviously, regional markets change and investment prospects change with them. Although Pittsburgh experienced dramatic decline in the 1970s and 1980s with the contraction of the U.S. steel industry, community leaders catalyzed a dramatic revitalization effort so that today the city's economic base is in health care, education, technology, robotics, and financial services. Old steel factory sites have been redeveloped as high-quality residential and commercial sites. In 2009 Pittsburgh was named the most livable city in the United States by *The Economist* magazine and the 29th most livable city in the world. So, although financing terms may reflect high perceived risk in out-of-favor markets, frequently the return on investment for pioneering efforts to revitalize compensates for that risk.

TENANT STRENGTH

Commercial real estate property value rests on the financial strength of the tenants. For office, industrial, and retail, some tenants categorized as "credit tenants" are viewed as creating a highly reliable rent stream, as the basis of project value. The synergy of tenant mix in a retail project is also important in creating customer traffic for a center.

A tenant such as Whole Foods Market, Trader Joe's, or even Starbucks adds value to a retail or mixed-use project by generating traffic. A tenant such as Microsoft or GE would be a solid credit tenant for an office property, and Walmart would be a prime credit tenant for an industrial property. Tenants such as these negotiate for lower rents because they understand the value they bring.

VALUE-ADD OPPORTUNITIES

Many older properties offer varying opportunities to add value through redevelopment, repositioning, or reuse. According to David Blitz of Nebo Capital, functional and market-driven obsolescence has driven the value of many enclosed shopping malls down to as low as $15 to $20 per square foot, which is a fraction of the development cost (excluding land). Many industrial facilities, auto dealer sites, and low-rise commercial sites are also underused and present redevelopment opportunities.

This market condition raises an opportunity for investment in value-added change that creates value by changing the use. As Michael Beyard noted in the January 2009 issue of *Urban Land*,

> *The world has changed fundamentally, and the current crisis should be a wake-up call for us to step back and address the serious shortcomings of our present retail land use and development policies, which have led to the industry's current overbuilding, obsolescence, and financial disaster.*

> *Communities must demand sustainable mixed-use development, higher commercial densities, green leasing, more redevelopment of obsolete spaces, and retail centers that make sense regionally as well as locally.*

Many of these of these obsolete sites are being redeveloped as mixed-use town centers with high-density housing, small retail shops, and public gathering space.

Much of this revitalization effort relies on public/private partnerships to address costs that cannot be supported solely from private investment. These costs sometimes include parking, infrastructure, or public space. They can also include co-investment programs through which the public sector invests in an amenity such as a theater, park, or pedestrian bike trail that creates value—which helps make the private investment viable.

Capital Markets and the Risk-Reward Evaluation

The Great Recession of 2008 will continue to affect commercial real estate financing for at least the next decade, if not beyond. Through the early 2010s, even with interest rates at historic lows, the $1.4 trillion "maturity wall" of commercial real estate loans coming due will affect banks' balance sheets and their appetite for loan origination. Valuation losses concentrated in some markets and in some sectors have unbalanced portfolio allocations, restricting capital deployment by managers into some sectors. Lenders and investors have become acutely sensitive to cycle risk and will shy away from new capital deployment in many markets until markets create more credible evidence of stability. Numerous unfinished office buildings and "broken condo" projects will supply the market for some time with distressed pricing and inhibit new development opportunities.

More than ever before, to be effective in attracting capital, a developer needs to understand conditions in the capital markets. Project financing is not just about project viability anymore but about how a project fits into the risk-reward profile of a capital source. And the developer needs to cultivate relationships with a broad range of sources to find the right fit.

Notes:

1. *Structured Investment Vehicles were first established in the late 1980s as a form of unregulated opportunity fund affiliated with a regulated sponsoring bank. The SIV issued notes and commercial paper paying low short-term interest rates to, in effect, borrow money and purchased mortgage securities at a higher long-term interest rate to, in effect, lend money. At their peak, SIVs totaled $400 billion in market value. The collapse of the mortgage-backed security market in 2007 caused all SIVs to become insolvent and either be taken back onto their sponsoring bank's balance sheet or declare bankruptcy and be liquidated. The last bank-sponsored SIV entered liquidation in October 2008, and SIVs are now virtually extinct.*

2. *Whether this perception occurred suddenly or grew over time is an interesting sidelight to the 2007–2008 collapse. As early as the fall of 2006, analysts at Credit Suisse First Boston began sounding alarms about "abnormal" default rates on mortgages issued in 2006 compared with those of earlier vintage.*

CHAPTER 6

Obtaining Financing for Development

To successfully obtain financing for a project, a developer approaching financing sources in the 2010s needs much greater understanding than ever before about real estate market conditions, capital markets, and underwriting criteria. This chapter describes how a developer accesses and communicates effectively with capital sources. It begins with a description of market conditions. It then describes how developers connect with capital sources. Finally, it describes the content of presentations to a capital source.

Market Conditions

Financing for real estate development in the 2010s has been transformed by the events of the late 2000s. Several pervasive market conditions are likely to dominate the next decade:

- *Capital is mobile:* As an asset class seeking capital, real estate competes more than ever with other investment sectors. Developers must understand how their projects compete with opportunities available in the broader capital markets. In addition, capital sources today are less constrained to investment and lending opportunities within their local market, despite the emphasis of smaller banks and insurance companies on relationship-based lending. Obtaining capital for a development, consequently, results from a competition with projects in other regions.

- *Significant differences in market conditions exist among regions:* As conditions improve, larger primary market projects will attract the greatest interest from money center banks and the revived CMBS market. Secondary markets will struggle until asset values are perceived to have hit bottom. Growth-constrained markets with strong economies will see quicker resumption of new development projects and will, in general, receive more favorable financing terms than markets with unconstrained growth and/or weaker economies.

- *Development is more complex physically and economically:* Development today is often more complicated because it is more urban, more mixed-use, and more financially difficult. This reality places a greater burden on the developer and his or her organizational and planning skills.

- *Development will lag in regions where property values are below replacement costs:* Development will have a difficult time competing for capital in the many markets where property values are below replacement costs. In these markets, projects that convert existing real estate to new uses will predominate, as will projects with public/ private gap financing.
- *Leverage is lower:* For existing properties, the financing equation is affected by uncertainty about where property fundamentals and values are trending. A strong stabilized NOI and a high debt-coverage ratio determine leverage, but investors are following those indicators only to the extent that they believe that markets are heading in the right direction and that they are getting a price that reflects long-term value.

Of course, market conditions will change with time, but the conditions that exist entering the 2010s have implications for how developers work with financing sources:

- Projects must meet strict underwriting criteria for debt-coverage ratio and lower leverage. The developer's track record and reliability are more important than ever before.
- Professional credentials in the form of academic degrees and certifications carry more weight than ever.
- The expertise of other professional disciplines on a development team is critical to successful financing of complex developments.
- Success in obtaining financing for development is more likely to be in growth-constrained markets that have less commodity competition, usually because of difficult entitlement processes and high development standards.
- Expertise in public/private partnerships is an important skill for addressing the economic viability and community fit of projects.

Atelier 505 is a mixed-use project in Boston, Massachusetts. It was the result of a public/private partnership between the Druker Company, Ltd., the city of Boston, the Boston Center for the Arts, and the Huntington Theatre Company. The 300,000-square-foot building includes 103 condominiums, restaurants, retail space, a parking garage, and a performing arts complex.

ANTON GRASSL

- Developing and maintaining long-term relationships with numerous lenders and investors is more important than ever in obtaining financing, because of the much greater importance of finding the right fit between a project and the risk-reward profile of a funding source. These relationships are no longer just local.
- Capital brokers will be more important in assisting developers in matching capital sources to projects. Some brokers specialize in debt, others in equity. They can help developers access whole-loan lenders and syndicates that would otherwise be difficult to find. They can provide guidance to developers on building relationships with financing sources, and they can help match funding sources to project characteristics.

Connecting with Capital Sources

Connecting with capital sources is no longer just a task in the predevelopment process; it now requires an ongoing effort to monitor conditions in the capital markets and to develop relationships with capital sources. This requirement is particularly challenging for new developers. This section discusses strategies for making those connections. Chapter 10 provides personal stories of how developers developed and maintained such relationships.

ACCESSING PREDEVELOPMENT AND DEVELOPMENT EQUITY CAPITAL

How does a developer connect with equity capital sources that are willing to fund the early, very risky phases of a development project? This is perhaps the most critical problem any beginning developer faces, and there is no simple, textbook solution to this challenge. Experienced developers with internal capital often fund this stage from their own working capital, because the risks to equity capital are very high. Attracting outside equity capital at this stage is as much art as science, as much salesmanship as analysis.

For a beginning developer, connecting with equity capital begins with career building and networking. The process begins at the start of a career, when an individual engages in a series of successful endeavors in business, preferably in a real estate business or a related field such as architecture, consulting, urban planning, or finance. Developers typically spend ten or more years working for others, learning, and making connections with a range of real estate business leaders. If they are successful in this early career, many of their colleagues in the real estate business community take note and doors start to open.

The beginning developer should be able to use a successful track record, together with salesmanship and communication skills, to make connections with various capital sources, especially high–net worth individuals known to invest in real estate in the local area. Establishing relationships with these individuals is critical. It likely will involve networking and socializing at real estate industry and local community events. In many cases, a beginning developer makes a connection through a successful working relationship while employed by a real estate firm; the developer can then tap into that relationship when he or she embarks on a development venture. High–net worth capital is often

What Do Private Equity Providers Want?

by Leslie Braunstein

As the nation's commercial real estate markets begin to recover from the effects of the Great Recession and debt financing has become more difficult to find, private equity has assumed a more prominent position in the capital stack. But accessing it is more complicated than simply walking into the local bank.

"Equity is always an essential part of doing a deal, filling the gap between debt and acquisition cost, but [it] is now more important than ever because debt sources are underwriting more conservatively than they did before the downturn, resulting in lower proceeds," explains Kevin H. Smith of Centerline Capital Group's mortgage banking group in Vienna, Virginia. "For smaller sponsors, it can be difficult to secure institutional equity without assistance."

Many real estate owners and developers take the first step into private equity financing by obtaining funds from traditional sources such as friends and family, high–net worth individuals, and personal resources. But as their horizons expand, they may begin looking toward institutional sources such as family offices, commingled dedicated real estate equity funds, pension funds and endowments, sovereign wealth funds, life insurance companies, and corporate investors, among others. Clearly, they must do their homework before approaching private equity providers.

"You really have to sell yourself," advises Doug Wilberding of CenterCap Group. "Tell us how you are going to execute the business plan and why you are better than the next guy."

"Come up with three takeaways that you present to capital providers," counsels Ashleigh Simpson of MetLife Real Estate Investment in Washington, D.C. "Remember that you are not the only one asking for money. Your expertise should align with what you are

trying to do." "It's all about the sponsor and choosing the right asset and investment strategy."

James Riordan of Baltimore-based Lupert-Adler Partners says, "Although we are a large fund, we do a lot of small deals; we start below $5 million, but our sweet spot is the $5 to $15 million equity outlay. We are most focused on distressed multifamily housing; we don't buy open-air retail centers unless we can tear them down and build something else." Riordan points out the "burden of capital," including extensive governance and reporting requirements.

"We invest for four funds, doing ground-up development through buying core assets," notes H. James Darcey of ASB Real Estate Investments, based in Bethesda, Maryland. "Our primary focus is on major gateway cities. Urban-oriented retail is a focus in the best markets. The deal size is from $10 to $100 million in equity; we are conservative, with 40 to 50 percent leverage."

Thad Paul of the Washington, D.C.–based Carlyle Group says that his firm typically holds properties for three to five years and will leverage up to 95 percent in some cases.

Taking a different tack is Michael Schonbraun of New York City–based Cerberus Real Estate Capital Management. "We are not scared of residential land or single-family home product in select markets where there are value-add components; our capital is flexible."

Philadelphia-based Grosvenor Investment Management also is focused on for-sale residential property, as well as apartment development and health care–related assets such as medical office space and senior care facilities, says managing director David Reiner.

Urban Land online magazine, January 26, 2011, urbanland.uli.org.

referred to as "country club money," and it is no secret that being a member of the right country club or business club—or serving on the right community board—can provide connections and ultimate access to such investor capital. Doctors, lawyers, stock brokers, financial advisers, and land owners are particularly good candidates to connect with in such settings. Partnerships with land owners can be especially fruitful if you like the land they own. And, of course, when trying to attract equity capital at the outset of a venture it is always a plus to have money or access to money already. Starting out with a partner can also be helpful; two heads and two sources of personal equity are usually better than just one when starting a venture.

As a project proceeds toward construction, the developer must obtain financing commitments for the development phase from equity investors to attract the debt for construction. For beginning developers, development equity capital includes the same capital sources just discussed but the list may need to be expanded to include larger equity investors, including pension funds, private equity funds, insurance companies, listed and unlisted REITs, and other real estate investment firms. These investors are more risk averse than the initial investors and will only enter a deal when a specific degree of certainty about project success has been achieved.

Developers often seek the help of capital market intermediaries, including firms such as CassidyTurley, Walker Dunlop, CBRE Capital Markets Inc., Jones Lang LaSalle, Colliers International, and Marcus & Millichap Capital Corp. When larger firms are looking to raise large amounts of equity capital for a new venture, investment banks are usually brought in to the process. Intermediaries engage in a range of real estate finance activities, including debt placement, investment sales, advisory services, private equity and joint venture transactions, corporate finance, structured finance, and loan sales and servicing. These intermediaries can be very helpful in arranging both equity and debt financing for real estate development projects.

For example, in August 2010, Holliday Fenoglio Fowler, L.P. (HFF) arranged both construction financing and joint venture equity for Jefferson at West Goshen, a 230-unit luxury multifamily community in West Goshen, Pennsylvania. HFF worked on behalf of the borrower, Jefferson Apartment Group, to secure the $22.85 million, 36-month construction loan through Wells Fargo's Real Estate Banking Group. AEW Value Investors II, a value-added real estate fund sponsored by AEW Capital Management, L.P., provided joint venture equity for the project. The project was scheduled for completion in 2011. Jefferson Apartment Group, founded in 2009 through the acquisition of JPI East, has acquired or developed more than 18,000 units with a value of more than $3 billion in ten states along the East Coast.

Experienced development firms embarking on a new project may use a range of equity sources, including equity from limited partner relationships, internal company equity, and equity raised through intermediaries, as outlined above. Even experienced developers need to constantly seek new relationships and equity partners, especially as their projects get larger and capital requirements increase. The largest and most sophisticated developers can tap into pension fund, insurance company, REIT, or private equity fund money to fund prime ventures. Many very large developers, such as Hines and Shorenstein, now develop, raise, and manage their own private equity funds that can be used to invest in their properties.

ACCESSING CONSTRUCTION AND PERMANENT FINANCING

Although relationships are important for attracting construction financing, a developer's track record and documentation are essential. The primary sources for small projects are typically local and regional banks. Money center banks are unlikely to lend for construction unless both the developer and the project are sizable and the developer has a good reputation. In some cases, multiple lenders may be involved in the financing, especially if the project is phased.

Permanent lending sources include insurance companies, banks, conduit lenders who securitize the loans in the CMBS market, mortgage REITs, and in the case of apartment development, Fannie Mae and Freddie Mac. Many of these sources are well-known industry names and can be accessed through mortgage brokers or other real estate service providers.

Although developing relationships with these capital sources is important, the quality of the property and its operating history and prospects are the essential elements that attract permanent financing. Permanent lenders make loans on the basis of loan-to-value ratios, debt-service coverage ratios, and other fundamentals, and they like to see stabilized properties with stabilized cash flows.

Developers may also need to seek mezzanine financing to fill a gap between traditional equity and debt financing. Numerous sources specialize in providing financing in the mezzanine and preferred equity space. They include banks as well as specialty firms such as Archon Capital and CapitalSource.

FINDING A BUYER FOR THE PROPERTY

Selling a property can involve personal relationships with investors, but generally property owners engage professional real estate brokers and intermediaries with experience in selling properties. Major national brokerage firms—such as CB Richard Ellis, Eastdil Secured, HFF, Cushman & Wakefield, Grubb & Ellis, Colliers, etc.—or local brokers are brought into the process, and the property typically is marketed by these firms or listed with commercial property listing services such as CoStar or LoopNet.

Presenting to Financing Sources

Obtaining financing commitments starts with the introduction of capital sources to the developer and the project early in the predevelopment phase. This early introduction enables the developer to educate the finance sources about the project's economic viability and the certainty of it receiving the expected entitlement. At the point that both of these issues are resolved, a financing commitment can occur.

With slight variations, the financing package for equity and loan addresses the same elements:

■ The development entity's experience, credibility, and financial capability;
■ The development project and the business plan; and
■ The entitlement process and the role of public/private partnerships.

EXPERIENCE, CREDIBILITY, AND FINANCIAL CAPACITY OF THE DEVELOPMENT ENTITY

As described in chapter 5, financing sources are as concerned with the trustworthiness and reliability of the developer and development team as they are with the transaction parameters. Consequently, the developer needs to describe experience in previous projects both for the development entity and for the key team members, especially the architect, contractor, marketing entity, and property manager.

Furthermore, the developer must demonstrate that the development team is credentialed and competent. The swash-buckling cowboy of yesterday has given way to the academically and professionally credentialed developer of today and tomorrow.

The balance sheet of the developer and of the contractor are important parts of the presentation, because these assets frequently are encumbered with recourse provisions to secure completion and lease-up guarantees. Of particular importance are the following issues:

- Do the developer and the team have experience with the type of project that is being proposed?
- What is the working relationship between the architect and contractor?
- What experience with problem solving does the development team have?
- What is the academic background of the development team? Are team members academically and professionally credentialed for the project?
- What are the critical risk issues in the project, and how does the experience of the development team make it suited to address these issues?
- What resources will the developer use to pay predevelopment costs before the project funds?

Having established the capacity of the team, the developer can then turn to the details of the project.

THE DEVELOPMENT PROJECT AND THE BUSINESS PLAN

The presentation of the project must address all the risks and all the determinants of viability. Each assumption in the financial pro forma must be verified and sourced, and a management strategy for identifying, quantifying, and mitigating risk must be presented.

Typically, lenders and institutional investors have proprietary software and presentation formats for presenting a project, and the development entity must ensure that information is transported accurately into these frameworks. The lenders also have a process for addressing the risks and understanding projects. It is best that the developer understand this process and adhere to the lender's process.

In presenting the project and the business plan for acquisition, entitlement, development, and sale, the developer must address five specific areas of concern:

- *Site:* This area of concern needs to address the terms for site acquisition, including cost and buyer's conditions to close. Included here should be information about the title, environmental and soil conditions, infrastructure and utilities, and the cost of any remediation strategies where they're needed. Nothing can substitute for a site visit. All parties involved in the project must walk the site.
- *Market analysis:* This area of concern usually requires an outside consultant to address the following questions:

- What is the rationale for the site and location to respond to the market?
- What is the competition, and what is the likelihood of competing projects diluting the market? That is, are there barriers to entry that will reduce the likelihood of competition?
- What are the customer profiles, and what is the best merchandizing or unit mix to respond to likely customers?
- What is the best marketing plan? How will this plan be implemented? By whom?
- What is the strength of preleasing or presales commitments?
- Are the income projections based on pricing and absorption supported by the market?

■ *Project and product design:* The presentation of the design should address how the product mix, product design, site layout, and architectural treatment respond to the market conditions, the community's entitlement process, and the ability to build cost-effectively.

■ *Cost analysis:* This area of concern should include verified construction costs and verified property management costs. Specific items to address:

- Preconstruction cost estimate and the process for updating this estimate;
- Construction period and special construction issues that need to be addressed, such as pre-ordering materials or unknown conditions that will create risk;
- The possibility of construction delays: causes, responses, and impact of delay on the carrying costs of the project and project economics;
- Construction management approach (in terms of the approaches described in chapter 4), accountability, and incentives for on-time and on-budget performance;
- Developer fees and their basis as market-rate payments for services provided;
- Marketing costs and verification as based on the market for services; and
- Property management costs and verification as based on the market for services.

Del Mar Station is a $77 million transit-oriented village in Pasadena, California. It was the result of a public/private partnership between Urban Partners, Archstone, and the Los Angeles Metropolitan Transportation Authority. It includes 347 residential units, 11,000 square feet of retail space, 1,200 underground parking spaces, and the restoration of the historic Santa Fe Train Depot.

©TOM BONNER PHOTOGRAPHY, COURTESY OF MOULE & POLYZOIDES

- *Financial analysis:* This area of concern should combine the income and cost analysis to identify risk factors and strategies for managing the downside as well as identifying upside opportunities. Specific items to address:
  - Key cost factors that need to be managed and their impact on project viability;
  - Income variability and strategies for maximizing income opportunities;
  - Market risks and strategies for minimizing downside possibilities; and
  - Exit strategy describing the holding period and trigger points for early liquidation.

ENTITLEMENT PROCESS AND ROLE OF PUBLIC/PRIVATE PARTNERSHIPS

Because the entitlement process is so complex in many places, the presentation should describe the risks and management of this process. A long entitlement process will make most project assumptions invalid because they will be out of date, so the developer must address how these assumptions will be updated as the entitlement process proceeds and how project viability will be reassessed with each update.

In addition, many projects involve some form of public/private partnerhsip. Public/private partnerships that involve financial participation by the public agency have become an increasingly important factor in meeting underwriting criteria from private capital sources. (Chapter 9 discusses these partnerships in detail.) The presentation should address the timing, reliability, and financial impact of a public/private partnership.

Conclusion

Connecting with and matching a capital source to a development project requires that the developer understand both the range of sources available and the investment criteria of the source, and how the underlying risks of the project match with these criteria. Presenting the opportunity to the source involves introducing the reliability of the project team as well as documenting the market, cost, and entitlement risks of the project.

CHAPTER 7

The Development Entity, Joint Ventures, and the Financing Structure

This chapter describes various types of development entities and real estate ownership structures, and the elements involved in structuring a joint venture transaction. It diagrams financing structures involving multiple capital sources, and it describes a typical distribution of profits to partners within a development entity.

A project development entity takes one of several legal structures and typically involves a joint venture among several individuals or other entities. The complexity of development entities and of financing structures has increased significantly with the increased use of capital from various sources—including pension funds, insurance companies, private equity funds, securitized loans, mezzanine loans, and REITs—and with the multifaceted nature of many projects.

Usually, a joint venture arrangement between an investment source and a development entity is the primary structure for a real estate development project. The joint venture stipulates the roles of each party and the priority of payment of profits in the waterfall to the investors, as described in chapter 2. The joint venture also stipulates reporting requirements and joint decision-making procedures on important issues, to meet the fiduciary needs of the investment sources.

Real Estate Entities

Three key factors affect the way development entities are organized:
■ Taxes,
■ Personal liability, and
■ Control.

The tax issues, as described in chapter 5, primarily concern the avoidance of the double taxation of profits that corporations experience when their corporate profits are taxed and then dividends paid out to shareholders are also taxed. In addition, some entities cannot pass depreciation or other losses through to shareholders.

Most types of entities shield the investors from personal liability associated with the development project, placing liability primarily on the developer. For some types of entities, less liability may result in less control.

Some entities allow the investors significant control, which may include removing the developer or exercising a buy-sell provision. Other structures, in which the investment is more liquid, provide opportunities for the investors to sell their shares and get out.

Real estate development entities take five primary forms:

■ Partnerships—general and limited,
■ Limited liability companies (LLCs),
■ S corporations,
■ Real estate investment trusts (REITs), and
■ Corporations.

Some are best suited to be organized around one or two projects; others are ongoing large entities that may form individual entities for specific projects.

PARTNERSHIPS

To avoid the double taxation problem, many real estate entities are organized as partnerships. A partnership is a reporting vehicle, not a taxable entity, because partnerships are not considered a separate entity for tax purposes. Therefore, all income, appreciation, depreciation, and other losses flow through to the investors in the partnership. Net income is taxed only once, when it is received by the investor.

In a general partnership, all the partners share the risks, rewards, and management of the venture. Any and all partners are liable (jointly and severally) for all the debts and obligations of the business. For this reason, wealthy individuals and other money partners do not typically enter into general partnerships for real estate ventures, preferring the protection of limited liability provided by limited partnerships.

Limited partnerships have historically been the form of ownership most widely used for real estate. A limited partnership must include at least one general partner and one limited partner, with the general partner (or partners) liable for the partnership's debts

Appleton Mills, in Lowell, Massachusetts, was developed by a limited partnership. The 1.9 million-square-foot project incorporates market-rate and affordable housing, as well as commercial and retail space.

ICON ARCHITECTURE, INC.

and other obligations and the limited partner (or partners) bearing no liability beyond its contributed capital. Participation by limited partners in the day-to-day management of the partnership is not allowed, and if it occurs the limited partners risk losing their limited liability status. The most common type of limited partnership involves a corporate entity established by the developer, who acts as the general partner and manager, and investors who are limited partners.

LIMITED LIABILITY COMPANIES (LLC)

An LLC combines the advantages of a nontaxable entity, limited liability for investors, and no restrictions on investors' participation in the management of the enterprise. An LLC also has considerably streamlined governance provisions. Virtually every state has adopted legislation that allows business organizations to be formed as LLCs.

In general, the members and managers of an LLC are not personally liable for the LLC's debts and obligations, regardless of the degree to which they participate in its management. A member's liability is limited to the amount of capital contributed. Accordingly, creditors may not recover any part of a claim from a member's personal assets if the LLC's assets are insufficient to satisfy it. The advantages of LLCs—flexibility in allocation of income and loss, flow-through tax benefits, limited liability, streamlined governance, and owners' participation in management—make this form of ownership very attractive for development and investment.

S CORPORATIONS

An S corporation, like an LLC, can pass corporate income, losses, deductions, and credits through to its shareholders, who are then assessed tax at their individual income tax rates. This allows S corporations to avoid double taxation on the corporate income.

The specific parameters required to qualify for S corporation status can make this entity cumbersome. An S corporation cannot, for instance, include other partnerships, corporations, or foreign investors. Banks, insurance companies, and international companies are also prohibited from organizing as an S corporation.

This form of ownership protects the shareholders from individual personal liability and was relatively common until the introduction of the LLC, which is now a more common form for entities organized around individual project development.

REAL ESTATE INVESTMENT TRUSTS

A REIT is a private or public corporation that accesses capital through the sale of shares, creating enhanced liquidity for real estate investment. If they meet certain technical requirements, REITs can elect to pass realized gains through to shareholders and take tax deductions for the distributions, thus avoiding a double tax. Otherwise, they are taxed as corporations. A REIT is required to pass through 90 percent of its income, which effectively limits its source of capital to investor capital.

A public REIT provides investors with an opportunity to invest in managed real estate, spread risk through diversified holdings, and acquire interests in properties that would ordinarily be beyond their means. The shares of a publicly traded REIT can be sold or transferred easily and thus are more liquid than other types of real estate holdings. However, the prices of REIT shares can also be quite volatile, as with other stocks in the stock market. A disadvantage is that tax losses are trapped inside REITs: they may not be passed directly to investors as they are by partnerships, LLCs, and S corporations.

A private REIT can be used to raise capital without the filing or disclosure requirements required of a public offering. An unlisted public REIT may be publicly traded but does not meet listing requirements on an exchange.

Often, a REIT is structured as the general partner in a limited partnership. The umbrella partnership REIT (an UPREIT) is used in many REIT initial public offerings to allow the company's principals to transfer property from private ownership to the REIT without triggering a valuation change and tax liability. The REIT, as general partner, controls the activities of the limited partnership as effectively as it would if it owned the properties outright. A variation on this structure is a downREIT, in which partnership units (held by a specially formed downREIT) are used as the medium of exchange for acquiring properties without triggering tax consequences. These structures both use a joint venture agreement to set forth the parameters of the transaction.

CORPORATIONS

In general, real estate entities try to avoid the double taxation of profits characteristic of many corporations. However, insulating shareholders against personal liability for the operation of the development entity is a primary advantage of the corporate form of organization. The corporation also has an advantage in raising capital and more flexibility than a REIT in retaining earnings and charging losses against profits.

Elements of a Joint Venture

A "joint venture" is a real estate investment agreement between two or more parties negotiated and tailored for an individual project.[1] It stipulates the operating rules for multiple partners operating within a legal entity, such as a limited partnership or LLC that is formed to implement the transaction. It is a contract that stipulates the business plan, ownership, governance (including reporting), capitalization, and revenue distribution among the partners. A joint venture has an operating partner, who manages the operation of the entity, and investors, who have a more limited role in operations. The operating partner is usually a development entity, so it could itself be an LLC, limited partnership, REIT, corporation, or other entity.

A joint venture can be formed to invest in a single specific property (a single-asset joint venture), a portfolio of properties (a strategic or programmatic joint venture), or an operating company (entity-level joint venture). Its business plan can focus on the full range of real estate investment activities including development, redevelopment, acquisition of a portfolio of properties, recapitalization of an existing real estate entity, and distressed property acquisition.

The single-asset joint venture is the model historically used by owners and developers to raise capital from friends and family and high–net worth individuals. It can pool funding from a variety of sources, including institutions, and provides the flexibility to tailor the business terms to the circumstances of a particular asset. This model works also for new relationships between developers and institutional investors, because it focuses on a specific property and provides the opportunity to test the relationship on a limited basis and modify it with experience. It is often the starting point for forming a longer-term, broader relationship moving toward a strategic or programmatic joint venture.

A strategic/programmatic joint venture has the advantage of creating a long-term relationship between an operating partner and investors, thus creating more certainty on capital availability. The investors seek operating partners who have demonstrated expertise in implementing the business plan of the joint venture. The governance provisions provide protocols for deploying the capital either to the strategic categories or deal by deal. In return for the long-term commitment of capital, the investors frequently seek exclusivity commitments from the operating partner. These joint ventures depend on the investors to meet scheduled capital contribution payments. The operating partner has a requirement for reporting frequently to investors. As with the single-asset joint venture, a strategic or programmatic joint venture can create a track record for an owner/developer to engage in entity-level activities.

An entity-level joint venture invests in a real estate operating company (REOC) by purchasing a portion of the company's business and fee streams. This could involve purchase of the company's common or preferred equity, with provisions for voting control over the company's activities. Depending on the scope of the REOC, this type of equity investment can involve a much broader scope of investments than the other two forms of joint venture. Typically, this form of investment is used for distressed companies facing liquidity shortages or potential bankruptcy.

Each joint venture is specific to the partners, the opportunities, and the investment objectives; there are no preset terms. As with most real estate contracts, the parties to a joint venture spend most of their negotiating time addressing a small number of issues related to what could go wrong. What happens if the investors become unhappy with the operating partner? What happens if an investor fails to honor a scheduled capital contribution? How much control do investors have over the day-to-day decisions of the operating partner? These questions and more require considerable time to resolve. However, although good contract provisions are critical to the success of a joint venture, the trustworthiness and reliability of the participants are the most important contributors to its success.

Frequently, the terms of the joint venture agreement evolve as a project evolves and new partners join the project. An initial agreement may establish a partnership for land acquisition and the initial predevelopment tasks. As the project obtains financing commitments, a new separate joint venture may add investors and the legal form may change. The new form may be a joint venture agreement between the original partnership and the new investors. Usually, the joint venture takes the legal form of a limited partnership or LLC. Sometimes, a joint venture is formed between a landowner and a development entity to allow the landowner to participate in a project as a development partner.

Here are the major issues to be addressed in a joint venture agreement:

■ Business plan,
■ Participants,
■ Governance,

- Capitalization,
- Revenue distribution among the partners, and
- General provisions.

For each major issue, there are numerous elements to address.

BUSINESS PLAN

The business plan can be general or specific, depending on the purpose of the joint venture. Its purpose is to ensure that all the partners have the same expectations for how capital will be deployed. It should address, at a minimum, the following topics:

- *Investment strategy:* The investment strategy should describe the property, properties, types of properties, or entity in which investment will occur in as much detail as necessary to create common understanding among the participants and should provide the flexibility to respond to unforeseen circumstances. Some of the options that the investment strategy could address include the following:
  - Development of a specific property;
  - Development of a range of properties that meet stipulated criteria;
  - Acquisition of a portfolio of properties that meet specific criteria;
  - Acquisition of a real estate operating company;
  - Development and sale or ownership of property separately or collectively for a specific use or mixture of uses; and
  - Creation of an entitlement on a property with sale before all or a portion of it is developed.
- *Timing and budget:* The total investment amount anticipated and the timing of anticipated expenditures. This section should also include a preliminary budget with a draw schedule that is coordinated with planned activities.
- *Financing structure:* The anticipated debt and equity structure, including anticipated senior and junior loans and possible mezzanine financing. Because a joint venture relies on loans, the financing structure description should provide some formula for determining the equity investment amount based on the leverage that is actually achieved. The operating partner's co-investment requirement should be clearly stipulated.

  As described in chapter 4, if the investment is a development project, the operating partner usually funds the predevelopment costs. These predevelopment dollars are high risk so investors who participate in predevelopment financing warrant receiving a premium return.
- *Holding period:* Because most joint venture investments are relatively illiquid, the business plan should stipulate an expected holding period for the assets and an expected liquidation date, so that the investors have clear expectations of how long their investment will be tied up.

PARTICIPANTS

In general, all the participants in a joint venture are separate business entities, but some may be high–net worth individuals or other equity investors, such as a private equity fund, REIT, pension fund, or endowment. It is important to consider the status of each participating entity. Some entities may be tax exempt and not need the pass-through of tax losses. If the joint venture is organized as a general partnership, partners probably want to invest through some entity of their own, to protect themselves from personal liability. Here are some specific topics to address:

- *Roles:* The role of the operating partner should be clearly defined in terms of expected tasks and delegation of authority. If the joint venture is the operating partner, then the specific responsibilities of each participant should be clearly defined. For instance, in such a joint venture, one entity may be primarily responsible for obtaining entitlements, another for working as a public spokesperson, another for securing loans and outside investors. If the joint venture includes limited partners, their responsibilities and roles should be defined within the parameters of the legal entity.
- *Guarantees and recourse:* If the project is a development project, there needs to be a stipulation of which partner (usually the operating partner) provides the performance guarantees and which partner is providing the assets for recourse.
- *Ownership:* Where the ownership of the assets is vested is important for distributing tax benefits from depreciation and other provisions. Usually, the ownership is vested in the limited partners, who then capture most of the tax benefits. The operating partner then holds a token percentage of ownership.
- *Liability:* Usually, the operating partner is assigned liability for the activities of the joint venture.

GOVERNANCE

The terms should reflect how the partners will share information, how decisions will be made, and who will make them:

- *Reporting:* Communication and information-sharing methods should be clearly described in terms of frequency and format of reporting.
- *Decision making:* How decisions are made and who is involved in making them need to be addressed. Within the parameters of the authority delegated to the operating partner in the role description, the terms should identify which decisions require the participation of the limited partners and spell out the procedures for making those decisions. Some key decisions may require concurrence from all members of the joint venture; others may require only a majority or super-majority. For instance, contracting for services below a certain dollar limit could occur within the authority delegated to the operating partner. Larger commitments may require a majority vote, and selling the project may require unanimity.

CAPITALIZATION

The terms should stipulate the expected outside limits of the capital contribution requirements and mechanisms for addressing delays in contributions and shortfalls in funding:

- *Contribution amounts and timing:* The total responsibility of each partner in both amount and timing must be specified, as should the responsibility of the operating partner for predevelopment expenditures and co-investment. The terms should stipulate the expected outside limits of the capital contribution requirements and how the participants will obtain additional funding if the project requires more in capital than the outside limits require. If a member of the joint venture is the land owner, then the value, or some agreed-upon method of valuing the land, should be stipulated.

- *Dilution provisions:* There should also be provisions for diluting a partner's share of profits if that partner fails to make a scheduled contribution on time. This provision should provide a penalty and reflect the cost to the project for obtaining alternative sources of capital.
- *Shortfall provisions:* Unpredictable costs and shortfalls in revenues test the strength and ingenuity of the joint venture. If expenditures exceed budgeted amounts, provisions should exist for meeting the funding shortfall. These provisions should address how this additional capital will be obtained and the amount of return it will receive.

REVENUE DISTRIBUTION AMONG THE PARTNERS

The agreement should stipulate how returns will be distributed and how fees will be calculated and distributed. Here are specific issues:

- *Preferred return:* The agreement should address the calculation of preferred return, taking into account when capital is deployed and when returns start to accrue. Returns are usually paid pari passu among investors on the basis of the amount invested, unless there has been a dilution of shares from a delay in making a contribution or there are priority payments for early investors who funded high-risk phases of the venture. A land owner who puts property in the joint venture as equity may also receive a priority distribution before other equity investors.
- *Promotional returns:* There should be a clear stipulation of the distribution levels for promotional return, showing clearly the trigger points for changing the distribution between the investors and operating partner.
- *Fees:* Frequently, investors and lenders authorize the operating partner to take "fee income" associated with services provided to the investment program. This income provides needed cash flow for a developer/operating partner before it receives a distribution from cash flow. Fee practices vary considerably among project types and investors. The typical generic fee income is a "developer fee," which is charged when project financing is successful and is usually paid along with the construction draw. Other fees include "acquisition fees," "marketing fees," and "construction management fees." Joint ventures may also pay incentive payments to the operating partner based on the performance of the assets. The carried interest incentive payments described in chapter 5 fall into this category; they are based on the increase in asset value after investors' principal is returned.
- *Clawbacks:* Many joint ventures also include clawback provisions that kick in at the point of asset liquidation. They are used to recover excess incentive payments made to the operating partner during the life of the joint venture. Upon liquidation of the investments, the cumulative profits are tallied and distributions received by the operating partner in excess of a certain percentage are deemed excess and returned to limited partners. These provisions apply when asset values decline at the point of sale below the levels that were the basis for the incentive payments.

GENERAL PROVISIONS

The agreement should address generic issues, including operations, confidentiality, disagreement, death, and bankruptcy. Here are some common issues in this category:

■ *Management services for the joint venture:* Sometimes, one of the parties assumes responsibility for accounting, tax filing, and other tasks. This is especially true if the joint venture is not anticipated to be an LLC or some other recognized business entity immediately. There should be provisions for transferring this function when necessary.

■ *Winding up:* As noted in chapter 5, disputes leading to termination typically are addressed with a "buy-sell" provision, which should be relied upon only in dire circumstances.

■ *Death:* The death of a key individual should also be addressed in a manner that allows the parties to the joint venture to continue with the venture by purchasing the share of the deceased party. Key-man life insurance is an option, though expensive. The process for valuing the share of the deceased party probably should involve some third-party appraisal.

■ *Confidentiality and public announcements:* Confidentiality and public announcements should be addressed, particularly if one of the members of the joint venture is a publicly traded company and must meet the disclosure requirements of the Securities and Exchange Commission.

Financing Structure

This section discusses various options for structuring a joint venture, a primary vehicle by which investors and operating partners create the means for deploying equity capital, raising debt capital, and implementing a real estate venture. Although joint ventures differ in investment focus and participants, figure 7-1 summarizes the major elements of an equity joint venture.

The addition of a lender or lenders to a real estate venture makes the financing structure more complex. Each financing participant wants a clear stipulation of the priority of payment and their remedies for recovery if there is a loan default. Figures 7-2 through 7-6 depict increasingly complex real estate transactions. It should be noted that these are illustrative; the actual percentages associated with each component of capital for project finance depend on capital market conditions at the time of project financing.

Figure 7-2 shows the relatively simple structure of a development project with one lender and a joint venture composed of one operating partner/developer and one investor. The joint venture is the borrower, though the provisions of the joint venture agreement may assign responsibility for recourse to the operating partner/developer. This recourse mechanism may also involve some combination of assets available to the developer and investor. The joint venture is organized as either an LLC or limited partnership. The lender keeps the entire loan on its books, and the joint venture agreement governs the distribution of profits between the developer and investor.

Figure 7-3 shows the added complexity of having a junior (subordinated) lender in the transaction. The joint venture is now responsible for two loans. Inter-creditor agreements must be in place between the primary and junior lenders to ensure clarity in the access of the primary lender to the project value. As with the simple structure, the recourse mechanism for securing the performance guarantees is stipulated within the joint venture.

FIGURE 7-1
Joint Venture Structure for Equity Deployment and Venture Management

Limited partnership or LLC governed by joint venture agreement
among operating partner/developer and limited partners

OPERATING PARTNER/DEVELOPER
One or more of:
- General partnership
- LLC
- REIT
- REOC
- Individuals

LIMITED PARTNERS (INVESTORS)
One or more of:
- High-net worth individuals
- Family and friends
- Private equity funds
- Pension funds
- Insurance companies
- Managed funds
- REITs
- Landowner

ROLE AND RESPONSIBILITIES
- Manages investment
- Assumes liability
- Co-invests in project
- Provides performance guarantees and recourse
- Provides project reports
- Receives service and incentive fees
- Receives share of preferred and promotional return based on co-investment
- Receives share of promotional return after limited partners' objectives are met

ROLE AND RESPONSIBILITIES
- Vested owners of the real estate investment (99%)
- Provide capital contributions on a stipulated schedule
- Participate in major decisions on capital deployment
- Receive preferred and a share of promotional return

Joint Venture Obtains Loans For Venture

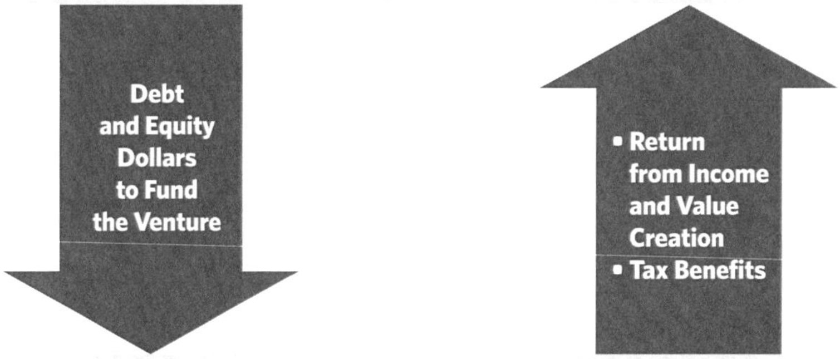

Debt and Equity Dollars to Fund the Venture

- **Return from Income and Value Creation**
- **Tax Benefits**

Real Estate Venture

FIGURE 7-2

Simple Joint Venture with One Lender and Developer/Investor

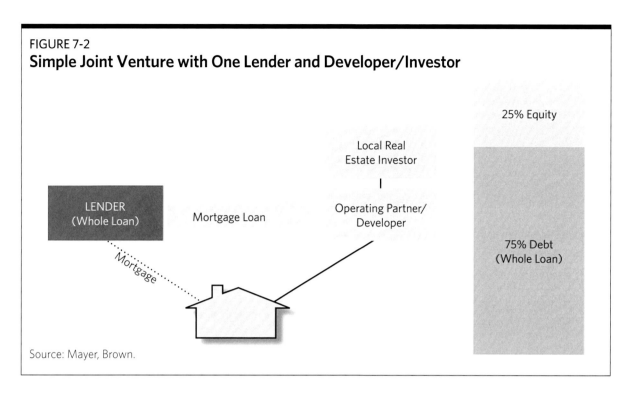

Source: Mayer, Brown.

FIGURE 7-3

Two Loans with Developer/Investor Joint Venture

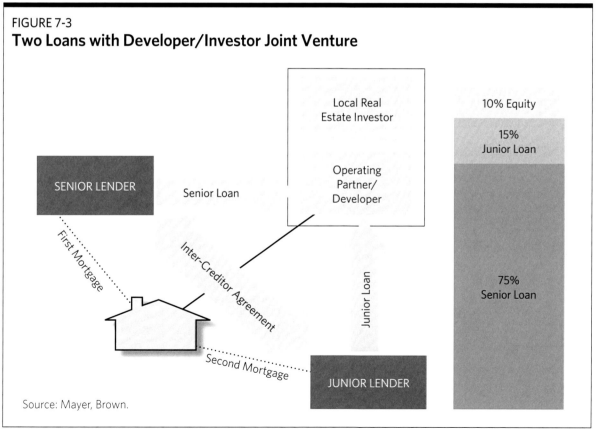

Source: Mayer, Brown.

FIGURE 7-4
Primary Lender with Developer, Investor, and Mezzanine Joint Venture

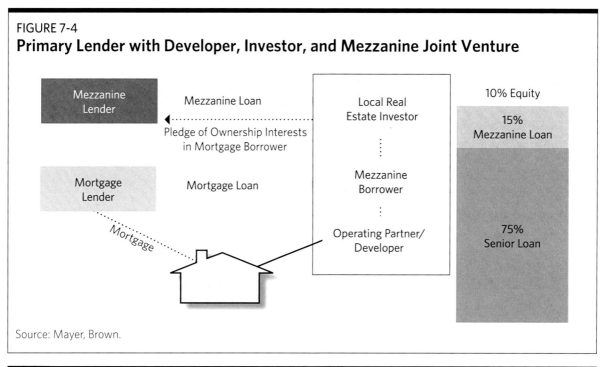

Source: Mayer, Brown.

FIGURE 7-5
Primary Lender with Developer, Investor, Equity Fund, and Mezzanine Joint Venture

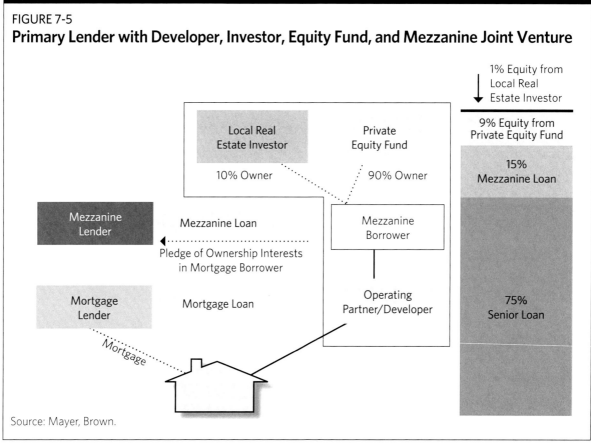

Source: Mayer, Brown.

Figure 7-4 shows the structure for a mezzanine lender in which the mezzanine borrower becomes party to the joint venture with repayment of the mezzanine loan secured by contractual provisions among the members of the joint venture. The principal and an interest payment is paid to the mezzanine lender out of sale or refinance proceeds. The mezzanine loan also has a return on equity component, which can be superior, equivalent, or subordinated to other equity investors, depending on what the parties negotiate. These contractual provisions may or may not be supplemented with a subordinated lien on the property; if they are, an inter-creditor agreement is needed to avoid confusion about the primary lender's position. Again, the recourse mechanism for securing the performance guarantees is stipulated within the joint venture.

Figure 7-5 adds another outside investor, in this case a private equity fund, to the structure involving the mezzanine lender. Here, the equity fund is part of the joint venture with a priority of payment, stipulated in the joint venture agreement, before the other investor. In this structure, as in the previous one, the primary and mezzanine lender are secured with a lien on the property; this means that they get paid principal and interest by the priority of their lien and then there is a distribution of equity return among the mezzanine lender, the equity fund, and the local investor based on an agreed priority of payment. Again, the recourse mechanism for securing the performance guarantees is stipulated within the joint venture.

Finally, figure 7-6 shows the tranching of a loan into priority payments levels for a securitized CMBS loan. If the project fails to meet total debt service on the loan, then the CMBS trustee must act to protect the interests of the bondholders. This may mean foreclosure, wiping out the position of the equity investors and developer, even if the default is small enough that a reduction in loan balance could enable the project to meet its loan payment obligations.

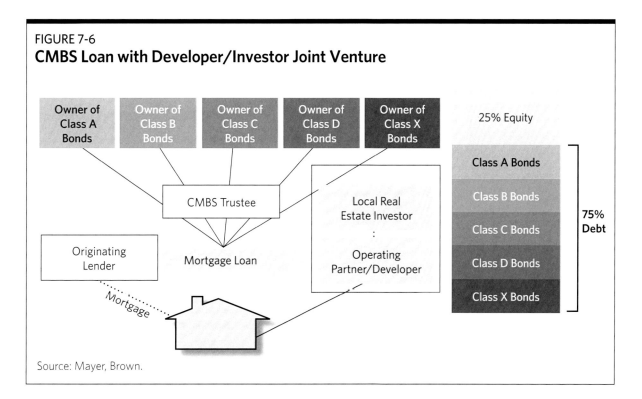

FIGURE 7-6
CMBS Loan with Developer/Investor Joint Venture

Source: Mayer, Brown.

PROFIT DISTRIBUTION TO THE DEVELOPMENT ENTITY

In a development project, the operating partner receives a distribution of project profits according to an agreed-upon distribution formula between equity investors and the developer. Figure 7-7 shows a typical allocation of profits, illustrating that for most projects this distribution occurs at two levels—first between the developer entity and the equity investor, and second among the parties to the development entity. Many development entities are, in turn, joint ventures of other individuals or entities. The figure shows the waterfall distribution between investors and developer described in chapter 2. After the waterfall distributions to investors have been satisfied, profits are available to provide returns to the development entity for distribution among its members.

As shown in figure 7-7, profits received by the development entity typically are divided among the members of the entity based on return to investment dollars and return to "talent." Depending on project profitability and the investment return requirement, the profits paid to the development entity will be distributed equally to each of these two categories.

This distribution is particularly relevant in partnerships or joint ventures in which different parties have different roles. Some may be limited partners who are simply investors. Others may have all the development skill and invest little money, contributing primarily talent. Negotiating the split of profits between investment return and talent return is a major effort associated with the formation of a development entity.

FIGURE 7-7
Distribution of Project Cash Flow Between Investors and Operating Partner/ Developer and Within the Development Entity

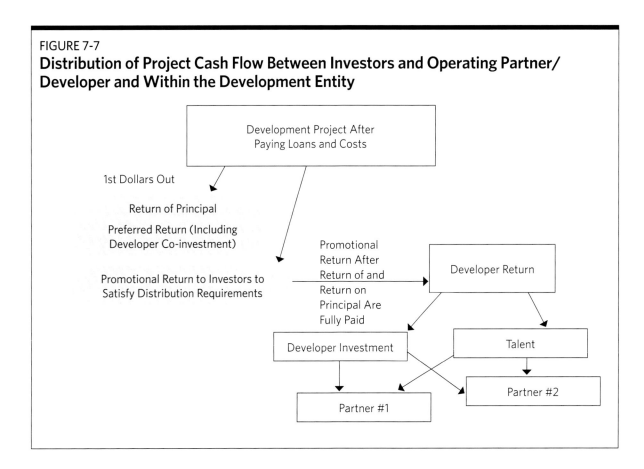

Once agreement has been reached on the percentage of profits that will go to repay investment, allocations from this flow typically are distributed proportionately to the amount of investment made by each partner; that is, pari passu. For example, an investor that put up 20 percent of the investment would receive 20 percent of the profits distributed to the investment side. It is not unusual to have a "penalty dilution" of the distribution of profits to the investment side if one member of the entity fails to make required contributions. As an example, if the agreement is that each partner will contribute half of a $4 million budget—that is, $2 million each—and one partner is short by $400,000, that partner's share of profit distribution would drop to less than the 40 percent of the budget that the partner ultimately contributed. To take this example further, a possible penalty dilution provision could require that a partner's failure to meet contribution obligations would cause the distribution percentage to fall 1.5 percent for each 1 percent shortfall. This provision motivates investors to meet their investment obligations.

Allocations to the talent side vary considerably depending on the mix of partners and the nature of the project. In general, they are allocated according to how the parties negotiate the distribution, which depends on a variety of factors:

■ The role of each party;
■ Which party controls the development opportunity;
■ Which party is "bankable" and can provide assets for recourse loans; and
■ Which partner has skills vital to the success of the project.

EXAMPLE: PROFIT DISTRIBUTION WITHIN A DEVELOPMENT ENTITY

This hypothetical example illustrates the distribution of profits within a joint venture and then within the operating partner/developer of the joint venture, as shown in figure 7-7. As an overview, consider that a development joint venture is composed of an operating partner/developer and investors. Profits are distributed from a real estate project as, in priority order, 1) return of equity to investors only, 2) preferred return on equity to investors only, and 3) promotional return distributed in a waterfall between investors and the operating partner/developer at agreed-upon percentages. Once the operating partner/developer receives its distribution of profits, then there typically is another distribution to the parties that make up the operating partner/developer.

This example involves a joint venture with an operating partner/developer that is also a joint venture. The operating partner/developer has two participants, a senior and junior partner. Their agreement is that any distributions made to the operating partner/developer are distributed equally between an investment category and a talent category. Distributions to the investment category are distributed between the two participants proportional to the amount of money they have invested in the larger joint venture. Distributions to the talent category are distributed 30 percent to the senior partner and 20 percent to the junior partner in accordance with the negotiated distribution.

The project is 81 for-sale townhomes and 20,000 square feet of commercial space with project value and costs as shown in figure 7-8. The example assumes that the commercial component is sold upon project completion.

FIGURE 7-8
Hypothetical Project: Development Summary

DEVELOPMENT PLAN

Total Land Area (Sq. Ft.)		180,000		
Residential[a]	Number	Sq. Ft.	Average Price	Total Value
Model 1	45	1,800	$675,000	$30,375,000
Model 2	22	1,400	$546,000	$12,012,000
Affordable	14	1,600	$320,000	$4,480,000
Total Residential	81			**$46,867,000**
Commercial, at Cap Rate of 7%				
Rental Rate/Sq. Ft.			$24	
Space		20,000		
Total Commercial				**$6,857,143**
Gross Project Value				**$53,724,143**

DEVELOPMENT COSTS

Residential		$16,500,000
Site Development		$3,570,046
Commercial		$2,200,000
Parking		$632,435
Land		$11,000,000
Construction Loan Interest	5.4% of construction and land costs	$1,923,041
Architecture and Engineering	4.5% of construction costs	$1,030,612
Construction Management	4% of construction costs	$916,099
Taxes	1% of construction costs	$229,025
Contingency	10% of construction costs	$2,290,248
Total Costs		**$40,291,506**

SALES

Residential Value		$46,867,000
Marketing	8.0%	($3,749,360)
Commercial Value		$6,857,143
Net Value		**$49,974,783**

a. Market sales: models 1 and 2 at $400 per sq. ft. and affordable at $220 per sq. ft.

FIGURE 7-9
Hypothetical Project: Financing and Estimated Return

COSTS	
Construction	$22,902,481
Design, Financing, and Contingency	$6,389,025
Land	$11,000,000
Total Nonmarketing Costs	**$40,291,506**
Net Sales Value	$49,974,783
Gross Return	**$9,683,277**

FINANCING PACKAGE	
Bank Loan at 65% of Nonmarketing Costs	$26,189,479
Equity Investment	$14,102,027
Total Financing	**$40,291,506**

SOURCE OF EQUITY	
Outside Investors at 90%	$12,691,824
Operating Partner/Developer at 10%	$1,410,203
Total Equity Investment	$14,102,027
Rate of Preferred Return	9%
Waterfall Percentage of Promote to Outside Investors	80%

DISTRIBUTION OF RETURN TO EQUITY SOURCES	
Outside Investors	
Preferred Return (for 2 Years): 18.81% Total Return on Outside Investor Equity	$2,387,332
Promotional Return: 80% of Gross Return After Paying Preferred	$5,624,548
Total Return	$8,011,881
Total Rate of Return, Annual	28%
Operating Partner/Developer	
Preferred Return (for 2 Years): 18.81% Total Return on Developer Co-investment	$265,259
Promotional Return: 20% (Remaining Gross Return After Paying Preferred)	$1,406,137
Total Return	$1,671,396
Total Distribution of Gross Return	**$9,683,277**

Figure 7-9 shows the financing structure for this project, which involves a loan for 65 percent of project costs (not including marketing), with the remaining costs coming from equity. The operating partner/developer provides a 10 percent co-investment on the total equity requirement. The equity investors (including the operating partner/developer based on the co-investment amount) all receive a 9 percent preferred rate of return over the two-year construction period and 80 percent of the promotional return after paying the preferred return. The operating partner/developer also receives 20 percent of the promote after paying the preferred return. Total return on the project is shown in figure 7-9.

FIGURE 7-10
Hypothetical Project: Distribution of Return

Distribution within Operating Partner/Developer	
Preferred Return[a]	$265,259
Promotional Return[b]	$1,406,137
Total Distribution	$1,671,396
Distribution as Return on Investment	
Amount of Total Distribution	$968,328
Share to Senior Partner	25%
Share to Junior Partner	25%
Total Percentage Distribution to Investment	50%
Total Rate of Return on Invested Capital	30%
Distribution to Talent	
Amount of Total Distribution	$703,069
Share to Senior Partner	30%
Share to Junior Partner	20%
Total Percentage Distribution to Talent	50%
Distribution among Partners	
To Senior Partner for Investment	$484,164
To Junior Partner for Investment	$484,164
To Senior Partner for Talent	$421,841
To Junior Partner for Talent	$281,227
Total Distribution among Partners	**$1,671,396**
Total Return to Senior Partner	**$906,005**
Total Return to Junior Partner	**$765,391**

a. Allocated all to cash investment.
b. Allocated between cash investment and talent based on percentage to each.

Figure 7-10 shows the distribution of the total return within the operating partner/developer, between the two development partners (a senior partner and a junior partner). As figure 7-10 shows, all of the preferred return on equity received by the operating partner/developer is distributed proportionally to what each partner invested to meet the co-investment capital requirement.

The remainder of payments to the operating partner/developer come from the promotional return. Half of this promotional return is paid as additional return on the investment side of the distribution. This distribution to the "investment" side of the development entity is distributed proportionally to the cash investment made by each of the development partners. The remainder of the developer's return on the project is distributed to the talent side. The senior partner receives 30 percent of the total distribution and the junior partner receives 20 percent. This percentage distribution is what the partners negotiated before proceeding with the project and reflects an agreement between them about the relative talent contribution that each makes to the project's value.

Note:
1. *This discussion of a joint venture benefitted from a webinar delivered by Steven Ott, University of North Carolina at Charlotte, entitled "Understanding and Navigating the World of Real Estate Private Equity."*

CHAPTER 8

Managing the Entitlement Process for Financial Viability

I n most U.S. communities the regulatory process for obtaining development approvals—entitlement—has become increasingly complex, frustrating, and time-consuming. Communities have responded to concerns about traffic congestion, poor air quality, overcrowded schools, lack of adequate infrastructure, design, energy efficiency, and sustainability with more oversight, more requirements, and, in general, more regulation. In many jurisdictions, requirements are not completely determined before a project goes through the entitlement process, creating considerable uncertainty about the duration and outcome of that process. For all these reasons, managing the entitlement process to achieve financial viability requires considerable skill and a thorough understanding of project economics.

The entitlement process has a very significant effect on a project's financial viability in a variety of ways. First, projects take more time to entitle than they used to, thus requiring more at-risk capital to be outstanding for a longer period. Second, project modifications during entitlement affect the project's value and cost and can significantly change its financial viability. Third, the scope of professional services required to address entitlement issues results in much higher processing costs than in the past. And fourth, uncertainty about receiving an entitlement increases the risk of losing predevelopment capital.

Typically, many independent regulatory authorities have a say in what happens in a project, thus compounding the complexity of the process. In the United States, almost 39,000 "general-purpose" local governments control land use within their jurisdictions. Another 13,500 local governments are special districts; many of them are key municipal service providers that overlap the service areas of the general-purpose governments and influence requirements for new development.

Each entity and its regulatory action has the potential to impose changes on a project to meet public and regulatory concerns. A developer must anticipate the possible changes and must have created a framework to accurately evaluate the financial impact of a change. Understanding what a change costs requires analyzing multiple development scenarios to anticipate how possible changes would affect a project's viability. The developer also must understand how changes to development conditions that have a cost may create value that offsets the cost.

Finally, because the public is a major participant in the entitlement process, a developer must understand how to make a case directly to, and establish relationships with, the public. The goals of a developer in managing an entitlement process should be to build trust and community ownership with the public and with officials.

Effective entitlement management is fundamental to a project's financial viability. This chapter describes how to manage the entitlement process to reduce its duration, manage modifications required by it, engage professional services cost-effectively, and avoid failure in achieving an entitlement.

Mapping the Process

Because the entitlement process can be so complex and time-consuming, successful developers understand the importance—from the beginning—of mapping the steps in the regulatory process and developing a comprehensive communication strategy to accompany the formal steps. Mapping and managing the process are fundamental to minimizing the time that entitlement will take.

General-purpose local governments exercise five categories of direct regulatory control, each of which relies on different sources of legal authority and each of which may have a separate, uncoordinated approval process, depending on how the jurisdiction manages its approvals:

■ *Land use control:* This category includes zoning, design review, and comprehensive plan compliance.

■ *Environmental review and conditions:* Many states require a separate environmental review process that imposes mitigation measures in order to receive environmental approval.

■ *Subdivision and parcel map conditions:* This review typically relates to access, transportation, and utility requirements for dividing property into multiple parcels.

■ *Infrastructure fees and dedications:* Fees capture the prorated cost of public improvements and are usually imposed by ordinances that are separate from other regulatory categories. Additional infrastructure dedication requirements can also be imposed as a condition of entitlement.

■ *Building code:* These regulations focus on the structural and safety aspects of building construction and, although locally administered, usually connect to a state or national set of uniform standards.

In addition to these five categories of direct control, two other categories of regulatory control affect many projects:

■ *Regional or state requirements:* Most states give regional transportation and utility providers authority to approve development projects through either separate or coordinated action with general-purpose governments. For significant projects, some states also require a state-level review.

■ *Federal requirements:* In some areas, federal requirements such as flood control or wetlands preservation may also affect entitlement conditions. These requirements may be incorporated into local development regulations or imposed independently of local action.

Effective management of the entitlement process starts before and continues during the due diligence period. It then continues throughout the predevelopment stage. The steps for effectively mapping and managing the entitlement occur at four points:

■ Before making an offer on a development site;
■ After an offer on a development site has been accepted;
■ During the due diligence period; and
■ As circumstances change.

BEFORE MAKING AN OFFER

Before making an offer, a developer should carry out the following tasks:

■ Get to know the land use jurisdiction. Visit several policy board meetings; research the history of land use decisions; read land use policy documents; talk to other developers about the jurisdiction; read the local newspaper; and join local civic groups and talk with citizens about their community.
■ Visit the planning department to understand the policy framework within which a development site is considered. Make a preliminary identification of issues and time frames for processing the entitlement.
■ Investigate development impact fees from all jurisdictions that levy fees, and ask a land use jurisdiction official to confirm the results of this research. Investigate whether additional public improvement costs will be required as a condition of development approval.
■ Investigate the requirements of regional, state, and federal influences on land use and understand how much interaction will be required beyond the local level. Build the evaluation of issues, time frames, fees, and other costs into the offer for the development site.

AFTER AN OFFER IS ACCEPTED

After an offer on a development site has been accepted, during the due diligence period, a developer should talk to all the key professional staff of the jurisdiction who will influence the entitlement result. The goal is to identify the issues more thoroughly and obtain greater certainty on the formal steps in the entitlement process. Specifically:

■ At the local agency planning department, discuss all aspects of the land use control and environmental review issues.
■ If the project requires a subdivision map, include the engineering staff in discussions.
■ In all the jurisdictions that levy development impact fees, talk with the relevant officials about the fees and prepare an estimate that is validated by an official from each such jurisdiction.
■ With the chief building official, discuss the plan check and building inspection process and develop realistic expectations about time and requirements.
■ Evaluate the involvement of regional, state, or federal interests that affect development conditions.
■ Engage the architect and other professionals, if necessary, in evaluating whether the issues raised during these discussions create unusual cost or processing difficulties.

- If any aspect of the more detailed research on the entitlement issues and process differs from the assumptions made in preparing the offer for the development site, evaluate whether this difference causes a reconsideration of the terms and conditions of purchase.

DURING DUE DILIGENCE

During the due diligence period, the developer should conduct the following tasks:

- Create a draft schedule of submittals and formal actions, and review it—first with the project architect and then with other professionals—to ensure it is realistic. Then review the schedule with the local jurisdiction's professional staff and ask them to comment. On the basis of these comments, create a final schedule and ensure that the project architect and other professionals on the project work to meet it.
- If the local entitlement process is separated into multiple processes, attempt to reach agreement with the professional staff on consolidating as many as possible for simultaneous processing. For instance, attempt to reach agreement that the public hearings for the zoning change, the subdivision map, and the environmental review can occur simultaneously instead of sequentially.
- Identify the issues that may have a significant effect on project costs or the timing of entitlement. Focus predevelopment budgeting and task management efforts on resolving these significant issues.

AS CIRCUMSTANCES CHANGE

Developers must continuously monitor progress and update the schedule as circumstances change. This includes the following tasks:

- Make sure that the project team is meeting its part of the schedule.
- If the staff of the local jurisdiction fails to meet its part of the schedule, inquire about the reason. If the jurisdiction's professional staff continues to fail to meet the schedule, raise this issue with a department head, chief executive officer, or elected official.

A final observation on mapping the process: the entitlement process is inherently unpredictable because of citizen participation and additional requirements that can result from it. Mapping the formal process of submittals and regulatory action is a first step to effective management, but the schedule must be dynamic. It must accommodate time to work with the public and to respond to related demands for project reconfiguration. The more research that a developer does before entering the entitlement process, the fewer surprises occur. Nevertheless, a successful developer stays flexible and responds when change occurs.

Managing Project Economics During Entitlement

Beyond having a firm grasp of the original project finances, the developer must understand the economics of options or reconfigurations that may be discussed or proposed in the entitlement process. Although the types of change that the entitlement process can impose are numerous, four types are most common:

- *Density:* These changes go both ways, with some communities seeking higher density to achieve sustainability goals and some reducing density because of public concerns.
- *Parking requirements:* Parking consumes land area and, if it is not surface parking, has a high cost.
- *Contribution to public improvements:* Communities sometimes try to extract contributions to public improvements where there is little or no connection between the development and the need for the improvement.
- *Project design:* Design approval, usually the last step in the entitlement process, can entail costly and impractical requirements for the project.

DENSITY

Three important issues can arise regarding project density, and the developer must evaluate them very carefully:

- First, more is not necessarily more. Denser projects may have a higher yield per acre, but they may have a lower return on costs. The optimal density for the project may be less than the maximum density allowed.
- Second, because density can be controversial, it creates uncertainty in the entitlement process. The public focuses on density as a major determinant of neighborhood character. High density requires height. It also increases traffic and parking demands. For residents in low-density communities, higher-density residential uses may imply higher crime. And density frequently brings a mix of uses that provoke public fears about change.
- Third, density entails extreme variations in construction costs. High-density projects typically require expensive parking structures or complex construction techniques, which can cause costs to be very high. To ensure that construction can be accomplished efficiently, the developer must pay careful attention to how the project is configured.

To understand the economics of different densities, the developer must recognize that higher-density projects usually carry a higher unit cost for construction and a higher total cost when parking is included. Moving from Type V construction (wood frame) to Type I (steel superstructure) means higher costs. Higher density makes sense when a project can sell or rent at prices that will cover these higher costs. A developer may attempt to build at higher density because the larger amount of development can produce a higher total profit.

Figure 8-1 illustrates the construction cost for a hypothetical 1,500-square-foot residential unit using the product types shown in chapter 1. Note how unit costs for residential development increase with density and product type. To simplify the analysis, land and indirect costs are not included here.

To take this analysis one step further, figure 8-2 shows the net dollar yield per acre in terms of sales value less construction and parking costs. (Again, to simplify the analysis, land and indirect costs are not included here.) Clearly, the higher-density projects produce higher total profit per acre even at the higher construction costs. Of course, higher total profit seems worth striving for—until one looks at the return on investment that this higher profit requires.

Figure 8-3 shows the cash-on-cash return at various densities, illustrating that as the density increases the percentage return on cost actually declines. Again, these costs do not include land or indirect costs.

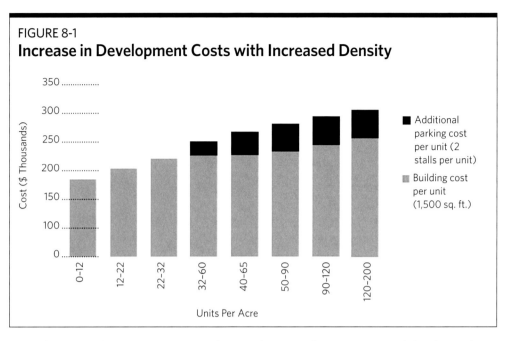

FIGURE 8-1
Increase in Development Costs with Increased Density

Cost ($ Thousands) vs. Units Per Acre

Legend:
- Additional parking cost per unit (2 stalls per unit)
- Building cost per unit (1,500 sq. ft.)

Often a developer gets so wrapped up in the original project proposal that he or she fails to examine alternatives that may better fit the community's wishes and could perform better economically as well. That is, he or she fails to complete a real option analysis. As the preceding discussion shows, careful analysis is needed to understand how changes in density may affect project viability. In many situations, lower density can produce a higher rate of return, even though the total return may be less. A project with a higher rate of return will more easily attract investors.

A significant variable in medium- and high-density projects is the cost of construction—in particular, the cost per square foot. Differences in configuration and site conditions affect construction costs. A major factor is whether the sellable or leasable space

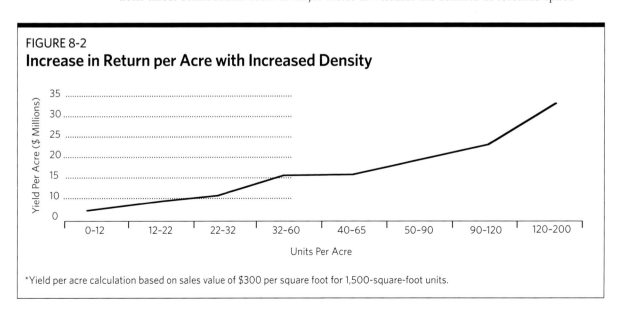

FIGURE 8-2
Increase in Return per Acre with Increased Density

Yield Per Acre ($ Millions) vs. Units Per Acre

*Yield per acre calculation based on sales value of $300 per square foot for 1,500-square-foot units.

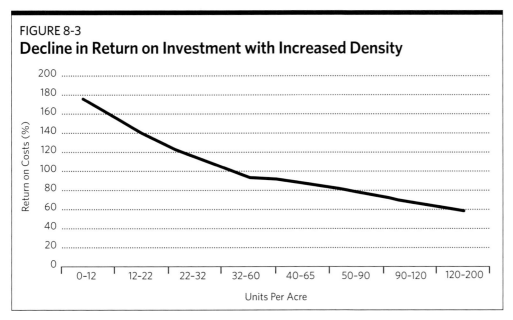

FIGURE 8-3
Decline in Return on Investment with Increased Density

Return on Costs (%) — Units Per Acre: 0-12, 12-22, 22-32, 32-60, 40-65, 50-90, 90-120, 120-200

captures economies of scale in spreading the relatively high cost of parking structures. Site conditions also play a significant role in cost variability, with some sites requiring expensive foundation work because of slope or soils conditions.

Figure 8-4 presents data on the actual construction cost per square foot of medium- and high-density (40 to 50 units per acre) residential projects in the San Francisco Bay Area. Note how costs per square foot and costs per unit vary without any correlation to the number of units. For medium- and high-density projects, it is critically important that the developer closely analyze the costs of the project and understand the factors affecting costs.

FIGURE 8-4
Variation in Construction Costs for Medium- and High-Density Residential Projects, 2005 to 2010

Units	Area (Sq. Ft.)	Construction Cost ($ Million)	Cost Per Sq. Ft. ($)	Cost Per Unit ($)
40	40,936	8.1	198	202,500
47	31,611	10.2	323	217,021
49	66,575	13.0	195	265,306
80	81,567	12.3	151	153,750
80	126,000	25.7	204	321,250
84	63,000	12.3	195	146,429
86	125,000	21.2	170	246,512
129	127,932	29.8	233	231,008
		Average	209	222,972

Source: Roberts Obayashi Construction, Dublin, California.

PARKING

Parking requirements are controversial. An "under-parked" project may add significantly to a parking shortage in the surrounding neighborhood. In addition, parking ratios have a dramatic effect on both project economics and project design. Depending on the density of a project, a high parking ratio requires either significant land for parking or significant costs for parking structures. Figure 8-5 shows some typical areas and cost per stall for different parking configurations.

As the project density increases, the total cost and the cost per stall of the parking increases, because denser parking requires structures or underground parking that will be expensive to build. An entitlement that reduces parking ratios below the standard (two stalls per residential unit and five stalls per 1,000 square feet of commercial space) lowers the cost of parking. However, it may result in a project that cannot be sold or leased because of a perception of insufficient parking for users' needs. The issues of cost and marketability must be evaluated very carefully.

FIGURE 8-5
Parking Costs and Area, Different Configurations

Parking Configuration	Cost Per Stall ($)	Area Per Stall (Sq. Ft.)
Surface	3,000	250
Under Podium	15,000	350
Structure	20,000	400
Underground	35,000	450

PUBLIC IMPROVEMENTS

Obtaining entitlements may also require developers to contribute to the cost of public improvements or other community objectives. Sometimes these contributions bear little, if any, connection to the impacts of the project in scope or cost. Sometimes a community group demands a contribution to an organization or to an improvement for the neighborhood. Sometimes the local government demands that the project pay for the entire cost of an improvement that serves the entire community.

If these costs are known before land is purchased, they can be built into the pro forma and reduce the residual land value. But frequently a concern raised during the entitlement process identifies a need—for, say, a signalized intersection, or a contribution to open space or schools, or an increased setaside of units for affordable housing. Unanticipated changes can have a dramatic effect on project costs and may make the project economically unviable. If a contribution has no connection (legally, no "nexus") to the project, as occasionally happens, the developer must evaluate what is right and what can be afforded and decide whether the cost and time required to fight the demand is warranted.

DESIGN

The design review process is typically the last step in entitlement before the application for a building permit. Frequently, this process can seem quite arbitrary; in many communities it is conducted by a committee of citizens who may have little, if any, familiarity with architectural issues. The reviewers may impose what appear to be superficial changes to the architectural look of the project that have significant cost implications. Or they may impose major changes to site utilization that have significant effects on the marketability of the site.

As the entitlement process proceeds, the community or the governing body may seek changes (concessions) that were not anticipated at the beginning of the process and which add cost but do not add value. It is critically important that the developer anticipate these items and know their cost. It is also critically important that the developer get something in return for making a concession. For example, if the residents in an adjacent neighborhood ask for lower density and the developer decides to make this concession, it is important that the developer do so in a way that commits the neighborhood residents to support the project. Such deals need to take place in the context of a working relationship in which the developer attempts to build community ownership of the project.

To summarize, the recommendations for managing the entitlement process to enhance project viability are these:

- Continuously monitor project financial viability. Update the project financial analysis throughout the entitlement process.
- Analyze the effect that density and parking have on project yield and on rate of return. Recognize that increased density and floor/area ratio come with increased construction costs per unit of development and therefore may result in a lower return on investment. Consequently, carefully analyze any incentive program that allows higher density of development in return for a public benefit, to ensure that the incentive offsets the cost.
- Anticipate what concessions the project may be asked to make. Identify early what additional costs may be imposed on the project. Do not make concessions without getting value in return; each concession should generate a reciprocal commitment.

Managing the Process

Bill Hudnut, former mayor of Indianapolis, congressman, and Senior Fellow at the Urban Land Institute, has this to say about the entitlement process:

> In the public process, the developer has to answer two fundamental questions about a project: Will it pencil? Can it be approved? Approval comes [more easily] if time is taken to work the grass roots. Attend public hearings. Listen. Learn what the public wants—and what it opposes. Be a problem solver, seek direction, perceive what the community needs, and show citizens how the project will fill that need. Do not just try to sell a project cold. Explain the proposal. Tell it like it is. Do not be obscure. Educate people. Co-opt the opposition. Do one-on-one visits. Meet with government staff, who can be an important resource; with elected officials, who will have to vote on the project; with activists and other vocal members of the public; and with the press. Give people a sense of ownership!

All this advice sounds fine, except that entitlement processing in today's political environment is highly vulnerable to the intervention of one individual or a small group who may have a narrow agenda that differs from that of the community at large. How does a developer overcome this vulnerability? The late Debra Stein, a land use attorney and an expert in the entitlement process, offered some guidance. She summarized the entitlement process as one that is focused on three audiences:

- Government;
- Community; and
- Media.

Stein counseled developers to research the priority focus of government decision makers as a first step for planning how to communicate. Some make decisions on the basis of whether the project meets published standards; for these decision makers, demonstrating compliance with standards is important. Others decide on the basis of community acceptance; for these, building a community constituency that supports the project is important.

Stein also encouraged developers to understand the communication styles of decision makers. For those who care about group harmony, it is important to foster cooperation. For those who are analytic, facts are important. For those who desire to lead the way, it is important to avoid rivalry. Developers should communicate with decision makers in a way that supports the decision makers' preferred styles.

For communicating with the public, Stein advised first identifying the different audiences that are stakeholders in the process. Recognize that each group cares about different aspects of a project and has different motives for opposing or supporting it. Stein identified four causes of opposition to projects:

- Misperceptions about what the project actually is;
- Perceived disrespect of the public or group by the developer, causing a loss of face;
- Conflicts of values, such as historical preservation or environmental awareness; and
- Conflicts of interest involving the negative effects of the project on opponents.

To address these issues, Stein strongly recommended communicating bilaterally whenever possible. To enable discussion and personal interaction, meeting with people in small groups is preferred. Large community meetings usually deal with so many issues that they offer only limited opportunities for solving problems. Preferred communication forums are open houses with small discussion groups, invitational events, and small meetings.

It is important, also, to have a decision maker—not a technician—represent the project in these meetings. This enlivens the dialogue because people take discussions seriously when they know that the representative can make changes based on their input. However, the representative must know the project and its economics so that he or she makes no commitments in these discussions that cannot be kept.

Having a Web site to describe the project is very important. It should encourage respectful, even-handed interaction and suggestions. And the developer should make sure that those who make suggestions receive responses.

Stein also stressed the importance of building support for a project to mitigate opposition to any aspect of the project. Obtaining written support is important, but having people testify in favor of a project can be the most critical way to manifest support. It takes work to obtain that support. Getting initial support, getting a promise to act on behalf of the project, and then getting follow-through on that promise requires building a personal connection with supporters. A developer who gets involved in the community by pursuing a genuine interest creates personal connections between the developer and members of the community that enable dialogue about projects that would never occur otherwise.

Stein's advice on making concessions—"Don't waste concessions"—is targeted to getting something for giving something. Frequently, the opportunity to make a concession is offered without a commensurate commitment by other parties. Concessions do not appease those who oppose a project irrevocably, so make concessions to groups that will reciprocate.

John Knott of Noisette Company, LLC, has pioneered a very sophisticated community-based entitlement process. His company spends many months working with neighborhood groups on project design. The initial phase consists entirely of listening, without preparing project proposals. He has trained his design team to work in small groups with community members and even to extend the drafting pen to community members as a way of soliciting their ideas.

H. Pike Oliver, who spent many years as a developer and is now a professor of real estate at Cornell University, had this to say about the entitlement process: "Entitlement processing is inherently interdisciplinary. It is not for passive personalities, but communicators are more effective than dominators." He offers the following advice:

■ Be optimistic.
■ Listen carefully.
■ Make no assumptions.
■ Expect problems.
■ Expect the unanticipated.
■ Never underestimate the psychology of the situation.
■ Be generous.
■ Be humble.

Optimism and openness work better than frustration and opacity. Frequently, going slowly gets things done faster. Listening creates greater understanding than asserting. Participating in other aspects of community life shows commitment. And sharing power creates more power. All these behaviors contribute to effectively creating public ownership.

Conclusion

Effective management of the entitlement process is fundamental to project financial viability. Managing time, managing concessions, defining clearly the scope of entitlement analysis and, most importantly, ensuring that the community takes ownership all contribute to financial viability.

CHAPTER 9

Public/Private Partnerships

This chapter describes the role that public/private partnerships can play in enhancing a project's financial viability. As development has become more economically and physically complex and as communities continue to face a growing inventory of underused, obsolete sites, public/private partnerships have emerged as vital mechanisms for both the public and private sectors. For developers, these partnerships can reduce entitlement risks. For many projects, they are crucial to aid with site cleanup, assembly, or access and circulation. They create value through co-investment by the public and private sectors. And, more frequently than ever before, they contribute public funding to the capital stack needed to meet underwriting criteria. On the public side, these partnerships provide a range of public benefits such as economic development, affordable housing, urban revitalization, sustainability, tax base stimulation, open-space preservation, and infrastructure finance. Yet, as important as these partnerships are, opportunities are missed and deals are badly made because the art of formulating and executing public/private partnerships is still relatively new and evolving.

This chapter addresses five questions about public/private partnerships:

- How are these partnerships being applied to projects today?
- How do communities prepare for these partnerships?
- How do communities and developers work together with such partnerships?
- What are the financing tools of public/private partnerships?
- What are the standards for successful partnerships?

Application

Public/private partnerships assist with the financial viability of development today in four ways:

- Provision of public capital for private projects;
- Reduction of entitlement risk by creating clear development standards before a developer enters the predevelopment process;
- Assistance with site issues including cleanup, assembly, and access and circulation; and
- Co-investment to create value for both the public and private sectors.

PUBLIC CAPITAL FOR PRIVATE PROJECTS

Richard Klawiter, of DLA Piper in Chicago, observes that the old paradigm of public financial assistance to private development was usually a simple pledge of tax-based incremental revenues generated by the project and limited to reimbursement of extraordinary costs. This revenue stream had little value for underwriting the capital needed for the project. He points to the incentive program that University Park, Illinois, used to attract a Clorox distribution facility as an example of this old paradigm. The city pledged to pay 90 percent of the future incremental taxes generated by the facility back to Clorox; however, the facility was self-financed by Clorox, and the payments from the city were not pledged to repay a portion of the capital.

Figure 9-1 summarizes several examples of projects that illustrate a new paradigm in which public capital is an important layer of a project's capital stack. Bonds, public revenue streams, and public land value now are routinely used to help a project achieve financial viability. These public capital sources are now routinely considered by private capital sources as part of their evaluation of whether a project meets underwriting criteria.

One example of this new paradigm is the Lakeside Steel Plant site conversion on Lake Michigan in Chicago, south of the Loop, described by Jeff Owen, of DLA Piper. This public/private partnership will convert a 150-acre former U.S. Steel plant into a high-density, mixed-use project with 13,600 residential units and 17.5 million square feet of commercial space. The $400 million in phase I costs of this project—a partnership between McCaffery Interests, U.S. Steel, and the city of Chicago—are financed with $300 million of private capital and $100 million of tax increment redevelopment bonds. The bonds will be repaid from tax increments generated by the project; the city of Chicago is providing an additional pledge of its general obligation taxing authority as backup security for repayment of more than half of these bonds.

Another particularly iconic project is the transit-oriented development at the Pleasant Hill BART station in Pleasant Hill, California, in the San Francisco Bay Area. This partnership took more than 20 years to put together, overcoming significant community concerns about density. The transaction involved leasing the transit station's surface parking lot to AvalonBay for residential development and the surrounding BART property to other developers for both commercial and affordable housing development. The long-term lease provides ongoing revenue based on project performance. The land is, in effect, an equity contribution to the project with a return coming from the lease payments. The redevelopment agency issued bonds to fund the replacement of the surface parking with a parking structure and also issued mortgage revenue bonds to provide debt financing for the residential development.

Mission Bay is another example of how public capital assists private development. Mission Bay is a mixed-use project converting a 400-acre shipyard into high-tech office space, residential units, and a university campus, using $400 million of land-secured bonds to finance the cleanup, parking, and other infrastructure. The low-cost municipal debt (secured by the land and with tax increment revenues) lowered the costs of debt and the tax increment revenues assisted the developers in paying this debt.

The public sector is also a source of equity for private development. James Keefe, president of Trinity Financial describes the Appleton Mill conversion project in Lowell,

FIGURE 9-1
Examples of Projects with Public Participation in Capital Stack

Project/Location	Developer or Contact	Description	Public Participation
Lakeside Steel Plant Conversion Chicago, IL	City of Chicago, U.S. Steel, and McCaffery Interests	• 150-acre steel plant conversion • $400 million total cost for Phase I • $300 million private financing • 13,600 residential units • 17.5 million sq. ft. of commercial	• $100 million of public financing supported by tax increment revenues and pledge of general obligation tax by city of Chicago
Pleasant Hill Bart Station Pleasant Hill, CA	Contra Costa County Redevelopment Agency	• 522 residential units • 290,000 sq. ft. of office • 35,900 sq. ft. of retail • 2,300 sq. ft. of civic	• Lease of transit surface parking lot to developer for 100 years • $57 million tax increment financing for parking and other infrastructure • $125 million of housing revenue bonds to finance residential development
Mission Bay mixed-use project San Francisco, CA	City of San Francisco Redevelopment Agency	• 400-acre conversion of old shipyard to high-tech office, residential, retail, and university campus site	• $400 million of land-secured bonds to finance cleanup and infrastructure • Redevelopment tax increment assistance to private and public development
Appleton Mills Lowell, MA	Trinity Financial Boston, MA	• 1.9 million sq. ft., mixed-use, transit-oriented • 725 market residential units • 480,000 sq. ft. of office and retail	• 4% tax credit equity: $26,282,806 • $13.6 million in tax-exempt loans
Pinole Valley Shopping Center Pinole, CA	Pinole Redevelopment Agency	• 70,000 sq. ft. renovation of a 1960s-era grocery-anchored neighborhood shopping center • Re-tenanting resulted in Trader Joe's and Walgreens as new anchor tenants • Developer obtained construction and permanent loan using ground lease value as equit	• Agency purchased shopping center from foreclosure in 2004 and, subsequently, two separate gas stations for total cost of $7.3 million • Leased entire site to developer at rent of 80% of net cash flow • With sale of shopping center, agency receives 80% of net sale proceeds after paying off permanent loan

Massachusetts, as a good example. This project converted a historic textile mill to a transit-oriented development with 725 residential units and 480,000 square feet of commercial space. The $47 million in project costs were financed in part through a combination of $26 million in low-income federal and state tax credits.

Public sector equity funding can also take the form of a public agency contributing or leasing land to a project and taking a promotional interest. The renovation and re-tenanting of the Pinole Valley Shopping Center in Pinole, California, included a lease of $7.3 million of the land value as equity for project financing. Project construction was funded entirely with a construction loan that was replaced with a permanent loan. The Pinole Redevelopment Agency receives ground rent on the land of 80 percent of the operations cash flow and, upon sale, will receive its capital contribution plus 80 percent of the net sale proceeds. By leasing the land at a rental rate tied to project performance, the redevelopment agency is, essentially, taking a promotional interest in operating cash flow.

ENTITLEMENT RISK

Many jurisdictions that are interested in high-quality development have realized that they can lower entitlement risk and increase private investment by taking the lead on creating a community-based plan. The city of Bellevue, Washington, is a great example. Beginning in 1981, the city involved all stakeholders in a process to convert its suburban downtown to a pedestrian-oriented town center. The city was able to build a community consensus and has followed with a number of specific plans for other areas, most recently in the Bel-Red Corridor between Bellevue and Redmond, where the plan focuses on job development in a new transit corridor. The Bel-Red Corridor plan is the largest mixed-use development opportunity in the state, planned for 10,000 new jobs and 5,000 new housing units. In 2008, Bellevue was named number one on the CNN Money list of the best places to live and launch a business. The citation noted, "It has a top-down and highly integrated land use and transportation process."

The city of Walnut Creek, California, is another example of a city with a pre-entitlement approach to reducing entitlement risk by developing and adopting specific plans for areas in and adjacent to its downtown. In the 1980s voters in Walnut Creek enacted an initiative to limit building height, in response to what the public felt was too much density from office development. The city engaged the community in creating a specific plan for the downtown that enabled development within the imposed height limits but that also reflected the community's desire for more retail and services. The city then took the extra step of performing an environmental impact analysis under the California Environmental Quality Act. The city has subsequently prepared several specific plans for areas adjacent to the downtown, all with the environmental impact analysis conducted by the city. The result is that development that is consistent with these specific plans goes through only two additional steps of entitlement—design review and building permit. As a consequence, Walnut Creek has developed as a major regional, high-quality office and retail center.

The Greenbelt Alliance of the San Francisco Bay Area recognized the importance of this approach to high-quality development in its guide called "Smart Infill," describing how communities can achieve higher-quality sustainable development:

> Involve the public to help development go forward smoothly, and share the benefits and costs fairly. Simplify the process for developers. By streamlining permitting and construction processes, getting departments to work together to promote infill, and ensuring requirements are consistent, cities can smooth the way for good development.

This advice, essentially, calls on communities that want good development to reduce the predevelopment risk for the type of development they want. Streamlining the entitlement process for development that meets the criteria of community-based policies achieves both these objectives.

SITE ACCESS, CLEANUP, AND RECONFIGURATION

Especially for conversion properties, public assistance is crucial to clean up a site, to improve poor access, and to reconfigure parcel lines that constrain conversion. Figure 9-2 summarizes two examples of jurisdictions engaged in such activity:

■ The city of Newark, California, is cleaning up a contaminated 223-acre industrial site with four property owners adjacent to the Dumbarton Bridge and a future transit line. The city's redevelopment agency is working with the property owners to ensure cleanup and plans to use tax increment and land-secured bonds to equalize costs among the property owners and fund the infrastructure for access and circulation needed for this new transit-oriented town center project.

■ The city of Dallas, Texas, has developed a strategy to rejuvenate a dead shopping mall in the South Dallas area. The Southwest Center Mall was built in the 1970s and rehabilitated in the 1990s. It now sits mostly vacant, because retailers have moved to newer locations nearby. South Dallas has a total of 44 square feet per capita of retail. The national average is 23 square feet per capita. The city is working with the property owners to address the biggest problem: there are six property owners, five of them major department stores and one the mall owner. Two of the major department stores remain vacant, since Dillard's and J.C. Penney left the center. To accomplish anything on this site, property ownership

---

FIGURE 9-2
Examples of Projects Involving Site Cleanup, Assembly, or Access

Project/Location	Developer or Contact	Description	Public Participation
Dumbarton Transit-Oriented Development Newark, CA	Newark Redevelopment Agency	• 223-acre former industrial site with multiple property owners. • Project involves cleanup, planning, and infrastructure finance to achieve a mixed-use town center adjacent to a future transit station	• Redevelopment agency coordinating cleanup efforts • Agency leading planning process • Agency using tax increment financing to address financing gaps • City to use land-secured finance for infrastructure
Southwest Center Mall Dallas, TX	City of Dallas Office of Economic Development	• Revitalization of regional shopping mall built in the 1970s to a town center • Substantially overbuilt retail market argues for mixed-use development program	• City to assist in consolidating property ownership from six current owners • City to form redevelopment project area to aid in financing improved access and circulation

must be consolidated by reconfiguring property lines. There must be a new, community-supported development plan that diversifies the uses beyond just retail, which is vastly overbuilt in the South Dallas area. And the 100-acre sea of parking lots and mall buildings must be reconfigured to improve access and circulation. The city is working with property owners to remove property lines and create larger, more usable parcels and is forming a tax increment district to fund the cost of improving access and circulation.

CO-INVESTMENT

The public sector creates value in a place whenever it provides access or amenities such as parks, theaters, or open space; these amenities enhance value for adjacent private development as well as for the public. Figure 9-3 summarizes several examples:

■ The Del Mar Station in Pasadena, California, is a mixed-use project of Urban Partners, Archstone, and Los Angeles Metro with all components—residential, commercial, parking, and transit—constructed simultaneously. It includes 347 residential units and restoration of

FIGURE 9-3
Examples of Projects Involving Public Co-investment to Stimulate Private Investment

Project/Location	Developer or Contact	Description	Public Participation
Del Mar Station Pasadena, CA	City of Pasadena, CA	• LA Metro transit stop • Restoration of historic train depot • 11,000 sq. ft. of retail • 347 units of residential • 1,200-stall underground parking garage	• Joint project of Urban Partners, Archstone, and Los Angeles Metro, with construction occurring on all project components at the same time
The Metropolitan Charlotte, NC	Pappas Properties	• $240 million mixed-use project • 390,000 sq. ft. of commercial • 205 residential units • 2,000 parking spaces • Restoration of creek to become a pedestrian/bike trail	• $8.9 million contribution to infrastructure • $8.0 million contribution to land acquisition and greenway development • $17 million in property tax rebates
Rancho Solano and Paradise Valley Golf Courses Fairfield, CA	City of Fairfield, CA	• Two professional public golf courses located in two large residential developments on land donated to the city by the developers	• City financed all costs of developing the golf courses and adjacent club houses using lease revenue financing • City franchises operation of courses to private operators • Golf course revenues fully support operations and debt service

a historic train depot with 11,000 square feet of retail. A four-level, shared, underground parking garage serves transit riders, commercial customers, and residents.

- The Metropolitan, developed by Pappas Properties in Charlotte, North Carolina, converted an obsolete shopping center built in 1959 by the Rouse Company into a mixed-use project with 205 residential units and 390,000 square feet of commercial. The city of Charlotte invested $8.9 million in infrastructure, $8 million in a creek restoration project to create a greenway and pedestrian/bike trail, and $17 million in rebates from future property taxes. This participation resulted from the project qualifying on a city "sustainability index" rating.
- The Rancho Solano and Paradise Valley golf courses in Fairfield, California, were financed by the city using lease revenue bonds. The land for the courses was donated by the developers of the adjacent residential projects based on the increased value that the golf courses created in the home sales. The courses, which are public, generate revenues sufficient to pay both the city's debt service and operations costs.
- Oklahoma City, operating in partnership with its downtown business improvement district (BID), has invested $140 million in downtown improvements since the partnership was started in 2001. In December 2009, voters approved an additional $777 million program of downtown improvements. The economic health of downtown Oklahoma City has improved dramatically as a result of these investments, with numerous residential projects and corporate headquarters relocations.

Community Preparation

The degree to which a public/private partnership proceeds effectively and efficiently for all parties depends, to a large extent, on how well a community has prepared for such a partnership. Developers should understand how communities prepare and what they should look for in choosing a community with which to engage. Communities should understand how to prepare to attract the development they seek.

A well-prepared community will have undertaken two key tasks: first, the creation of a community vision that achieves public benefits from private development and, second, the development of the institutional capacity to implement public/private partnerships. A successful visioning process involves all stakeholders—residents, developers, businesses, community groups, environmentalists, etc. It must first come to a consensus on the desired public benefits. Communities now seek a range of public benefits from private development; among them:

- Revitalization of declining areas,
- Competitive jobs,
- Preservation or enhancement of local employment and businesses,
- Infrastructure resources,
- More tax revenues,
- Better-quality development,
- Reduction of greenhouse gas emissions,
- Green buildings,
- Mixed-use infill and transit-oriented development,
- Affordable housing,

- Amenities (such as performing arts centers, parks, open space, golf courses, and stadiums), and
- Asset management.

Creating the institutional capacity and governmental tools to engage in public/private partnerships takes time and should be rooted in the community-based planning process. It must include training programs that teach the public professional staff and policy makers skills in and knowledge about real estate economics and the development process, and familiarity with the types of partnerships and how to craft them. It should also include creating policies that enable the financing necessary for infrastructure or public facilities such as a theater or parks.

Of great importance, the community must create the institutional tools to be able to enact the business terms for public/private partnerships. Communities should consider three types of institutional tools:

- *Partnership entity:* Such an entity has the legal ability to engage in partnerships on behalf of the community. It usually is a redevelopment agency and sometimes a development corporation.
- *Financing programs:* Accessing municipal debt on behalf of private projects requires putting policies in place to ensure that this tool is used responsibly.
- *Business improvement district:* Such entities exist throughout the country as semi-governmental associations of businesses focused on improving the economic vitality of local areas.

PARTNERSHIP ENTITY

In most states, general governments (cities, counties, and townships) are restricted from engaging in activities not directly related to health or safety. As a consequence, general governments typically cannot sell land or other assets for less than fair market value, usually as determined at a public auction. They are also typically prohibited from investing in real estate projects through direct investment or guarantees of private debt. These restrictions usually require that the community use some other related entity, usually a redevelopment agency or a nonprofit development corporation, to engage in deal making. Such an entity operates under a separate set of statutes from the general government and may have a separate governing board.

FINANCING PROGRAM FOR INFRASTRUCTURE OR OTHER PUBLIC FACILITIES

Another area of preparation involves the use of tax-exempt financing for infrastructure or other public facilities that may be associated with a public/private partnership. Because interest payments on municipal bonds are exempt from federal income tax and also from state income tax for taxpayers within the state of issuance, the interest rate on such bonds can be 2 or 3 percent below that of conventional financing. Also, because municipal debt typically attracts longer-term holders of bonds, it can be issued with a longer amortization period than is typically available in conventional financing.

There are numerous types of municipal finance, each with its own legal authority for issuance and repayment sources. In general, capital markets that buy municipal bonds impose credit conditions on the issuers that are conservative and that lower risks. However, use of these tools requires skilled professional staff and knowledgeable policy makers who craft responsible policies for the use of municipal debt as a first step.

BUSINESS IMPROVEMENT DISTRICTS

A BID is a fundamental tool for enhancing and maintaining the economic vitality of an area with multiple businesses and multiple property owners. BIDs have grown in use throughout the United States as older business districts have organized to compete with large, single-ownership retail projects. A BID provides many of the same services and management that a large shopping center under one owner provides, except a BID must deal with numerous property owners and a much broader spectrum of businesses. The United States has over 1,000 of these districts; New York City has 64, the most of any city.

These districts typically have a board of directors composed of business and property owner representatives from within the district. The larger BIDs hire professional management. They typically engage in five primary activities: promotional events such as farmers markets or arts festivals; advertising; enhanced municipal-type services, such as garbage collection or more lighting than provided by the community; parking management; and services to enhance the effectiveness of businesses in the district, such as training in merchandising or display. Successful BIDs also influence the retail tenant mix by providing incentives to property owners for leasing to retailers that enhance the retail synergy within the district. Although BIDs are governed by private boards, they usually have the authority to levy tax-like assessments above what the businesses would otherwise pay in property taxes and utility fees.

STAPLETON AIRPORT REDEVELOPMENT: AN EXAMPLE OF COMMUNITY PREPARATION

Perhaps the iconic example of community preparation occurred in Denver, Colorado, with the redevelopment of Stapleton Airport, Denver's primary airport since 1929. With Stapleton scheduled to close, the community engaged in a six-year planning process before seeking proposals from developers. Forest City was selected as the developer and negotiated a public/private partnership over three years, leading to a set of obligations for funding infrastructure and implementing the community plan that are summarized in figure 9-4. The community agreed to form tax increment and tax benefit districts that would reimburse Forest City for the cost of installing the infrastructure as development and value increases occurred. This project has won numerous awards for incorporating sustainable development principles. It has held its value even during the Great Recession because it is viewed as a livable and desirable place to live and work.

This example illustrates how a community can prepare and implement a development program that includes the institutional capacity necessary for implementation, thus creating tremendous community benefits and private value using a public/private partnership.

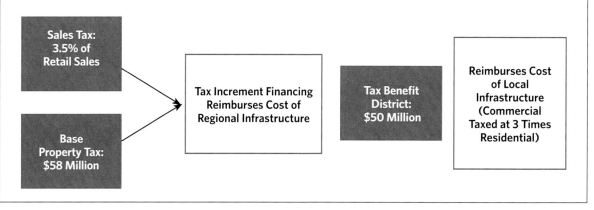

FIGURE 9-4
Stapleton Airport Business Terms

Forest City Obligations
- Purchase 2,935 acres at appraised value of $79.4 million + CPI increase
- Pay $15,000 per acre for parks impact fee, totaling $44 million
- Purchase a minimum of 1,000 acres every 5 years for 15 years (935 acres in final year)
- Develop according to the Stapleton Development Plan
- Make $5 million downpayment
- Advance all funds for major and local infrastructure

City of Denver Obligations
- Complete zoning for the entire site
- Establish tax increment financing for major infrastructure
- Create tax benefit districts for local infrastructure
- Complete environmental remediation
- Complete demolition of buildings and runways
- Reimburse Forest City for infrastructure as funds are generated from tax increment financing and tax benefit district (that is, as value/development occurs)

Sales Tax: 3.5% of Retail Sales

Base Property Tax: $58 Million

Tax Increment Financing Reimburses Cost of Regional Infrastructure

Tax Benefit District: $50 Million

Reimburses Cost of Local Infrastructure (Commercial Taxed at 3 Times Residential)

How Communities and Developers Work Together

Working with a developer can start with a formal selection process, such as a request for proposal (RFP) or request for qualifications (RFQ). It can also result from a developer controlling a site and working with the community to create mutual gain. However the process starts, for it to succeed it must lead to a business relationship between the public agency and developer that is based on mutual trust and on community ownership of the development project.

There are challenges to achieving this trust and ownership:

■ *First, each sector has different perspectives on time:* for the public sector, time allows greater public understanding and acceptance; for the private sector, time is money. Reconciliation occurs when the public sector properly prepares and streamlines entitlement for a development that meets its standards. The private sector must also understand and embrace the need to "go slow to go fast." Community acceptance is fundamental to project success, and the time needed to achieve it cannot be shortchanged.

■ *Second, the two sectors really have different ways of measuring project success:* for the public sector, success means achieving public benefits; for the private sector, success means financial viability. For the partnership to succeed, each sector must recognize the legitimacy of the other's objectives.

- *Third, the sectors have very different financing sources:* the public sector has access to non-project-related funding from taxes, fees, public debt markets, and focused incentive programs; the private sector relies solely on the economic viability of the project for financing. Increasingly, private capital sources look to public financing sources as a component of the capital stack to meet underwriting criteria.
- *Finally, the sectors respond to different constituencies:* the public sector is accountable to the community; the private sector is accountable to investors. If these two constituencies cannot recognize mutual interests, the partnership will fail.

Overcoming these different perspectives requires addressing fundamental stereotypical views that each sector has of the other: The public sector often views the private sector as not caring about the community; the private sector views the public sector as not understanding project finance requirements. Both sectors must explicitly address stereotypes.

The process of building a relationship between a developer and a public agency is really a process of building trust while conducting due diligence on each other. The developer looks at the public agency to ensure that it has reasonable expectations, clear goals, reasonable processing requirements, and competence in holding up its end of an agreement. The public agency looks at the developer for reliable performance, financial capacity, the ability to anticipate and solve problems, and the fairness of the developer's other partnerships. This due diligence takes time and should continue throughout the process of planning the project and negotiating the partnership.

NEGOTIATING A DEAL

When the parties have completed the initial due diligence on suitability or selection has occurred, formal negotiation can begin. It is important that the parties treat the negotiation process as a problem-solving exercise, not a hard-bargaining situation. For the negotiations to be successful, the economics of the project and the public benefits that it will achieve must be clearly articulated. The overarching objectives of the negotiation process should be to build trust, create a shared vision, make a fair deal, and create community ownership.

An important part of building the relationship is the open-book style of negotiating—in other words, the sharing of relevant economic information about the project so that the public understands the fairness of the business terms. If the public is investing in the project to address an economic gap, documentation must show the basis for arriving at the amount of the investment. If the developer is buying land from the public agency, documentation must show that the price paid reflects the fair value of the land for the use anticipated by the project. In general, the open-book style will require third-party verification of the fairness of the deal to the public agency.

The open-book style does not mean that proprietary information or confidential financial data need be disclosed publicly. Where such data must be provided, it can usually be disclosed to third-party consultants and kept confidential under local public information laws. This issue requires careful legal research to ensure that the terms under which proprietary or confidential information is provided can be relied upon.

One significant concern in using the open-book approach is that information about financial returns will become known. The developer should not be ashamed that a project needs an adequate return to attract private investment and to compensate the developer for the time and skill devoted to the project. The open-book approach will assure, however, that windfall profits in excess of what is needed to attract capital and fairly compensate the developer will be distributed fairly between the public agency and the developer.

ULI's *10 Principles of Successful Public/Private Partnerships*[1] articulates many of the concepts for working with developers that are discussed here:

■ Properly prepare for public/private partnerships.

■ Create a shared vision.

■ Understand your partners and key players.

■ Be clear on the risks and rewards for all parties.

■ Document a clear and rational decision-making process.

■ All parties must do their homework.

■ Secure consistent and coordinated leadership.

■ Communicate early and often.

■ Negotiate a fair deal structure.

■ Build trust as a core value.

We now turn to the details of applying public sector tools and crafting the business terms of a public/private partnership.

Public/Private Financing Tools

As discussed in the section on community preparation, there are important financial tools that a public agency can use in a public/private partnership. Both the developer and the community should be familiar with these tools because they are the essence of the partnership. Six tools are discussed in the following sections:

■ Redevelopment agencies;

■ Municipal bonds;

■ Land assembly and conveyance;

■ Grants and incentives;

■ Affordable housing subsidies; and

■ Tax credits.

REDEVELOPMENT AGENCIES

With its broad financing powers, a redevelopment agency is a primary tool for enabling public/private partnerships. Redevelopment agencies receive funds through property taxes deriving from the increase in property value within a redevelopment project area since its formation. These revenues are called "tax increment revenues" and go exclusively to the redevelopment agency to pay for debt associated with investment in the project area. Figure 9-5 illustrates how a tax increment is distributed from the increase in value within the project area. Tax increment financing, if it is sufficient, is used as a source to repay tax increment bonds from the tax-exempt municipal market.

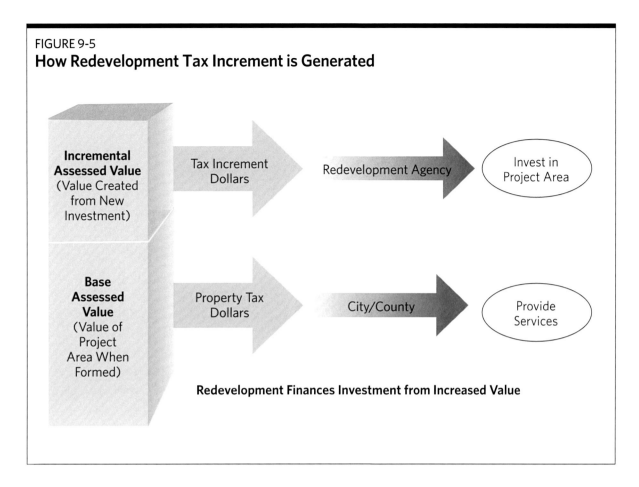

FIGURE 9-5

How Redevelopment Tax Increment is Generated

Incremental Assessed Value (Value Created from New Investment) → Tax Increment Dollars → Redevelopment Agency → Invest in Project Area

Base Assessed Value (Value of Project Area When Formed) → Property Tax Dollars → City/County → Provide Services

Redevelopment Finances Investment from Increased Value

Redevelopment agencies try to partner early with a private development entity that can help ensure that acquisitions and development plans respond to market opportunities. Today, agencies routinely also guarantee debt payments on project components and may even make direct equity investments in a project, as well as convey land at its residual land value.

Because redevelopment is often controversial, a developer should be extremely cautious in establishing a partnership with an agency until due diligence has been conducted on the competence and reputation of the agency. Part of the controversy comes from the authority that redevelopment agencies have had to exercise eminent domain to acquire property. A 2005 U.S. Supreme Court decision that sustained the action by the redevelopment agency of the city of New London, Connecticut, to acquire two single-family owner-occupied homes to make room for a mixed-use development adjacent to a business park inflamed national political opposition to the use of eminent domain by redevelopment agencies. (The decision is frequently called the Kelo decision, after the name of one of the families whose homes were acquired.) Subsequently more than 40 states enacted legislation to severely limit or completely curtail the use of eminent domain by redevelopment agencies for conveying property from one private owner to another.

Another reason that redevelopment is controversial is that many overlying taxing agencies (school districts, cities, and counties) believe that redevelopment agencies capture tax increment revenues that would accrue regardless of redevelopment investment. These agencies therefore may oppose redevelopment efforts because those efforts are seen as denying them property tax revenues they need for ongoing operations.

Finally, establishing a redevelopment project can be time-consuming and require extensive documentation to make the necessary findings of need. Given the numerous public hearings and technical determinations, a community needs to start early to create institutional readiness for public/private partnerships using redevelopment agencies. Redevelopment agencies remain an important institutional tool for public/private partnerships. A competent public redevelopment agency that understands its limitations can contribute considerable resources to many aspects of a public/private partnership.

MUNICIPAL BONDS

For public/private partnerships, the primary types of municipal debt are tax increment financing and land-secured bonds. Other types of municipal financing may also be used with public/private partnerships depending on the circumstances.

LAND-SECURED BONDS

Land-secured bonds are issued by a public agency to pay for infrastructure (streets and utilities) for land development projects or for parking for urban infill projects. They are repaid through special taxes or annual assessments on the benefitting properties. For parking bonds, a public agency can also use parking revenues to offset annual installment payments by property owners.

Land-secured bonds provide a low interest rate because the interest paid to bondholders is exempt from both federal income tax and state income tax in the state where they are issued. This exemption results in an interest rate in most market conditions of between 200 to 300 basis points less than that of private financing. In addition, financing periods are longer (up to 30 years) than those for private financing, resulting in lower annual debt service. The amount of interest savings is very dependent on market conditions and the structure of the bond issue.

These bonds have some risk: If annual installments are not paid, they become a lien on the property ahead of private debt and the public agency must foreclose to recover delinquencies. This action wipes out private lenders and equity investors. Private lenders and equity investors therefore look very closely at the amount of such debt and the repayment program to ensure that the municipal debt does not overleverage the project.

A public agency must prepare for using this tool for the benefit of private development. It must develop policies not unlike those of a private lender, stipulating lien-to-value ratios and the types of projects that are eligible.

In the mid-1980s, as a result of the savings and loan crisis, banks stopped lending for infrastructure costs for land development projects, and land-secured financing became essentially the only means for financing such infrastructure. Many communities used this tool unwisely and issued too much debt for the wrong types of projects. In the early 1990s, many of these transactions resulted in defaults and foreclosures on projects that could not support the annual payments.

Today, communities usually allow a ratio of no more than 1 to 3 of bonds on raw land value (the value of land before improvements). Many communities prohibit the use of this tool for developing residential land, allowing its use only for business or industrial parks, because public agencies do not want to contend with the difficulties of having to foreclose on homes.

OTHER BONDS

A public agency can also use many legal structures to issue bonds, the proceeds of which can be used in the context of a co-investment strategy to synergize private development. Examples of co-investment by public agencies that create private value include highway interchanges, parks, plazas, theaters, and streetscapes. Perhaps the iconic contemporary co-investment project is a sports stadium financed with public bonds on the premise that such investment stimulates private investment around the stadium.

All municipal financing is heavily constrained by federal regulations that limit the extent to which private parties can benefit. These regulations are generically called the "private activity" limitations. For some types of municipal bonds, such as mortgage revenue bonds, the limitations are in the form of annual limits on the total amount of issuance. For other forms of municipal debt, there is usually a limit that no more than 10 percent of the issue can benefit a private party. The rules are too complicated to describe completely here; using this form of financing requires the involvement of specialists.

Here is a short list of the types of municipal debt that can be used with a public/private partnership:

- *Revenue bonds:* These bonds are repaid from the revenues of a separate utility such as an airport or a water or sewer enterprise. They are commonly used for public facilities that catalyze private investment.
- *Mortgage revenue bonds:* These bonds fund residential mortgages and are repaid from the stream of mortgage payments. The mortgages can be for single-family or multifamily projects. Of the annual amount authorized by the federal government, each state gets an allocation. Each state then has a process for distributing its allocation among competing issuers.
- *Lease revenue bonds:* This type of financing is repaid from revenues of a facility leased to a public agency. Usually, the bonds are issued in the form of certificates of participation that securitize the revenue stream. The public agency may sublease or franchise the facility to a private organization to carry out the facility's mission. For instance, a theater could be subleased to a nonprofit theater group and revenues from that sublease could offset any payments that the public agency would need to make from its own resources for bond service. Another example is a revenue-generating public golf course operated by a private operator under a management contract. Use of these bonds is restricted solely to financing public facilities, but these facilities (theaters, parks, golf courses, stadiums, etc.) frequently generate adjacent private development.
- *General obligation bonds:* These bonds are secured by the full faith and credit of the issuing entity. As with general obligation bonds, use of these bonds is restricted solely to financing public facilities, but these facilities can frequently generate adjacent private development.

Forest City developed Stapleton on Denver's old airport site. Stapleton's infrastructure was built using bonds issued on tax increment finance districts.

STEVE LARSON

LAND ASSEMBLY AND CONVEYANCE

Land is frequently the medium of exchange in public/private partnerships, despite the controversy that it has generated in the use of eminent domain through redevelopment. Properly used, land assembly and site conveyance are key components of a public/private partnership.

A development site with multiple property owners faces a challenge: each owner desires to maximize the value of its own site, which may, because of its small size, have a value-to-area ratio higher than that of the entire development. This challenge may require the use of public funding to cover the economic "gap" resulting from land costs that are higher than the residual land value for the project.

How the land assembly is conducted needs careful consideration. Usually, it is better to have the private developer acquire the land. Eminent domain may be appropriate but should be used only with great care.

For a development site already owned by a public agency, the terms for conveyance will greatly affect project viability. During predevelopment, the public agency can hold the site, thus lowering the predevelopment risk. During the entitlement process, the public agency can stipulate the use of the site and, through the terms of conveyance, require the developer to meet a performance schedule. Failure to perform by the developer usually results in reversion of the site to the public agency. The price and terms for the sale or lease for a partnership of this type should reflect the residual value of the land for the use intended.

Land conveyance also provides opportunities for public agencies to convert assets to income. Some public agencies prefer a long-term lease instead of a sale, opting for long-term income instead of a lump-sum payment. Other public agencies recognize that if property is sold, the asset value from the site can be redeployed for other public purposes.

Often, the value of a site at the time of conveyance is discounted because of high project risk. For instance, public land conveyed for business park development may have a low value because of the expected length of time for market absorption; however, if users occupy space faster than expected, the project may exceed its pro forma value. Agencies faced with comparable situations may convey a site at low or no cost but provide in the partnership agreement for sharing the enhanced value if the project succeeds beyond initial expectations.

In some situations, the residual land value of the site may be negative, because of the intended use. For instance, infrastructure or other costs necessary for project viability may be high. In such situations, conveyance may require a direct investment by the public agency in the project to cover the economic gap and ensure project viability.

GRANTS AND INCENTIVES

Grants and incentives are provided at the local, state, and federal levels. Here are some examples of local incentives:

- *Density bonus for affordable housing*: Many communities provide incentives for developers to construct affordable housing by allowing higher density as a means to offset the cost of the affordable housing.
- *Streamlined processing for "green" buildings:* As a way to motivate developers to incorporate green building standards into project design, many communities streamline the plan check or entitlement processing of projects that have outside certification (for instance, from the Leadership in Energy and Environmental Design program of the U.S. Green Building Council).
- *Reduced parking requirements:* For projects that are transit oriented or located in the community's central business district, requirements to incorporate parking can be reduced or eliminated.

For some project types—affordable housing, for instance—numerous state and federal grant and incentive programs provide economic assistance. As an example, HOME funds and Community Development Block Grant funds are commonly used to buy down project costs so that a project can deliver low-cost housing. Often, these programs require that the project conform to strict operating covenants that include annual reporting on the income level of the assisted tenants and income and expense statements showing appropriate management practices. These programs are often used along with federal tax credit programs.

AFFORDABLE HOUSING SUBSIDIES

Numerous mechanisms exist to aid in the development of affordable housing, all of which create a funding source for direct investment that lowers the economic gap between development costs and the hurdle rate of return. This direct investment can be funded from federal or state tax credits (described below), federal or state grant funds (such as HOME or Community Development Block Grant funds), or local direct investment. Each funding source has its own programmatic business terms.

Inclusionary housing, a requirement to set aside a percentage of the project's units as affordable, is becoming the norm in many metropolitan areas that have high housing costs.

These programs are usually tied to density bonuses or financial assistance. Their implementation involves issues of eligibility, compliance monitoring, property maintenance, and, if the units are for sale, the distribution of gain upon resale.

TAX CREDITS

Three federal income tax credit programs can assist with the financing of real estate projects that create public benefits. The federal tax credits are often used in conjunction with similar state tax credits programs. Each program targets different types of projects and has a different allocation process. Usually, these programs are used along with other public/private financing sources as a part of the overall capital stack. The programs provide either low-cost equity or debt to a project that meets program criteria.

LOW-INCOME HOUSING TAX CREDIT

This program provides equity funding for residential projects that have set aside a percentage of units for low-income renters. It is administered by the U.S. Department of Housing and Urban Development through a designated agency in each state. States receive an annual allocation of tax credits based on state population equal to about $2.00 per capita.

The credits are allocated on the basis of how well a project meets criteria stipulated by federal law and implemented in the state agency's allocation program. These criteria generally involve an assessment of whether the project serves the lowest-income families and is structured to remain affordable for the longest period of time. In addition, 10 percent of each state's annual housing tax credit allocation is set aside for projects owned by non-profit organizations.

Typically, the credits provide equity funding for as much as 30 to 50 percent of total development costs. By funding the equity, the program lowers developer equity requirements and enhances effective leverage. The tax credits result in a dollar-for-dollar credit against federal tax liability every year for ten years. The amount of the annual credit is based on the amount invested in the affordable housing. Although the credits amortize over ten years, the project must comply with the performance conditions for serving low-income residents for at least 15 years. Failure to comply results in a revocation of the tax credit.

Developers may claim the tax credits directly, but most sell the tax credits to raise equity capital—either directly to an investor or through a syndicator that assembles a group of investors. Selling the tax credits results in a discount from face value to reflect the transaction costs and the demand for tax credits. The discount means that the project will receive fewer proceeds than the face amount of the credits.

The purchaser of the tax credit becomes a member of the property ownership entity, by becoming either a limited partner or a member of a limited liability company. The developer remains responsible for managing the project and the partnership, while the investor remains in a passive role.

Typically, the investor receives all the benefit of the tax credit over the ten-year amortization period and also receives a distribution of profits and losses according to the investor's percentage ownership interests, based on the waterfall distribution. Typically, the developer receives a large share of any positive cash flow, often structured in the form of fees for services such as partnership management, incentive management, or investor services.

Accessing this capital source requires knowing which state agency provides the tax credit allocation and being familiar with the application procedures and evaluation criteria. Information about available allocations, designated state agencies, and evaluation criteria is available at www.hud.gov.

NEW MARKET TAX CREDITS

This program provides low-cost debt funding for investment projects in designated low-income areas. It is administered by the U.S. Treasury Department's Community Development Financial Institution Fund, which distributes a total of $3 billion to $4 billion annually to individual "Community Development Entities" (CDEs), which, in turn, fund loans or investments ("Qualified Low-Income Community Investments") in "Qualified Active Low-Income Community Businesses." Figure 9-6 depicts this flow of funds.

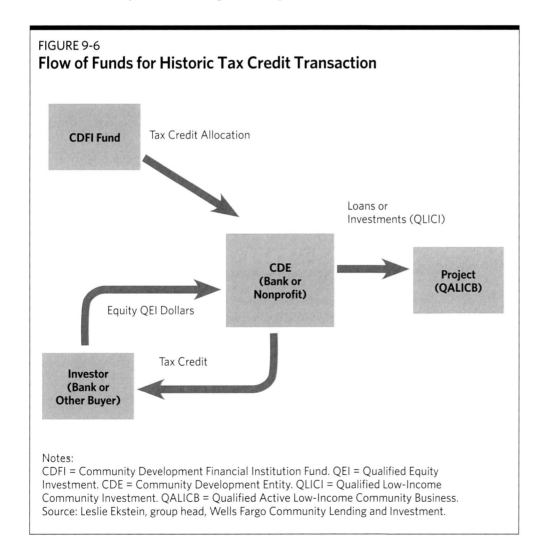

FIGURE 9-6
Flow of Funds for Historic Tax Credit Transaction

CDFI Fund — Tax Credit Allocation →
CDE (Bank or Nonprofit)
Loans or Investments (QLICI) → Project (QALICB)
Equity QEI Dollars
Investor (Bank or Other Buyer)
Tax Credit

Notes:
CDFI = Community Development Financial Institution Fund. QEI = Qualified Equity Investment. CDE = Community Development Entity. QLICI = Qualified Low-Income Community Investment. QALICB = Qualified Active Low-Income Community Business. Source: Leslie Ekstein, group head, Wells Fargo Community Lending and Investment.

The range of projects eligible for New Market Tax Credits is much broader than for the low-income housing program. In general, the credits can fund commercial real estate, including community facilities such as charter schools, clinics, and museums, as well as mixed-use residential rental projects where the nonhousing income exceeds 20 percent of the total operating income.

The investment must occur in a low-income area that satisfies at least one of these criteria: median income less than 60 percent of that in the region; a poverty rate greater than 30 percent of the national average; or an unemployment rate that is 150 percent of the national average. Investors receive a 39 percent tax credit in the project amortized over seven years, with a 5 percent per year amortization in years one through three and a 6 percent amortization in years four through seven.

The CDEs are typically commercial banks, primarily national and regional banks, motivated by community reinvestment goals and the desire to broaden their client relationships. In addition, many cities and redevelopment agencies serve as CDEs along with other tax credit syndicators, provided they agree to serve a role on the board of directors of the project. The banks typically invest in their own allocations, while the other CDE entities must monetize the tax credits through outside investors.

The New Market Tax Credit program lowers the cost of debt for a project by two or three percentage points. It also essentially increases leverage with lower-cost debt, thus reducing borrower equity.

HISTORIC PRESERVATION TAX CREDITS

This program, administered by the U.S. Department of Interior's National Park Service in conjunction with state historic preservation offices, provides a 20 percent federal tax credit for qualified historic preservation. Projects must be certified as historic structures by the Park Service and meet the Interior Department's standards for rehabilitation. The tax credit allocated to the project is amortized in one year. Projects that qualify for this program can include residential and commercial uses.

All the tax credit programs require that project sponsors become knowledgeable about the administering agencies and project criteria. They tend to have higher transaction costs than either conventional private or public financing, so the transaction size must be large enough to dilute the higher costs. They also take longer to implement than conventional financing sources, so their lead time must be taken into account for timely funding.

Deal Standards

A developer should pay close attention to the manner in which a public agency presents and vets a public/private partnership to ensure that the deal will meet standards of defensibility and soundness in public forums. A deal that blows up because it is not fair to the public agency can be extremely costly.

Public/private partnerships are usually incorporated into a written contract that stipulates the responsibilities of each party for investment, the accountability measures, and the distribution of project revenues. Such a contract is similar to a joint venture contract that

RODRIGUEZ ASSOCIATES ARCHITECTS & PLANNERS, INC.

Solara is an affordable housing development in Poway, California. Developed by Community Housing Works, the project is the first zero-energy new home development in the state. The city provided a 99-year ground lease, a construction loan, and a permanent loan. Photovoltaic costs were almost entirely financed with state rebates and federal tax credits.

covers the same issues among private parties, but a public/private partnership contract is usually more complex and is constrained to a far greater extent by legal restrictions than a private contract.

Where a partnership involves public financial participation in a project, it is critically important that communities and developers base the partnership on a mutual understanding of the real estate economics and of what the markets will support. The understanding of market support should be validated by an outside third party, because the public reacts negatively to what it considers unfair windfall benefits to the private sector.

Many partnerships are quite complex and require considerable expertise, time, and effort to complete. Several issues add to this complexity:

- Most states have statutes prohibiting a "gift of public funds," so any transaction in such states requires that a negotiated (that is, not publicly auctioned) asset or land sale have an analysis and a public report documenting that the transaction does not unfairly create windfall profits to a private party. Such documentation should be based on a valid analysis of real estate economics showing that returns to the private developer are reasonable given the project risk and the cost of the benefits provided by the project.

- Public/private partnerships also usually entail constraints on how construction or other implementation of the project is accomplished, requiring, for instance, local hiring, "prevailing wages" (wages stipulated by a state agency), or minority business enterprise participation. These constraints complicate operations and may increase costs.

■ Federal statutes closely regulate how municipal debt (debt issued at tax-exempt interest rates, described in more detail below) can be used to assist a private party and how quickly the proceeds of such debt must be spent (usually three years) without threatening the tax-exempt status of the debt.

■ Federal rules stipulate how tax credits can be applied to help finance a private project and require ongoing compliance reporting.

These and other complexities require that a developer engage additional experts as part of the development team. Each state has different rules, and each type of partnership will have different parameters to optimize.

Here are suggested standards for ensuring that a public/private partnership is defensible and fair:

■ *Confirm competence:* Ensure that both the private and public partners have the competence, credentials, and capacity necessary for the project.

■ *Price the benefits:* Connect the public benefits to their costs.

■ *Align interests:* Both parties should have skin in the game; that is, just as with a private project, the developer should co-invest.

■ *Share success:* Provide a return to each party commensurate with the risk and the return hurdle required to attract capital. If the project succeeds in providing a return beyond that needed to attract private capital, the public agency should share in the windfall.

■ *Have a holding period for returning the public investment:* Do not treat public capital as a handout. Provide a way for the public agency to get its investment out of the project upon refinance or resale. If the project succeeds, then the public investment can be returned and reinvested in creating other public benefits.

■ *Have a stop loss for the public agency:* Public agencies should not be put in the position of obligating themselves to open-ended liability for project losses or reinvestment requirements. This liability is untenable from a public policy viewpoint. There must be mechanisms such as letters of credit or performance guarantees which ensure that the public agency does not end up spending funds on an empty bag.

■ *Validate the market:* Base the deal on valid real estate economics parameters. Ensure that the deal reflects current market rates of return and financing terms. The deal should be comparable to a private sector transaction. Benchmark fees to third parties in the market.

■ *Use an open book:* Document all transactions and make them transparent to the public.

■ *Get third-party verification:* Involve an outside expert in real estate economics to provide third-party verification of fairness.

■ *Build in accountability:* Document terms in writing. Monitor performance during implementation. Provide ongoing monitoring, reporting, and auditing. Create default conditions and consequences. Follow through with consequences.

■ *Recognize that things will go wrong:* The options for dealing with things that go wrong include declaring the project in default, delaying performance requirements, or restructuring the deal. It is difficult to determine in advance which choice makes the most sense, so contract provisions that cover all eventualities are impossible to create. When things go wrong, the performance of the developer to that point and the nature of the relationship between the parties govern what happens.

- *Keep it simple:* Complexity is the enemy of a fruitful relationship. By making the deal open, transparent, and easy to understand, the partners create a relationship of trust and mutual gain.

   Three last points: To form partnerships that create value, developers and communities must

- *Make deals based on the real estate, not wishful thinking:* Communities and developers need a valid mutual understanding of the real estate economics and of what the markets will support.

- *Build trust and ownership:* Who is involved in the partnership is as critical as what the project is. Developers and communities must take the time to use the open-book approach and to develop relationships of consistency and trust.

- *Do the hard work competently:* Public/private partnerships are complicated and require resilience and persistence to establish. They require a competent team that includes the developer, the community, and financing sources who take the time and make the effort to craft complex deals.

Note:

1. *Corrigan, Mary Beth, et al.* Ten Principles for Successful Public/Private Partnerships. *Washington, D.C.: ULI–the Urban Land Institute, 2005.*

CHAPTER 10

How Developers Get Capital

This chapter describes the experiences of developers and finance experts and how they have built and maintained working relationships as market conditions changed. The descriptions are based on conversations and correspondence with the developers and finance experts quoted in this chapter. Biographical and contact information for all those interviewed is appended to this chapter.

Developers finance their first projects in many ways. But common values and communication are always the foundations for building relationships of trust with investors. As developers succeed in their early projects, they establish a track record of reliability, leading to longer-term relationships with capital sources. The capabilities of a developer's team are critical to its reliability.

Development and capital markets today require new skills and knowledge; the challenge that developers face during the next decade is how to acquire the new competencies that will be vital to acquiring capital. Developers must add financial experts to their team who can ensure that transactions terms are sound. They must learn new product types, new technology, understand rapidly changing market conditions, and new demands from communities.

Getting Started

According to conventional wisdom, developers who are just starting out rely on "friends and family" as investors for their first projects. Then, as David Blitz, president of Los Angeles-based Nebo Capital, points out, "It is important to establish a track record, otherwise friends and family will drop away and the better-capitalized sources will be uninterested."

Experience shows that the course that developers take in their initial capital acquisition results from how they enter the development business. As Jeff Hudson of George Elkins Mortgage Banking Company in Los Angeles describes it, developers often start as passive investors (who, perhaps, earned money in another business or inherited wealth) who then move from observer to actor; in other words, they learn the business through investing and then go out on their own. Or they may have expertise in some aspect of development, as a tenant leasing broker, architect, or contractor, for example. This expertise establishes credibility for investors and may also provide access to tenants that will lease the finished project. Another model sees individuals from established development firms going out on their own. Another is when a successful builder sees the margins in development and integrates vertically to include not only building and construction but also development. Moving from a specialty to the broader area of development represents a significant departure from the specialist's core competencies and requires broadening relationships, skills, financing sources, and financing products. In all cases, the quality and values embodied in the developer's first project influences the choice of capital sources at the start and in the future. No developer succeeds without a search for investors who share his or her values.

Monte Ritchey of The Conformity Corporation in Charlotte, North Carolina, describes the funding of his first development project, highlighting how he leveraged initiative and values to investment by outside sources:

> My first "proper" development was the Williamson (a 30,000-square-foot historical mixed-use project) in Charlotte, North Carolina. The capital requirements were only $540,000. I had $40,000. Having crystallized most of the vision for the development and much of the science, [I found that] the money needed to make it happen was not rolling in. I was feeling sorry for myself, when it dawned on me that the phone was not going to ring with news of "checks in hand."

> I started making calls. I reached out to a former landlord. I knew this individual owned a lot of property in the neighborhood that I planned to develop the Williamson in. I also knew that he had been a former city planner and that he would speak the language that I was so passionate about. He would appreciate that I felt what I was saying. He was the first $250,000. In this case, I at least knew him.

> The second $250,000 came from a gentleman who owned properties I'd always admired. You can spot an attentive owner, and this individual had assembled an interesting block of holdings that he cared for in ways that were readily apparent. I'd never talked to him before. I was directed to his voice mail. I left a message that went something like this, "I've always admired your property. I believe you and I view the world in the same way. Here are a few small projects I've done near your property (they were houses and a quadraplex, all rehabs). Please have a look. In the spirit of full disclosure, I am calling to pitch you for capital. If I do not hear back, I will know that you have no interest." He did call back and did invest $250,000.

Ritchey goes on to describe that his first project generated an 18 percent rate of return on capital. For subsequent projects, he has kept about half a dozen repeat investors who invest directly with him in amounts of $50,000 to $200,000 with no syndicate or fund manager. Ritchey's experiences highlight how important the issue of shared values is to attracting capital from high-wealth individuals, but it also highlights how important it is that these investors have some familiarity with the type of project—in Ritchey's case, historical mixed-use development.

Luis Belmonte, of Seven Hills Properties, in San Francisco, describes another path to entering development—through the portal of sweat equity. Belmonte started small, worked hard, and advanced to leadership roles in large leading national development firms. In 1968, Belmonte returned from two years of service in Vietnam with $5,000 in savings (probably the equivalent of $50,000 today). He purchased and rehabilitated a San Francisco apartment building, getting in at the beginning of an emerging renaissance in that city. He subsequently purchased and rehabbed several more buildings. Almost all were "seller carry" purchases, with the prior owners holding a mortgage and Belmonte collecting the rents to pay them and generate sufficient cash to fund rehabilitation. Much of his capital was "sweat equity"; he performed the work, using scavenged materials (he characterizes this period as his "dumpster diving" period). Belmonte ran this business for three years and then graduated to a career with large development companies, building connections with lenders such as insurance companies and high-wealth equity investors.

Dan Kingsley, of San Francisco-based SKS Investments, entered the development business by leveraging his experience as an employee of a major investor/builder to become a founding partner of a successful investment/development firm. In 1992 he and two partners, one from a development firm and another from investment banking and consulting, founded SKS Investments. Their first projects were the purchases of two office buildings, with high–net worth individuals as the investors. Success there broadened their capital sources to include institutional investors, who invested directly. SKS has over 20 properties in its current portfolio, many of which it developed, and it has several trophy office buildings in its pipeline.

SKS focuses on sustainable, office-based, mixed-use projects, in and around San Francisco, and Kingsley's move from working for another firm highlights how important market knowledge and relationships are to success. Success in the office market depends on understanding the needs of and, in many cases, having personal relationships with major tenants. It means relationships with the office brokerage community. And it means having an intuitive understanding of the office market and where it is going in terms of which types of tenants are expanding and which are contracting.

Before forming his own North Carolina–based development company in 1999, Peter Pappas had experience as a partner in another development firm as a real estate broker, in land development and with tax-free exchanges. Pappas's investors are high–net worth individuals who coinvest with him to acquire a development site for entitlement. Upon the granting of the entitlement, these investors are offered the opportunity to stay in the project, with the land value serving as all or most of the equity for the development. Most of Pappas's investors have stayed in his deals for development and invest with him in other projects.

Pappas's specialty is mixed-use projects that have a significant retail component. This challenging sector requires strong relationships with retail tenants and brokers, relationships that take years to develop and which Pappas formed through his experience in land development and his last employer before forming his company. One of his projects, the Metropolitan in Charlotte, North Carolina, is anchored by Target, Trader Joe's, Marshalls, Staples, and Best Buy.

Brian Jackson is senior vice president of EYA, a high-density, residential/mixed-use, infill developer in the Washington, D.C., metro area. Mixed-use infill development is a challenging sector, especially because it usually involves affordable or mixed-income residential. The skills involve working in public/private partnerships as well has creating a track record for quality product in revitalizing neighborhoods. Jackson describes EYA's capital sources as "relationship-focused investing."

EYA was formed in 1992 by partners who had experience in other development firms. They found their first investor, the Sanyo Corporation, through an equity broker. Sanyo saw investment in residential real estate as a means to foster its appliance sales business, but its investment with EYA was grounded in the strength of the local market and the strong experience of the development team. After the success of this first project, a family-owned real estate company, Westfield Realty—the landlord for the office building where EYA's offices were located—became EYA's sole capital investor. Jackson reports that EYA developed about $800 million in projects with Westfield. The relationship was "very open book," and since Westfield was just up a few floors up, project issues were resolved by "riding the elevator up to talk." According to Jackson, the relationship was so strong that there was no formal partnership agreement.

EYA's Capitol Quarter features 208 townhomes in a mixed-use neighborhood near the Capitol, in Washington, D.C. Westfield was sold in 2005 on the retirement of the principals in the company. After West-field's sale, EYA interviewed several equity sources and selected JBG Companies, a developer and equity fund group based in Chevy Chase, Maryland. (JBG is the developer of the project highlighted in the case study for chapter 1.) As with Westfield, the relationship with JBG has grown to be very strong, but with differences. Because JBG is a fiduciary managing seven equity funds, Jackson reports that JBG's approach is more disciplined and analytic than West-field's and that EYA has found itself benefiting from that more rigorous approach.

Jackson also describes EYA's banking relationships as "relationship focused." EYA worked exclusively with Wachovia for all its projects up to 2008. When Wachovia was taken over by Wells Fargo, EYA decided to look for a new lending relationship and discovered, somewhat to its surprise, a tier of "super-regional" banks focused on EYA's market and interested in working with the company. Consequently, EYA now has multiple lenders participating in projects instead of just one.

Curt Johansen describes Triad Development's capital sources as value-driven investors. Johansen came to the company in the mid-1990s from a background in the homebuilding industry, where, as he describes it, "Money had stopped caring about the product, becoming obsessed solely with financial return. The result was homebuilders diversifying into financial products, economies of scale, and commodity production." At Triad he found investors seeking economic, social, and environmental returns, or, in his words, "investors who connect the capital to the product."

Johansen's initial project with Triad, beginning in 1996, was a troubled land development project in Vallejo, California, called Sky Valley. It had been partially constructed with significant construction defects and had financing for the infrastructure through municipal debt that was defaulting. The owners were a Japanese homebuilder and a Chicago-based opportunity fund. Triad's investor-driven approach fundamentally changed the project's character. First, it re-entitled the project for fewer residential units by reducing the number from 1,500 to 1,200. It added a retail component and increased the amount of open space. It diversified the housing designs and density. It brought in high-quality talent to fix the construction defects, which included significant shortcomings in the street construction. Based on this approach, it was able to refinance the $44 million of defaulted land-secured municipal debt.

It helped, of course, that all these changes occurred just in time to capture the run-up in real estate values of the early 2000s. But, even with the fortunate timing, Johansen's experience highlights how important a project's outcomes are becoming in attracting capital to real estate development. Investors increasingly seek financial returns from projects that incorporate long-term values of place, community, and livability. Whether this investment strategy of focusing on the character of the project is just a smart financial assessment that quality projects have less risk or whether it reflects a desire to seek return from social and environmental dimensions is difficult to say.

The value-driven investment ethic that Johansen describes is confirmed in various ways by other interviewees. Peter Pappas says that his investors strongly endorse his development philosophy of creating value through building projects with a sense of place and of community. They believe that these kinds of projects simply achieve a higher return. Monte Ritchey says his investors invest with him because his projects are in "good locations and have higher intrinsic value." Dan Kingsley's firm focuses on transactions "that would be difficult for the majority of real estate operators to execute. At the same time, SKS has a keen interest in the triple bottom line—positive social, environmental, and financial returns." Brian Jackson's firm has a "vision of building innovative urban neighborhoods to the highest standards," and they have numerous awards recognizing their projects. Clearly, the values embodied by the product influence the ability of the developer to attract investment.

Building Relationships

Roger Staiger, managing director of Stage Capital, LLC, in Columbia, Maryland, emphasizes that relationships with capital sources are about transparency, consistency, intelligence, and simple courtesy:

> The worst thing one can do to an investor is NOT lose their capital but rather lose their capital and not understand how the capital was lost, providing zero explanation. Successful relationships in business and society are about utilizing simple skills. State your goal, state the process, report regularly on progress, and if/when there is a problem, run at the issue—NOT from the issue. No one likes surprises. Finally, the key to building relationships: just do honest work and word of mouth will provide its own marketing.

Relationships are also about knowing what your capital sources care about. Luis Belmonte, in his colorful language, offers three pieces of advice about building relationships with capital sources:

- *Find the hot button on the other side and press it repeatedly.* What are investors interested in? Is it return on capital? Or knowing if something will go wrong? Or receiving regular status reports? Whatever it is, make sure you push it!
- *For institutions, pay attention to the politics.* Have an ear inside the investment committee. Know about what is going on at the office. Be ready to empathize or run for cover. Know the who of the what.
- *Recognize the relationship as important.* Is the investor putting the money out with someone they like? Loan brokers can help, but the personal relationship with the capital source is the key.

Clearly, Belmonte is describing how important it is to understand and respond tow the needs and personality of the capital sources.

Dan Kingsley's advice echoes both Roger Staiger and Luis Belmonte and expands on their comments to focus on the importance that the developer's competence has for an investment source. Here is what he believes are the critical behaviors for attracting capital:

- *Demonstrate your understanding of the market:* The developer must recognize the entitlement risk and how to achieve value in the face of community opposition.
- *Demonstrate your understanding of the construction risk:* Delivering on time and on budget requires a commitment of time and patience.
- *Do not promise what you cannot deliver:* Protect against the downside and avoid promoting the upside.
- *Be organized and professional:* Provide accurate information in an easy-to-read format. Communicate with partners in a common language.
- *Act with integrity and reliability.*
- *Understand the risk/reward needs of the investors.*

Kingsley's principles are echoed by Elizabeth Conahan of Bethesda, Maryland–based Walker & Dunlop. She says, "The top considerations that capital sources have are the quality of the individual and the quality of the product." Track record, reliability, integrity, competence, and professionalism are clearly fundamental to building and maintaining relationships, along with communications skills and the art of creating realistic expectations.

The relationship between EYA and JBG described by Brian Jackson is an example of mutual benefit for "finding the buttons and pushing them repeatedly." JBG has caused EYA to examine its project choices more closely to exclude projects outside its core competency and to examine more closely something that JBG calls "optionality," to maintain flexibility in project direction. JBG also encourages greater analysis of the sensitivity of a project to different market, timing, and cost scenarios. Jackson says that this discipline has strengthened EYA's ability to manage important aspects of the project.

Monte Ritchey's advice reinforces the notion of a feedback loop from investor to developer:

> *We communicate monthly with our investors—narrative and financials. Consider the notion that your capital has valuable ideas. While you must maintain control of the ship, always welcome feedback from capital. When faced with the science of your agreements with investors and the nagging feeling that you should share the wealth, if dealing with individuals, share the wealth. You'll be paid back tenfold on reputation and repeat investments.*

In addition to listening, many interviewees stressed the importance of aligning interests to creating strong relationships with investors. Peter Pappas said, "Investors invest in my projects because the deal is fair. My profits come from project value; fees cover overhead expenses only." Brian Jackson described much the same compensation program for EYA, saying, "EYA gets paid on the profit from selling the units instead of taking development fees. This further aligns our interest with our investors."

In a financial world where equity, hedge, and opportunity funds have created high fee-compensation norms, the concept of a developer getting paid from the success of the project may seem novel or obsolete. Investors, however, value developers whose interest is aligned with theirs and who are fair.

The importance of aligning interests, finally, highlights the relationship that capital has with the skills of a developer. Jeff Hudson comments that a developer's skill is sometimes taken for granted but that sophisticated investors in real estate understand how valuable a developer's skills really are. He says, "Most people think that real estate developers are not as smart as bond or stock traders. Everyone thinks of themselves as in real estate because they own a house. In fact, real estate development is a lot more complicated and involves a greater creation of value than bonds or stocks."

And in the perception of most of the interviewees, the skills of the developer are even more critical to value creation than ever before. Elizabeth Conahan has had extensive experience as a capital broker, and she has seen these challenges. Her comment is, "Developers need to be a lot smarter. The ones succeeding in today's markets are really smart." Perhaps Monte Ritchey's comment best addresses the important connection that lies at the heart of a relationship between a capital source and a developer. "Development is a set of skills. Capital is static. It does nothing when not attached to human skill." Finally, a comment by Jeff Hudson resonates as an important trait of a successful relationship between capital sources and developers. "Successful developers have humility. They know how to articulate their weaknesses and mitigate them. They affiliate with people who overcome their weaknesses."

Skills for Acquiring Capital in the 2010s

All the interviewees agreed that attracting capital to development in the 2010s will be harder, requiring not just more financial sophistication but also new competencies to address the changing development environment. Capital sources seek reliable performance and that requires competence leading to relationships of trust.

What skills does a developer need in the 2010s to be able to act reliably and to attract capital? To answer this question, it is worth reviewing briefly where capital markets have come from in the past 20 years as a prelude to describing the skills that a developer will need in the 2010s. Fundamental changes to capital finance for real estate began in the late 1980s and early 1990s and continued through the 2000s. These changes, described in chapters 2 and 5, included different tax treatment; securitization of loans through CMBS; the entry of REITs, opportunity funds, hedge funds, and private equity funds into real estate; and the dramatic lowering of cap rates in the mid-2000s. Many interviewees described the result of these changes as the creation of a "transactional" environment characterized by short holding periods and high velocity of sales. The changes go beyond an emphasis on transactions; they include more sophisticated asset allocation strategies by sector, region, and class and strategies such as hedging and options that manage risk and, potentially, enhance returns.

Developers now need to know more about capital markets to be effective in dealing with capital sources. Roger Staiger describes the new capital market norm as a "chase for efficiency" with real estate being only one of many investment choices and consequently needing to compete effectively with other asset classes on dimensions of risk, liquidity, and return: "Real estate investment today is as much about its competitive position as an asset class as it is about shovels in the ground. The old world of real estate investment never required a high level of sophistication in capital markets. Today is different." He continues with advice to developers to understand the criteria that capital sources use to make funding decisions:

> Developers today face a much more complex environment in dealing with the question, "Is there available capital for a development project and at what margin? Understanding banking underwriting is critical, and understanding how loans are priced is required to best negotiate with a financing source. One must not only know and understand one's own margins but also those of counterparties, i.e., banks. When this is understood, the best financing terms are achieved to the mutual benefit of all parties.

Luis Belmonte, some 25 years senior to Staiger, describes the effect of a change in real estate finance that occurred in the late 1980s with the Tax Reform Act of 1986: "It was the Grand Canyon of real estate finance. We all fell in the river and came up on the other side of the canyon to a fundamentally different regime for real estate investment." He character-izes pre–Reform Act real estate investment as follows:

> The big issue for tax-oriented syndicates was sheltering income from taxes through depreciation and lower capital gains rate. It was about "goosing the write-off" because the marginal tax rate for ordinary income was 70 percent. Many investors would look only for return of principal and a modest preferred return.

These neighborhood-oriented shopping centers in suburban Portland, Oregon, are typical of the retail projects developed by Luis Belmonte's San Francisco–based firm, Seven Hills Properties. The firm has also developed residential, office, and industrial properties.

Or, as Jeff Hudson remarks, "Prior to 1986, real estate was a gimmicky investment. It became much more fundamental after 1986."

Reflecting on these changes, Elizabeth Conahan says,

> In the old days there were no REITs or individual retirement accounts. Early investors built [residential] projects through HUD loans. Many started small as family businesses and grew into large homebuilders, who then found they had to compete for capital on the basis of short-term return horizons. Today, even most insurance companies (there are exceptions) have shortened their horizons. The vulture ethic has made long-term ownership hard.

Peter Pappas, commenting on the transaction environment, had this to say:

> We build to hold but with the cap rate compression from 2000 to 2006, we were compelled by our investors to sell some of our properties. The transactional considerations affect but should not drive the primary vision. The transaction should be about maximizing value, not about quick turnover.

Real estate, in other words, will need to compete for capital when many investors are still looking for the quick turnover. David Blitz comments, "In today's market, everyone is still looking for the pre-2008 yields, but the reality is that there is less leverage and they can't be achieved. In addition, co-investment and recourse are back." But, as Dan Kingsley describes, the transactional ethic has created a divide among investors:

> There are two classes of operating partners in development: the first are cycle players who buy low, sell high, and rely on good fortune instead of skill; and second, are value players who create long-term value using real skill. The institutional investors we work with are adopting a different yardstick for measuring risk and return. Prior to 2008, there was insufficient appreciation of the cycle risk. This is changing to a long-term value ethic.

Curt Johansen offered these thoughts on principles developers should follow in conceiving and executing projects that will attract capital:

- Development is not a transaction.
- Land is not about technology, it is about creating place and about making communities that work.
- No more externalities! Shift to a value-driven approach!
- A growing percentage of capital is seeking long-term value creation. It is a new era for real estate investing.

The 2010s will continue the trip up the "other side of the canyon." It is important to reflect on the skills a developer will need to operate effectively within Kingsley's "long-term value ethic." To do so, developers first need to recognize that the change to real estate is not just in the capital markets. It includes all dimensions of real estate. If a developer is going to establish a track record of reliability and enjoy the relationships of trust vital to attracting capital, the developer must recognize the importance of obtaining skills that respond to current conditions. Here are some of the key areas that developers will need to focus on if they hope to achieve reliable performance:

■ Through entitlement, communities are demanding more benefits from development. Developers need to better understand how to create community ownership so they can reliably deliver viable projects.

■ Every real estate sector is changing at a rapid pace. Here are examples:

▮ Retail, historically the fastest changing sector, has moved from lifestyle to entertainment to town to whatever may come next.

▮ Office users are demanding more energy efficiency and more sophisticated technology.

▮ Hospitality has absorbed fractional ownership and is testing new urban product types.

▮ Residential products are changing to accommodate transit-oriented development and new customer groups such as empty nesters. Developers are testing new parking ratios, new amenity packages, and new technologies.

▮ Industrial buildings are more sophisticated and locations are changing.

■ Development is physically more complex than ever, making construction a challenge.

■ Tenants in all sectors are demanding "green buildings" or "zero energy" buildings.

■ Heating and cooling districts, a configuration of the early 20th century, are making a comeback as a means of increasing energy reliability and efficiency.

■ Sustainable development requires that projects address the social and environmental aspects of development as well as the economic ones.

■ Development is more urban, involving challenges of repositioning and redeveloping obsolete sites, multiple sector involvement, and, frequently, public/private partnerships.

■ Markets are more volatile and more regionally differentiated, creating both more risk and more opportunity.

■ In many markets, replacement costs will continue to exceed valuations, making development opportunities scarce.

■ Capital sources are more diverse, underwriting criteria more sophisticated, and financing structures more complex, with more tiering of project revenue streams to multiple sources of capital.

As chapter 1 describes, the developer is the conductor of a chaotic and multi-disciplinary process, albeit one that depends on exogenous forces, especially market demand and capital availability. With the fundamental differences in real estate entering the 2010s, developers' teams must change to respond to the new challenges. A major enhancement should be the addition of a finance expert who is paid an hourly rate and not compensated as a percentage of a financial transaction. This does not rule out the use of capital brokers; in fact, capital brokers are needed more than ever in this environment. However, current conditions argue for the team to have a financial professional who looks to the interests of the developer without having the conflict of being motivated simply to see the transaction close. This expert should understand underwriting spreads and capital options, in order to help the developer negotiate a lower-margin deal in capital markets, where real estate now competes more directly with other asset classes in terms of return, risk, holding period, and liquidity.

Other evolutions in a developer's competencies will also enhance the developer's reputation for reliability and thus competitiveness for capital. As discussed in chapters 6 and 7, academic and professional credentials are more important than ever. As discussed in chapter 4, new models of design and construction can enhance on-time, on-budget performance for physically complicated projects. Staying current on the fast-moving changes in development trends, product types, and market conditions is fundamental to a developer's competency.

Building these new competencies requires that developers work harder than ever to stay informed and develop the relationships that connect the developer with resources. Here are suggested approaches for effectively attracting capital to projects in the 2010s:

■ *Participate in multidisciplinary professional organizations:* Broadly scoped professional organizations, such as the Urban Land Institute, help developers create relationships and increase knowledge of development trends throughout the industry. To obtain the maximum value from such organizations, developers must get involved in the organization's activities at both the regional and the national levels.

■ *Participate in sector specialty organizations:* Each sector has its own specialty organization that monitors trends and fosters professional relationships. For retail, the International Council of Shopping Centers (ICSC) provides a wealth of technical information and regional and national networking. For industrial or office development, the National Association of Industrial and Office Properties (NAIOP) performs these functions.

■ *Focus on the community:* To not be viewed as outsiders whose projects are only about money, developers need to join the community. This means participating and engaging and responding in a manner that creates community ownership of the project.

■ *Obtain professional certificates:* Attending classes in finance, capital markets, and industry trends helps developers understand and keep abreast of language and trends. Obtaining certifications increases developers' credentials for attracting capital.

■ *Stay close to customers:* Each sector has its primary customers that developers must know and understand. Retail, office, and industrial users enter projects as tenants or buyers with developers they know and trust. Developers should cultivate relationships with potential customers, usually starting through the professional sector organization.

■ *Real estate broker relationships:* Good brokers and brokerages know the market and can assist developers in securing customers and understanding market conditions.

■ *Capital brokers:* Capital brokers can provide invaluable assistance in today's capital markets for both debt and equity.

Competence, reliability, and relationships are the foundations for successfully attracting capital to a real estate project. Focusing on value, building relationships of trust, understanding capital markets, and constantly gathering new information on what constitutes long-term value are all behaviors that will position a developer to succeed in attracting capital.

Appendix A: Bios of Interviewees

Luis A. Belmonte
Seven Hills Properties
San Francisco, California
lbelmonte@sevenhillsprop.com

Luis Belmonte is a partner in Seven Hills Properties and was formerly executive vice president of AMB Property Corporation (NYSE: AMB). At AMB, he was responsible for more than $1 billion in global development and redevelopment activities and directed the asset management operations for 50 million square feet of the firm's U.S. portfolio. Before joining AMB, Belmonte spent 16 years with Lincoln Property Company as partner in charge of industrial development in northern California, constructing more than 18 million square feet of buildings valued in excess of $750 million. His early career included apartment redevelopment work in San Francisco for D.H. Overmyer Company and service as a junior officer in the U.S. Navy during the Vietnam war. Belmonte has a BA degree in political science from the University of Santa Clara and did graduate studies in political science at the University of California–Berkeley and the University of Chicago. He is a member of the Urban Land Institute and past president of the San Francisco Chapter of NAIOP, and holds a California real estate broker's license. Belmonte is a nationally recognized workout consultant, expert witness, and sought-after speaker in the real estate industry.

David Blitz
Owner, Nebo Capital, Inc.
Los Angeles, California
david@nebocapital.com

Before forming Mount Nebo Capital in 2001, David Blitz served as a director at Belgravia Capital and its successor firm, and as a partner in a private real estate investment banking firm. Blitz served as a senior vice president of Imperial Bank, where in the 1980s he originated and structured over $200 million of construction and term loans and in the 1990s restructured over $250 million in nonperforming loans, including real estate only (REO) sales. His 27 years of real estate experience include acquisitions and dispositions, capital markets, asset management, development, and financing. Blitz has also held positions with the New York Life Insurance Company and earlier, after earning a degree in architecture from Cooper Union, practiced for five years as an architectural project manager in Santa Monica, California.

Elizabeth Conahan
Walker & Dunlop
Bethesda, Maryland
econahan@walkerdunlop.com

Elizabeth Conahan is a consultant for Walker & Dunlop. She has completed more than $2.5 billion in commercial real estate transactions. She counts among her clients many of the premier real estate owners and developers in the Washington, D.C., area. Before joining Walker & Dunlop, Conahan was a principal and division manager for AMRESCO and a senior vice president for NationsBank. She also worked for UST Corp., Citicorp, and Shawmut in various real estate capacities.

Conahan is a member of the Urban Land Institute and the Mortgage Bankers Association and also served as chairperson of the ULI Washington District Council. She is also a board member of THEARC (Town Hall Education Arts Recreation Campus) in Washington, D.C. She holds a degree from Chestnut Hill College and performed graduate work in urban planning at Boston University.

Jeffrey Martin Hudson
George Elkins Mortgage Banking Company
Los Angeles, California
jhudson@gemb.com

Jeffrey Hudson, chief executive officer of George Elkins Mortgage Banking Company, began his professional career in real estate finance with a southern California–based mortgage banking firm in 1978 and became president of it in 1985. During his 14 years there, and since joining George Elkins, Hudson arranged more than $10 billion in financing of a range of property types, including office, industrial, retail, apartment, hotel, mobile home park, and mini-warehouse. He structured loans throughout the country that ranged from $1 million to over $300 million.

He joined the George Elkins Company in 1992 as senior vice president and general manager of Mortgage Banking. In 1993, he was made president and in 1995 chief executive officer of the company. In 1996, he and investors purchased the mortgage banking division, retaining all correspondent relationships, servicing, and division employees. In 2007 George Elkins became a wholly owned subsidiary of MMA Financial.

Hudson graduated from the University of California at Santa Barbara in 1974. He subsequently attended Woodland School of Law, where he received his doctorate of jurisprudence in 1978. The state of California admitted him to practice in 1978, and the following year he was admitted to practice before the Supreme Court. Also in 1979, Hudson received his certification to teach law, banking, and finance at the community college level.

He is a member of the California State Bar, the California Mortgage Bankers Association, the Mortgage Bankers Association of America, the Commercial Real Estate Secondary Market and Securitization Association, and the Apartment Owners Association. He is a member of the faculty of the Practicing Law Institute in San Francisco. He is on the board of directors of Kennedy Wilson International. As a member of the National Real Estate Forum, Hudson has been awarded the professional designation of certified real estate financier. He also holds a California real estate broker's license.

Brian Allan Jackson
EYA LLC
Bethesda, Maryland
bjackson@eya.com

"AJ" Jackson is a partner with EYA, LLC, a Washington, D.C. area urban infill development company and *Builder* Magazine's 2009 Builder of the Year. Currently, he serves as senior vice president of land acquisition and development and is leading EYA's participation in more than $750 million of public/private development partnerships, including the following:

■ Capitol Quarter, EYA's portion of the Arthur Capper/ Carrollsburg HOPE VI redevelopment in Washington, D.C.;

■ The redevelopment of the historic National Park Seminary in Silver Spring, Maryland, into a mixed-income community;

■ EYA's partnership with the Alexandria, Virginia Redevelopment and Housing Authority to create more than 500 units of mixed-income housing; and

■ A 90-acre, mixed-use/mixed-income, transit-oriented redevelopment partnership with Montgomery County, Maryland.

In addition, Jackson is a member of EYA's Executive Committee as well as its Investment Committee and directs strategy and planning for the firm. He has a decade of experience working with public-sector organizations on real estate and public policy issues.

Before joining EYA, Jackson served as chief of staff at the U.S. General Services Administration, the single largest owner and operator of real estate assets in the United States. While at the GSA, he played key roles in several high-profile development projects as well as in the GSA's response to the 9/11 terrorist attacks and the anthrax attacks in Washington, D.C.

Curt Johansen
TerraVerde Ventures Advisory, LLC
Petaluma, California
curt@terraverdeventures.com

Curt Johansen began his career as a California land development manager in the 1980s. He founded a construction company with 11 employees, building 12 to 15 high-end custom homes annually. He managed the development at Silverado Country Club in Napa, California, and has consulted for clients interested in entitling and building high-quality communities. One of his early accomplishments was the completion of The Vintage Club in Indian Wells, California, an award-winning, 712-acre community.

In 1997 Johansen became executive vice president of Seattle-based Triad Communities, L.P. and for more than 12 years managed the firm's California development portfolio. His flagship project was Hiddenbrooke, a mixed-use community featuring diverse neighborhoods with 1,200 residences, local-serving retail, recreational amenities, and over 700 acres of parks and open space. He also conceived, designed, and entitled the transit-oriented plan for downtown Vallejo, recognized in 2006 by the American Planning Association as the finest large-scale infill Specific Plan in California.

Johansen has entitled more than 3,000 residential units in the San Francisco Bay Area. His passion for sustainability led him to develop the Angwin Ecovillage, a leading triple-bottom-line community in California. Located in Napa County, this mixed-use, renewable-resource community will feature a 35-acre CSA organic farm amid 225 acres of preserved agriculture, solar and geothermal energy use, eco-literate education, a comprehensive transportation demand management program, reclaimed wastewater use for all outdoor needs, green building to LEED Silver equivalent or above, and diverse affordable housing—all while dedicating 90 percent of the land to permanent conservation easements.

Johansen is a founding partner of TerraVerde Ventures, LLC, and its advisory arm, TVVA. With its partners, TerraVerde is creating a portfolio of communities that balance economic prosperity, environmental protections, and social responsibility.

Johansen currently chairs the Planning Commission for the city of Petaluma, California. He is a founding board member of the California Infill Builders Association Council, is on the Urban Land Institute's Socially Responsible Investment Council, and participates on numerous other regional committees promoting sustainable communities. Johansen is publishing his first book, on the union of sustainable development philosophy and best practice. He is frequently invited to speak about market-driven sustainable communities.

Daniel Kingsley
SKS Investments
San Francisco, California
dkingsley@sksinvestments.com
Daniel Kingsley is a founder of SKS and has 29 years of experience in commercial real estate, primarily in real estate development. Over the course of his career, he has participated in the planning, entitlement, design, and construction of more than 8 million square feet of Class A office, hotel, and mixed-use building development. From 1985 until founding SKS, Kingsley was a vice president with Maguire Thomas Partners, one of the nation's five largest investment builders during the 1980s, headquartered in Los Angeles, where he participated in the development of over 3 million square feet of office space. He received a BS degree from the University of Oregon, an MBA degree from the Wharton School of the University of Pennsylvania, and an MS in regional planning degree from the University of Pennsylvania.

Peter A. Pappas
Pappas Properties
Charlotte, North Carolina
ppappas@pappasproperties.com
Peter Pappas founded Pappas Properties in 1999 after seven years as a partner at The Harris Group. While there, he led his team in developing a number of successful projects including Phillips Place; Ballantyne, a 2,000-acre, mixed-use community; Morrocroft, a 178-acre multiuse project; and 330 South Tryon. Before joining The Harris Group, Pappas was a vice president with The Bissell Companies and president of its land development subsidiary, Investment Mortgage Company.

Monte Ritchey
The Conformity Corporation
Charlotte, North Carolina
mritchey@conformitycorp.com
Monte Ritchey is president of the Conformity Corporation, a Charlotte, North Carolina–based real estate development company specializing in mixed-use and historic preservation projects. Ritchey is also president of Accord Construction, an unlimited-class general contracting company. The work of the Conformity Corporation is focused on respect for the human condition and breaking through known models to discover new solutions. Acknowledging the value that historic structures can provide to a venture, the Conformity Corporation routinely looks for opportunities to combine preservation with new infill.

Ritchey is an expert in tax-advantaged rehabilitation, having completed more than half a dozen certified projects. The most recent was the Rutzler, the largest of the remaining multifamily structures in Charlotte's Elizabeth neighborhood (a National Register District). Recent infill projects include the Williamson, SteelHaus, and Elizabeth Village, all predominately residential projects with supporting retail and office components. Each is in a National Register District within three miles of the city's core.

Today, in partnership with Lowe's Companies, Inc., the Conformity Corporation is completing Southborough, which includes Lowe's flagship store and a related mix of uses in the SouthEnd, a transit-oriented BID in Charlotte. Southborough is the subject of a ULI Case Study. Conformity's work enjoys a continuing stream of top honors and awards from professional organizations including the American Institute of Architects, the American Society of Landscape Architects, the Counselors of Real Estate, and Preservation North Carolina. Conformity's work has been the subject of numerous white papers and presented in classrooms at both the Harvard Graduate School of Design and the Massachusetts Institute of Technology's Department of Urban Studies.

Ritchey is a member of the Urban Land Institute, the International Council of Shopping Centers, and Preservation North Carolina. He serves on the board of International House, is involved in the Charlotte Chapter of ULI, and serves on several citizen advisory committees for the city of Charlotte.

Roger Staiger III
Stage Capital, LLC
Columbia, Maryland
rstaiger@gwmail.gwu.edu
Roger Staiger's areas of expertise include global portfolio management, real estate capital markets, derivatives and risk management, and financial modeling. He is currently managing director at Stage Capital, LLC, a real estate and management consulting firm. Stage Capital provides consulting and risk management services for clients nationwide on real estate issues including financial structuring and restructuring, loan modifications and strategies, asset repositioning, and portfolio management.

Formerly, Staiger was a fund manager for a development/construction fund in New York. He was a portfolio manager for the Ultra LongView Construction Loan Fund, a $1.25 billion portfolio which invests in all commercial asset classes nationwide. His professional experience includes multiple years as chief financial officer for a mid-Atlantic regional developer and builder. Before that, he was managing director with Constellation Energy, for both the gas and electric retail commodity divisions ($240 million annual revenue). Previously, he was the finance executive for Clark Construction, a privately held national commercial builder, and a senior quantitative analyst for Columbia Energy.

Staiger holds faculty positions at the Johns Hopkins University, Georgetown University, and Loyola University of Maryland, and leads executive seminars for ULI. He has spoken around the world on U.S. real estate investment and management topics; his most recent presentation was in Doha, Qatar, to the Arabian Academic and Finance Ministry.

Staiger is a recognized real estate expert. His articles have been published in *Developer* magazine and by the National Association of Realtors. *LiveValuation* magazine regularly features articles by Staiger focused on statistics trends in residential real estate. He regularly appears on television and radio, and in newspapers.

Staiger earned his BS degree in electrical engineering from Bucknell University. He earned his MBA and his MS in finance degree from George Washington University and his MA degree in international transactions from George Mason University.

Appendix B: Glossary

Absorption rate. The estimated pace at which units or square footage in a development project will be leased or sold in the market. Usually used when preparing a forecast of the sales or leasing rate to substantiate a development plan and to obtain financing.

Acquisition, development, and construction (ADC) loan. A loan that finances acquisition, development, and construction of a real estate development project. ADC loans enable a developer to buy land, install infrastructure, and build improvements. Developers applying for ADC loans typically have leases or presales in hand, along with conditions or commitments for takeout financing.

Adjustable interest rate. A variable interest rate on a debt (loan, bond, or mortgage) that adjusts periodically based on an index such as ten-year Treasury bonds or the LIBOR.

Amortization. Paying off the principal amount of a loan over the term ("killing" the debt). An amortization schedule shows the schedule for paying off the principal amount of the debt along with the periodic interest payments that constitute the total debt payment.

Anchor tenant. A retail tenant that is usually large, is often well-known, and attracts traffic to a retail shopping center, benefiting the smaller, less well-known retailers. A regional shopping center may have several anchor tenants.

Bonds. A debt security issued by a borrower and denominated in whole dollar amounts, such as $5,000, $10,000 or $100,000. The bonds represent an issuer's commitment to pay principal and interest to the bondholder over a maturity period.

Buy-sell provision. A provision of a joint venture agreement that allows for an orderly dissolution of a partnership in which one party estimates the value of the partnership and the other party has the option to either purchase or sell its share of the partnership at that value.

Capital. Money or property invested in an asset such as real property to produce a return from interest, periodic profits, or increase in asset value.

Capital market. The network of individuals, institutions (banks, insurance companies, equity funds, etc.), and brokers through which capital is obtained for investment in assets.

Capital stack. A description of the layers of capital invested in a project, starting from the lowest-risk interest-bearing debt, moving up to performing debt, then to equity that receives a return based on the financial performance of the project. The stack is described as a risk continuum: the top of the stack contains the highest risk and seeks the highest rate of return, and the lower-risk layers (or tranches) below seek lower rates of return.

Capitalization rate. An indicator of investor perceptions of current market conditions for the availability of capital and the perceived financial strength of a particular real estate project in terms of the reliability of its income and its potential for price appreciation. The "cap rate" is calculated as the net operating income, or NOI, divided by the value of the property. It is frequently applied as a way to estimate a project's future value, by dividing a projected NOI by an assumed cap rate. Investors who evaluate an investment over a holding period will apply a "going in" cap rate to evaluate project value upon acquisition and then estimate a "terminal" cap rate at a future time that will estimate value at the time that a property is expected to be sold.

Carve-out agreement. The agreement that spells out assets that are not included as security for the guarantee of a loan in the event of a default on a loan that provides recourse to the assets of the operating partner of a development project.

Cash-on-cash return. The property's annual net cash flow divided by the net investment, expressed as a percentage. It is typically calculated by dividing before-tax cash flow by the amount of cash invested. Cash-on-cash does not include property appreciation, which is a non–cash flow item until the year of sale.

Certificate of occupancy. A document issued by the building department of a local jurisdiction that certifies that a building and/or the leased area that was under construction has been inspected and found to be completed sufficiently to be suitable for occupancy.

Co-investment. Typically, the amount of investment required of the developer or operating partner to align the interests of the investors and the developer. This amount varies from 5 to 15 percent of the total equity requirement for the project.

Collateral. Assets pledged as security to the lender to secure repayment of a loan in case of default.

Commercial mortgage–backed securities (CMBS). Bonds issued by a trust to which a pool of commercial loans has been conveyed. The bonds are secured and paid by the value and income from the commercial loans. They are paid in a priority order resulting in "tranches" of bonds, with the higher-priority tranches rated as more secure and the lower-priority tranches rated as less secure.

Common area maintenance (CAM) charges. Charges issued to the tenants of a commercial real estate project in addition to the base rent to pay for the maintenance or operation of the common areas such as lobbies, parking lots, and utilities used by all tenants. These charges can include the costs of landscaping, outdoor lighting, parking lot sweeping, insurance, and property taxes, among others.

Conduit lenders. Another name for lenders that originate loans and then reconvey those loans to a pool for securitization, such as a CMBS pool. Any lender that converts a commercial mortgage into a security rather than retaining the mortgage in its portfolio can be classified as a conduit lender.

Construction loan. A short-term loan, usually from a bank, that finances the construction of a project. The loan proceeds are drawn as construction continues, so the entire amount of the loan is outstanding upon project completion. Construction loans usually carry variable interest rates and fund a share of total project costs between 55 and 70 percent.

Contingency cost. An amount added to estimated project costs that accounts for the unknowns or unexpected expenses that are likely to occur and that cannot be estimated precisely at the early stages of a project. The contingency estimate declines as a project proceeds, as more reliable and complete information is obtained and unknowns are eliminated.

Corporation. A formal business association with a publicly registered charter that recognizes it as a separate legal entity with its own privileges and liabilities distinct from those of its members.

Credit tenant. Usually a publicly traded or large private entity, most often a national retail chain, that is expected to create a highly reliable rent stream for a shopping center.

Debt capital. The portion of the investment capital for a project that is borrowed.

Debt coverage ratio (DCR). An underwriting standard used in determining the amount of a loan that will be provided to a real estate project. It is measured as the ratio of the annual net operating income (NOI) from a property to the annual cost of debt service on the maximum allowable loan. To calculate the DCR requires knowing the loan terms (amortization period, interest rate) and obtaining a reliable estimate of future (typically the next year's) NOI. A typical DCR might be expressed as 1.2, meaning that NOI is 120 percent of debt service costs.

Debt service. Periodic payments on a loan, with a portion of the payment for interest and the balance for repayment (amortization) of principal.

Deed of trust. A legal document that is recorded as an exception to title for a real estate property, granting a trustee the right to foreclose on the property if payments on a debt are not made.

Depreciation. In real estate, a decrease or loss in property value due to wear, age, or other deterioration of the improvements. In accounting, depreciation is a periodic allowance made for this real or implied loss.

Developer. An individual or organization that manages all aspects of a real estate development project. These aspects can include site acquisition, entitlement, construction, and close-out. A developer manages the efforts of key specialists, such as architecture, construction, engineering, marketing, and legal services.

downREIT. An organizational structure that makes it possible for REITs to buy property using partnership units. It has the same effect as an UPREIT; however, the downREIT is subordinate to the REIT. The UPREIT and downREIT enable principals that transfer their ownership from private to public (through REIT acquisition or IPO) to retain the historical cost basis on their books.

Due diligence. Investigation before finalizing a contract to purchase real estate of all relevant conditions of a property including ownership, boundaries, soils, environmental, regulations, market conditions, and financial considerations. Frequently, this investigation entails the efforts of outside experts.

Due diligence period. A period of 30 days to 6 months or more during which a developer conducts due diligence.

Easement. An exception to title on real property that provides for another use on portions of the property such as a water line, maintenance of public works, or access by others across the property.

Economic viability. A measure of when a project produces sufficient profit to repay capital sources and provide adequate compensation to the developer for the time and skill invested.

Effective gross income. The total income from a property generated by rents and other sources, less an appropriate vacancy factor estimated for the property, expressed as income collected before expenses and debt service. Effective gross income is a metric commonly used in developing the property pro forma to evaluate the value of investment property.

Entitlement process. The process of obtaining approvals from land use jurisdictions for the right to develop property for a desired use. This process includes a range of governmental actions ranging from environmental review to zoning to building permitting. The process also includes substantial interaction with citizens who may be involved in influencing the decisions of local elected officials.

Equity. The component of development capital provided by investors who obtain their return on and of capital primarily from project performance. This component typically is not secured by recourse to the property. The terms under which it is invested are usually stipulated in a joint venture agreement.

Fixed interest rate. An interest rate that does not vary with market conditions over the life of the debt.

Floor/area ratio (FAR). The ratio of the floor area of a development project to the land area of the development site. A low floor/area ratio implies that a significant portion of the site is not covered by a building and, usually, is set aside to accommodate surface parking that relates to the use of the building. For instance, a one-story building covering one-quarter of a site, with the rest of the site used as a surface parking lot, would have a FAR of .25.

Forbearance. A circumstance, usually stipulated in a legal agreement, under which a lender delays foreclosing on a real estate project that may be in default on a loan. The default could be a "technical" default, in that the underlying property value may have dropped below the underwriting criteria of the lender but the property still generates sufficient income to make loan payments on time. Lenders may forbear on "non-performing" loans as well, to allow time for properties to recover from poor market conditions.

Foreclosure. The legal process by which a lender forces the sale of a property that has defaulted on its loan to provide funds to pay off the loan. This process can be complicated if a property has multiple loans and lenders, each of which has a different priority of payment. Sometimes a "junior" lender will pay off the primary lender to obtain control of the property and to avoid the complete loss of its loan through foreclosure by the primary lender.

Forward commitments. A commitment for terms of a future loan on a real estate project. Forward commitments minimize the risk of changes to the cost and availability of the loan before the time at which the loan actually funds.

Gap financing. A broad category of project financing that ranges from mezzanine financing to public/private partnerships. The "gap" is the difference between the debt and equity. Gap financing may involve financing to cover a short period of time or to fill the void between equity and debt capital available to a project.

General partnership. A general partnership (as opposed to a "limited" partnership with a single operating partner) is a development entity in which all partners share the risks, rewards, and management of the venture and are liable for the debts and obligations of the business. A partnership, general or otherwise, is a reporting vehicle and not a taxable entity; therefore the tax liability associated with net income accrues solely to the members of the partnership.

Guaranteed investment contract (GIC). A written guarantee to an investor of a certain yield for a defined period of time. This type of contract is frequently used in a financing program in which the lender prepays interest on a loan and the prepayment is set aside in a GIC that creates income exactly sufficient to pay interest as it is due. GICs are used in a number of industries (such as insurance and institutional finance); the direction of payment and receipt differ.

Hard costs. Construction and land costs, as distinguished from "soft" costs such as financing, design, and legal costs, which vary based on the magnitude of the hard costs.

Hedge funds. A high-risk, opportunistic investment fund that seeks high returns. It is open only to qualified investors or institutions. Hedge fund managers aggressively seek investment opportunities, taking advantage of valuation differences, and earn a performance fee based on both current estimates of return and, at liquidation, a final tally of return over the investment period.

Hurdle rate. Minimum expected rate of return a developer or investor requires to determine that a project is financially viable. The dimensions for measuring return for a development vary widely among developers and investors; they can include return on cost, internal rate of return, cash on cash, and many others. The hurdle rate is the minimum rate for the dimension that the developer or investor is using.

Impact fees. Fees imposed by a local government on a new real estate development to cover capital infrastructure costs that the new development may create; for instance, costs for expanding schools or roads.

Institutional investor. Organizations that pool large sums of money, investing in securities, real property, and other investment assets. Institutional investors include pension funds, endowments, foundations, banks, and insurance companies.

Integrated project delivery. A collaborative development approach in which the developer, architect, and contractor work as a team focused on minimizing costs and overruns through collaboration and information sharing, sharing the risks and rewards of project success.

Interest-only loan. A loan which, for a set term that is usually less than the total term of the loan, requires only interest payments on the balance outstanding. The principal amount of the loan is repaid at its maturity date, which may be months or years from the loan origination date.

Internal rate of return (IRR). The discount rate at which a stream of income over time (including the return of principal) produced by an investment has zero net present value (that is, the yield to the investor). This dimension of return is the most accurate measurement of project viability, but its measurement requires detailed and accurate information on costs and income that may be unavailable in the early phases of a project.

Joint venture. A real estate investment entity whose scope and organizational structure is defined in an agreement among the parties. A joint venture may be a legally separate entity such as a partnership or limited liability corporation (LLC) or a simple association. The joint venture agreement is tailored to the circumstances and needs of the participants; it stipulates the operating rules for the partners and, if desired, creates the legal entity to implement the transaction.

Letter of intent (LOI). A letter from the developer to the land owner setting forth the proposed purchase price for the land and timing for the close of escrow. Also, a letter from a tenant or user indicating an intent to lease or purchase a portion of a commercial project.

Leverage. The ratio of debt to cost used for financing an investment.

Lien. A legally recorded exception to title on real property which gives the holder of the lien the right to foreclose on the property in the event that the owner defaults on a loan.

Limited liability company (LLC). A hybrid business entity, often well suited for companies with a single owner, that possesses characteristics of both a corporation and a partnership. The primary characteristic an LLC shares with a corporation is limited liability, and the primary character-istic it shares with a partnership is the availability of pass-through income taxation.

Limited partnership. Historically the form of ownership most widely used for real estate. A limited partnership must include one general partner and one limited partner, with the general partner liable for the venture's debts and other obligations and the limited partner bearing no liability beyond its contributed capital. Income and tax losses from the limited partnership pass through the entity without taxation directly to the partners, who assume all the net tax liability.

Liquidity. The degree to which cash is available for use. It also measures how easily noncash assets can be converted to cash.

Loan-to-cost (LTC) ratio. A ratio that lenders use as one of several underwriting criteria for lending on a real estate project. The LTC measures the ratio of loan amount to project costs, where costs are limited to categories allowed by the lender.

Loan-to-value (LTV) ratio. A ratio that lenders use as one of several underwriting criteria for lending on a real estate project. The LTV measures the ratio of loan amount to project value, where value is based on appraisal protocols of the lender.

Maximum supported investment. The total amount that the developer can afford to spend, including land, while still achieving the hurdle rate.

Mezzanine debt. A type of debt that combines elements of both debt and equity, called mezzanine because it is typically between equity and debt in the capital stack. Like debt, it typically is paid interest, but unlike debt, it is rarely secured by a lien on the property. Like equity, it frequently receives a return based on project performance, typically higher than debt but lower than equity returns.

Money center banks. Banks located in capital market centers such as New York, Chicago, or Los Angeles, which have large asset bases and focus on large projects.

Net operating income (NOI). Cash flow from rental income on a property after operating expenses (property taxes, maintenance, and insurance) are deducted from gross income.

Net rents or triple net rents (NNN). Gross rents after deduction of the three main operating expenses of property taxes, maintenance, and insurance. Net rents and CAM charges produce net operating income.

Nonrecourse loan. A loan that, in the event of default by the borrower, limits the lender to foreclosure on the property and does not include recourse to the assets of the borrower as additional security for the loan.

Operating cash flow (OCF). Net operating income less debt service. OCF is the amount available for distribution to investors to produce return on and return of principal invested.

Operating expense ratio. The ratio of operating expenses to either potential gross income or effective gross income.

Operating expenses. Recurring costs for property ownership, such as janitorial services, management fees, utilities, as well as taxes, insurance, and reserves.

Opportunity funds. An investment option for institutional and high–net worth investors that target properties with high-risk/high-return profiles.

Pari passu. A Latin phrase that means "of equal steps," used to indicate that each investor is paid in accordance with its share of the total capital invested.

Percentage rent. Rent based on a percentage of retail sales over a certain level that is charged in addition to the base rent. Also known as overage rent.

Permanent loan. The long-term mortgage on a property.

Predevelopment costs. Costs that are incurred before construction starts, such as those for architects, consultants, entitlement processing, nonrefundable land deposits, developer staff time, and preconstruction management.

Preferred return. A minimum annual internal rate of return paid to investors before distribution is made to the developer or operating partners. The developer or operating partners participate in preferred return in amounts proportional to the co-investment amount.

Prime rate. The interest rate at which commercial banks set their base lending rate; originally the interest rate at which banks lent to favored customers.

Private equity fund. A collective investment offering used for making investments, often in high-risk/high-reward scenarios such as short-term turnaround properties; limited to qualified investors and institutions.

Pro forma. A financial projection of revenues, expenses, financing, and capital events for a real estate project.

Promotional return. The accrued obligation for distribution to investors from the operating cash flow and/or capital event proceeds after payment of return of principal and preferred return.

Purchase and sale agreement. Formal document that sets forth the business terms of a sale, including the buyer's conditions for close of escrow and the seller's performance requirement for buyer payments.

Rate of return. Annual rate of return calculated as an internal rate of return, gross return (total received compared to total invested), return on costs, return on sales, and or any of many other measures of return.

Real estate investment trust (REIT). An entity that sells shares publicly or privately that combines the capital of many investors to acquire or provide financing for all forms of real estate. Much like a mutual fund, REITs offer investors the benefit of a diversified portfolio under professional management. A corporation or trust that qualifies as a REIT generally does not pay corporate income tax and must meet minimum distribution requirements of annual income.

Real estate operating company. A company that invests in real estate and whose shares trade on a public exchange.

Recourse. The right of a lender, in the event of default by the borrower, to recover against the personal assets of a party who is liable for the debt and against other investments in real estate if the party is a firm.

Refinancing. The replacement of an existing debt obligation with a debt obligation under different terms.

Residual land value. The difference between the maximum supported investment and total project costs excluding land.

Return on equity. A percentage measure of the return on the amount invested by equity investors.

S corporation. A corporation that does not pay any federal taxes. The corporation's income or losses are divided among and passed through to its shareholders, who must report the income or loss on their individual income tax returns.

Site plan. A detailed engineering drawing of proposed improvements for a parcel. A site plan typically shows building footprints; streets; parking; sewer and water lines; electric, gas, and other utilities; landscaping; easements; and certain natural features.

Soft costs. Project costs that vary with the amount of "hard" costs. Soft costs include those for architecture, engineering, construction management, financing, and other third-party charges associated with real estate development.

Sovereign wealth fund. A non-U.S., state-owned investment fund composed of financial assets such as stocks, bonds, property, precious metals, or other financial instruments.

Speculative development. The development of a project without presales or preleasing that instead is marketed to customers only after completion. Also known as "spec" development.

Stabilized income. The ongoing predictable income of a project after the lease-up period is completed. The lease-up period may be as long as several years after project completion.

Subordinated debt. Debt that carries a lower-priority claim on the issuer's income or assets than that of other (senior) debt should income or asset value fall below the amount needed to support the senior debt.

Subordination, Non-Disturbance, and Attornment (SNDA) Agreement. An agreement that gives the lender the right to foreclose if the developer defaults, while preserving the rights of the tenants to remain as long as they pay rent.

Syndication. The process of acquiring and combining equity investments from multiple sources (for example, syndicating units in a limited partnership).

Tax increment financing. A public financing method (usually enabled by establishment of a redevelopment agency) that is used for investment in community redevelopment projects by applying future gains in taxes in the defined redevelopment area to finance improvements that facilitate private investment.

Tenant improvement allowances (TIs). The amount that a landlord or property owner pays toward finishing a commercial tenant's space. TIs vary widely based on the desirability of the tenant and market rental rates.

Terminal capital rate. A rate used to estimate the resale value of a property at the end of the holding period.

Title report. A document issued by a title company that lists exceptions to title for a property, including loans recorded against the property, liens, easements, and deed restrictions on potential purchase.

Tranche. A segmentation of securities by seniority and risk. Higher-rated tranches receive priority payments from the income of the underlying pool of loans; lower-rated classes receive lower priority and offer higher yields.

Triple net rents (NNN). Rental revenues that do not include the three major occupancy costs: taxes, maintenance, and insurance.

Umbrella REIT (UPREIT). Organizational structure in which the assets of a REIT are owned, for tax purposes, by a holding company.

Vacancy and collection allowance. An assumed reduction in estimated income that allows for vacancies and collection problems that may arise.

Waterfall. A cascade of flow of profits from a real estate project, in which higher-tiered investors receive return of principal and preferred return, while the lower-tiered creditors receive distributions from profits after the first tier.

Index

Italic page numbers indicate figures, photos, and illustrations. Bold page numbers indicate case studies.

A

Abnormal default rates, 119*n*

Absorption rate: hurdle rate, 60–61, *61*; land values and, 179; market analysis, 13, 19–21, 128; mixed-use projects, 74

Accredited investors, 104–5

Acquisition: capital acquisition, 187–97; fees, 138. *See also* Land acquisition; Land value for acquisition

Acquisition, development, and construction (ADC) loans, 30, 41–42

Affordable housing: 800/900 North Glebe Road project, **22–24**; grants and incentives, 179–80, *183*; public/private partnerships, 163–64, 169

Anchor stores, 189

Apartment buildings: close-out requirements, 11; density, 16; valuation, 33

Appleton Mills (Lowell, Massachusetts), *132*, 164–65

Architects: entitlement process, 153–54; predevelopment costs, 10, 41; selection, 85–91

Archstone, *128*, 168

Argus real estate software, 39

Arlington County, VA, 800/900 North Glebe Road project, **23**

Asset allocation model, 110

Atelier 505 (Boston, Massachusetts), *122*

AvalonBay Communities, 107

B

Baby boom, 6

Banks: capital markets and, *99*, 99–101, 119; community development entities (CDEs), 181; construction loans, 30; debt yield ratios, 34; financing terms, 194; foreclosures, 100; foreign banks, 111; interest reserve, 41; relationship-based lending, 121, 126, 191; shadow banking, 95; underwater loans, 96; undesirable loans, 103

Belmonte, Luis, 188–89, 192, 194, 198

Bel-Red Corridor plan (Bellevue-Redmond, Washington), 166

Beyard, Michael, 118

Bid documents, 81

BIDs (business improvement districts), 169, 171

Blind pools, 104

Blitz, David, 118, 187, 195, 198

Bond types, 176–77

Boom cycles, non-sustainable, 117

Boston Center for the Arts, *122*

Brokers, capital, 123, 196–97

Brokers, real estate: developers and, 66, 197; national brokerage firms, 126; for site owners, 70

Budgeting: business plan, 78; contingency planning, 48–49, 84; due diligence, 72, *73*, 154; joint ventures, 136; management, 78; shortfall provisions, 138

Building codes, 152

Building inspection process, 153

Business improvement districts (BIDs), 169, 171

Business plan: budgeting, 78, 136; financing presentation, 127–29; joint venture presentation, 136

Buyers: conditions of sale, 71–72; finding, 126

Buy-sell provisions, 113, 139

C

Calculations. *See* Mathematical formulas

California Environmental Quality Act of 1970 (CEQA), 166

CAM (common area maintenance) charges, 47

Capital acquisition, 187–97; getting started, 187–91; relationship building, 192–93; skills for 2010s, 194–97

Capital brokers, 123, 196–97

Capital events, 39, 44, 121

Capitalization, 137–38

Capitalization (cap) rates: cash flow analysis and, 55, *55*; CMBS issuance, 102, *102*; initial and terminal, 39; as market condition indicator, 35–38, *36–38*; in mid-2000s, 194; multifamily residential, 116; NOI evaluation, 35–38, *36–37*, 50–51, *50–52*; retail, 116

Capital markets for real estate, 93–119; banks, *99*, 99–101; capital market conditions, 93–96, *94*; capital sources, 13–14, 96–111, *97*, *98*; CMBS, *101–2*, 101–3; fiduciary principles, 111–14; foreign investors, 111; government credit agencies, 111; hedge funds, 106–7; high–net worth individuals, 104–5, *105*; life insurance companies, 109; mutual savings banks, *99*, 99–101; ongoing connections, 123–26; pension funds, 109–11; private equity capital, 103–11; private equity firms, 105–6; property characteristics, 116–19; regional strength, 117–18; REITs, 107–9, *108*; risk-reward evaluation, 119; savings and loans, *99*, 99–101; sector risk, 116, *116*; syndicates, 104–5; tenant strength, 118; 1031 TIC investors, 104–5; value-added opportunities, 118–19

Capitol Quarter (Washington, D.C.), *190,* 199

Capital stack: leverage effects, 40; mezzanine debt, 32, 46–47; private equity, 124; public/private partnerships, 163–64, *165,* 173; risk-yield relationship, 97, *97;* tax credits, 180; waterfall distribution and, 29

Carve-out agreements, 42

Case-Shiller index, 95

Cash flow (CF): cap rates, 35, 38–39; fee income from, 138, 181; leveraged cash flow, 55; negative cash flow, 48; OCF, 35; permanent lenders, 42

Cash-on-cash returns: density changes, 155–56, *156;* project hurdle rate, 59–61, *61*

CDEs (community development entities), 181–82

Clawback provisions, 138

Cleanup, 167–68

Clorox distribution facility (University Park, Illinois), 164

Close-out, 10–11

CMBS. *See* Commercial mortgage–backed securities

Co-investment: as developer requirement, 13, 31, 43, 91, 112–13; public/private partnerships, 119, *168,* 168–69, 177

Commercial mortgage–backed securities (CMBS): bank size, 101; Congressional Oversight Panel report (2010), 103; developed in 1990s, 5; financing in 2010s, 194; joint venture loan, 143, *143;* large development projects, 100; life insurance companies and, 109; market impact, *101–2,* 101–3; as recent investment strategy, 93

Commingled funds, 104–5

Common area maintenance (CAM) charges, 47

Community Development Block Grant, 179

Community Development Entities (CDEs), 181–82

Community Development Financial Institution Fund, 181

Community Housing Works, *183*

Community issues: developer relationships, 68–69, 160, 172–74, 197; entitlement process, 80, 151–52, 160; information gathering, 13; land acquisition, 68–69; public/private partnerships, 169–72

Conahan, Elizabeth, 192–93, 195, 198

Concessions, 159–61

Condominiums: close-out requirements, 11; risk/return, 20; valuation, 33

Confidentiality, 139

Congressional Oversight Panel, 96, 99–100, 103

Construction: constraints, 183; costs, 13, 69; documents, 81; financing, 30–31, 42, 126; management fees, 138

Construction Users Roundtable, 83

Contingencies, 48–49, 62–63, 84

Contractor selection, 85–91

Core-asset investors, 114

Core-asset real estate portfolios, 109

Core-plus investment category, 114–15

Corporations, 134

Cost analysis concerns for lenders, 128

CoStar listing service, 126

Costs: categories, 62; construction management, 81–84; contingencies, 48–49, 62–63, 84; entitlement process, 154; estimation, 48–54, *49*

Country club money, 123–25

Credibility of development entity, 127

Credit tenants, 42, 118

Cycle players, 195

D

Darcey, H. James, 124

DCR (debt service coverage ratio), 33

Deals: negotiations, 173–74; standards, 182–85; typical structure, 45

Debt: funding, 41–43, 45; structure, 30–32, *31;* yield ratio, 34

Debt service coverage ratio (DSCR or DCR), 33

Del Mar Station (Pasadena, California), *128,* 168–69

Density: bonus for affordable housing, 179; entitlement process, 155–57, *156–57*

Deposits to site owner, nonrefundable, 71

Design: costs, 10; development, 81; entitlement process, 158–59

Design-bid-build model, 82

Design-build model, 82–83

Developers: beginning developers, career building, 123–25; broker relationships, 66; capital market understanding, 119; co-investment requirement, 91, 112–13; community relations, 68–69, 160, 172–74, 197; competence and financing success, 192; developer fee, 128, 138; discipline, 83; distribution of returns, 31–32; entitlement process management, 159; lender relationships, 42–43, 123–25; liability, 132; professional credentials, 122, 127, 197; removal for cause provision, 113; site owner relationship, 70–73; skills, 6, 14–16; trustworthiness, 112

Development equity capital, 123–25

Development process, 3–27; absorption, 19–21, *20;* case study, **22–27;** close-out, 10–11; complexity after market collapse, 121; conditions, 13; customer issues, 19; developer skills, 14–16; development, 9–10; development sectors, 16–21; financial viability, 13–14; information, 12–13; operation, 10–11; predevelopment, 8–9; project, 127–29; real estate overview, 3–6; relationships, 14; return, 19–21, *20;* risk, 6–8, *7,* 19–21, *20;* sectors, 16–21; stages, 8–11, *9;* values, 12

Development team relationship, 127

Dilution provisions, 138

Discount rate, 35

Dishnica, Richard, 9

Dispute resolution process, 42

Distressed companies investments, 135

Distributions, 43–45. *See also* Waterfall distribution

Double taxation, avoiding, 107

Dow Jones U.S. Real Estate exchange-traded fund (ETF), 95

DownREITs, 108–9, 134

Due diligence: after PSA, 71; budgeting, 72, *73*, 154; entitlement process, 154; land acquisition, 72–74, *73*; market review, 79; redevelopment projects, 175; renegotiable conditions, 72

Dumbarton Bridge (Newark, California), 167

E

Early project costs, 7

Easements, 67, 78–79

Economic contribution of development, 3, *4, 5*

Economic restructuring, 118

Edge cities, 17

Effective gross income, 33

800/900 North Glebe Road project (Arlington, Virginia), **22–27**

Emergency Economic Stabilization Act of 2008, 96

Emerging Trends in Real Estate (ULI): *2006,* 101; *2009, 93; 2011,* 117

Eminent domain, 175, 178

Entitlement process, 151–61; after offer acceptance, 153–54; before making offer, 153; circumstance changes, 154; density, 155–57, *156, 157*; design, 158–59; due diligence period, 154; environmental review/conditions, 152; federal requirements, 152–53; management, 159–61; mapping, 152–54; parking, 158, *158*; project economics, 154–59; public improvements, 158; public/private partnerships, 129, 163; risk, 166

Entity-level joint venture, 135

Environmental remediation, 79

Environmental review/conditions, 152

Equity: funding, 13, 43–45, *44,* 45, *51*; investors, 29–30, 114–15; structure, 30–32, *31*

Equity REITs, 107

ETF (exchange-traded fund), 95

Exchange-traded fund (ETF), 95

Extend and pretend practice, 96

EYA (Washington, D.C.), 189–91, 193, 199

F

FAR (floor/area ratio), 16

Federal Deposit Insurance Corporation (FDIC), 99

Federal Housing Administration (FHA), 11

Federal National Mortgage Association (Fannie Mae), 95, 111

Fees for services provision, 114, 138

Ferguson, Niall, 94–95

Fiduciary principles, 111–14

Finance, 29–57; capacity of development entity, 127; capitalization (cap) rates, 35–38, 36, 37, 38; cost estimation, 48–54, *49*; deal structure, typical, 45; debt funding, 41–43; debt structure, 30–32, *31*; equity funding, 43–45, *44, 51*; equity structure, 30–32, *31*; finance structure, hypothetical, 45–56, *46, 49–52, 56*; financial viability, 13–14; internal rates of return (IRRs), 38–39, *39, 52*; leverage, 40, *40*; project funding, 41–45; project return, 38–40, *56*; project valuation, 33–38, *34*; return evaluation, 54–56; tasks, 84, *86–89*

Financial analysis: concerns for lenders, 128; land acquisition, 69–70; skills, 15

Financial Industry Regulatory Authority, 95

Financial pro forma. *See* Pro forma preparation

Financing for development, 121–29; business plan, 127–29; buyer, finding, 126; capital sources, 13, 123–26, 173; construction financing, 126; credibility of development entity, 127; development equity capital, 123–25; development project, 127–29; entitlement process, 129; experience of development entity, 127; financial capacity of development entity, 127; market conditions, 121–23; permanent financing, 126; predevelopment equity capital, 123–25; presenting to financing sources, 126–29; public/private partnerships, 129, 174–82

Financing structure: joint ventures, 136, 139–49, *140–48*; profit distribution example, 145–49; profit distribution to development entity, 144–45

First deed of trust, 42

Floodplain considerations, 67

Floor/area ratio (FAR), 16

Florida, Richard, 117

Focused studies, 81

Foreclosures: CalPERS investments, 110; commercial mortgage–backed securities properties, 103; land-secured bonds, 176–77; REO properties, 100

Foreign Investment in Real Property Tax Act of 1981, 111

Foreign investors, 111

Forest City, 171, *178*

Formulas. *See* Mathematical formulas

For-sale projects, 33, 126

Forward commitments, 42

Freddie Mac (Federal Home Loan Mortgage Corporation), 95, 111

G

Gap financing. *See* Mezzanine debt
Gates, Jerome, 43
GDP (gross domestic product), 3, *4*
General obligation bonds, 177
General partnerships, 132
George Elkins Mortgage Banking Company (Los Angeles, California), 187, 198
Gift of public funds, 183
GMAC Mortgage, 20
Governance, 137
Government: credit agencies, 111; entitlement process, 160
Graaskamp, James, 12
Grants, 179
Great Recession of 2007–2008: debt yield ratio, 34; decade-long effects, 119; over-concentration perils, 117; real estate dynamics, 6. *See also* Real estate collapse
Green Building Council (U.S.), 179
Green building incentives, 179
Gross rents, 47
Growth-constrained markets, 122

H

Hazardous waste, 67
Hedge funds, 106–7, 194
High–net worth individuals, 104–5, *105*, 111
High-risk investment strategies, 115
Historical preservation tax credits, 182
Holding period provisions, 113–14, 136
HOME funds, 179
Housing and Urban Development Department, U.S., 180
HUD loans, 195
Hudnut, Bill, 159
Hudson, Jeff, 187, 193, 195, 198
Huntington Theatre Company, *122*
Hurdle rate, 59–63, *61*, 74, 113, 179
Hybrid REITs, 107

I

ICSC (International Council of Shopping Centers), 197, 201
Impact fees, 153
Incentives, 138, 179
Inclusionary housing. *See* Affordable housing
Income-valuation blend, 114, *115*
Industrial projects: close-out requirements, 11; defined, 16; requirements, 19; valuation, 33

Information: inputs, *67*, 67–70; investment, 77–78
Infrastructure: fees/dedications, 152; financing, 170–71
Initial cap rate, 35, 39
Inspection process, 153
"Integrated Project Delivery: A Guide" (AIA), 83
Integrated project delivery model, 83–84
Inter-creditor agreements, 97
Interest reserve, 41
Intermediary finance institutions, 125
Internal rates of return (IRR), 38–39, *39, 52,* 60
Internal Revenue Code Section 1031, 104
International Council of Shopping Centers (ICSC), 197, 201
Investment strategies, 114–15, 136
IRR. *See* Internal rates of return

J

Jackson, Brian, 189–91, 193, 199
Jefferson at West Goshen (West Goshen, Pennsylvania), 125
Job superintendent duties, 90
Johansen, Curt, 191, 195, 199–200
Joint control with stakeholders, 112–14
Joint ventures, 131–49; business plan, 136; capitalization, 137–38; contribution responsibilities in, 137–38; corporations, 134; death provision in, 139; decision-making authority, 137; defined, 134, 149*n*; elements of, 134–39; financing structure, 139–49, *140–43*; general provisions, 139; governance, 137; guarantees, 137; investor control in joint ventures, 131–33; limited liability companies (LLCs), 133; ownership of assets, 137; participants, 136–37; partnerships, *132,* 132–33; profit distribution, *144,* 144–48, *146–48*; real estate entities, 131–34; REITs, 133–34; revenue distribution among partners, 138; role definition, 137; S corporations, 133; tax issues, 131–33
Junior debt. *See* Mezzanine debt

K

Keefe, James, 164
Kelo decision (*Kelo v. City of New London* (2005)), **175**
Kennedy, Patrick, 12
Key-man life insurance, 139
Kingsley, Dan, 189, 191–92, 195–96, 200
Klawiter, Richard, 164
Knott, John, 161
Knott, Michael, 106

L

Lakeside Steel Plant (Chicago, Illinois), 164

Land acquisition: capital investment, 21, 74; due diligence, 72; financial viability, 13; joint ventures, 135; predesign, 72, 81; value determination, 7

Land assembly/conveyance, 178–79

Land development: defined, 16; land-secured bonds, 176–77; risk/return, 21; use, 152–53

Land valuation for acquisition, 59–75; community support, 68–69; construction costs, 69; costs, 62–63; due diligence, 72–74, 73; financial analysis, 69–70; hurdle rate, 59–61, 61; information inputs, 67, 67–70; market assessment, 68; negotiation with site owners, 70–73; pro forma model, 74–75, 74–75; project and product design, 69; purchase and sale agreement (PSA), 71–72; purchase steps, 71; residual land value, 63–65, 64–65; site analysis, 67–68; site selection, 66–70, 67; supported investment, 62–65, 64–65

Leadership in Energy and Environmental Design, 179

Lease revenue bonds, 177

Lease-up reserve, 48

Legal services, 90–91

Legal skills, 15

Lenders. See Capital markets for real estate

Letter of intent (LOI), 71

Leverage: decrease after market collapse, 122; defined, 29–30; investment strategies, 114, 115; leveraged IRR, 38; mezzanine debt, 32; returns on equity, 40, 40

Liability, 137

Liens. See Title issues

Life insurance companies, 109, 125

Limited liability companies (LLCs), 43, 133

Loans: loan-to-cost (LTC) criteria, 29, 33; loan-to-value (LTV) criteria, 29, 34, 100; non-recourse, 42; rates, 116, 116; segmentation, 42; terms, current, 100

Local government control, 152

LOI (letter of intent), 71

LoopNet listing service, 126

Los Angeles Metropolitan Transportation Authority, 128, 168

Low-Income Housing Tax Credit, 180–81

LTC (loan-to-cost) criteria, 29, 33

LTV (loan-to-value) criteria, 29, 34, 100

M

Management: of entitlement process, 159–61; services, 139; skills, 16

Market, real estate: in 2010s, 121–23; analysis concerns for lenders, 127–28; assessments, 68, 79, 90; 800/900 North Glebe Road project, 23; regional differences, 121; support, 13; unexpected changes, 10; validation, 79–80. See also Real estate collapse

Marketing fees, 138

Marketing program, 79

Material costs, unexpected increases, 10

Mathematical formulas: cap rate, 35; hurdle rate, 60; IRR, 38–39; maximum supported investment, 62; present value, 35; project value, 36; residual land value, 63

Maturity wall, 96, 119

Mechanical, electrical, and plumbing (MEP), 82

Mechanic's liens, 42

Media and entitlement process, 160

The Metropolitan (Charlotte, North Carolina), 169, 189

Mezzanine debt: CalPERS investments, 110; capital events, 39; capital sources, 97, 97; defined, 32; lenders, 142, 143

Misallocation (pension funds), 110

Mission Bay mixed-use project (San Francisco, California), 164

Mixed-use development: absorption rate, 74; Appleton Mills, 132; Atelier 505, 122; Del Mar Station, 128, 168; 800/900 North Glebe Road project, **23–24**; financing difficulties, 116; infill development, 189–90; Mission Bay, 164; as new sector, 17–19; for obsolete spaces, 118–19; pro forma example, 74–75, 74–75; public/private partnerships, 119; tenant strength, 118; valuation, 33; Williamson project, 188

Model homes, 11, 20

Mortgage-backed security pool, 42

Mortgage REITs, 107

Mortgage revenue bonds, 177

Multidisciplinary professional organizations, 197

Multifamily housing, 16, 17

Municipal bonds, 176–77

Municipal debt, 184

Mutual savings banks, 99, 99–101

N

National Association of Industrial and Office Properties (NAIOP), 197, 198

National Association of Real Estate Investment Trusts, 95, 107

National Council of Real Estate Investment Fiduciaries (NCREIF), 37–38

NCREIF (National Council of Real Estate Investment Fiduciaries), 37–38

Negotiated model, 82

Negotiations: developer's skills, 14–15; with site owners, 70–73

Net operating income (NOI): cap rate determination, 35, 39; DCR and, 33; project value determination, 36

Net rents, 47

New Market Tax Credits, *181,* 181–82

Nexus contributions, 158

NNN (triple net rents), 47

NOI. *See* Net operating income

Non-recourse loans, 42

O

OCF (operating cash flow), 35. *See also* Cash flow

Office building projects: close-out requirements, 11; requirements, 19; urban and suburban, 16; valuation, 33

Oliver, H. Pike, 161

Open-book negotiation style, 173–74

Operating cash flow (OCF), 35. *See also* Cash flow

Operation of finished project, 10–11

Opportunity funds, 194

Opportunity properties, 104

Overage rent, 47

Owen, Jeff, 164

P

Pappas, Peter, 189, 191, 193, 195, 200

Paradise Valley golf course (Fairfield, California), 169

Parcel map conditions, 152

Pari passu, 30, 43–44

Parking: 800/900 North Glebe Road project, **25**; entitlement process, 158, *158*; ratios, 158; reduced parking requirements, 179

Parkmerced (San Francisco, California), 110

Partnerships: joint ventures, *132,* 132–33; partnership entity, 170

Paul, Thad, 124

Penalty dilution, 145

Pension funds, 109–11, 125

Percentage rent, 47

Performance guarantees, 42, 112

Performing debt. *See* Mezzanine debt

Permanent financing, 30–31, 42, 126

Personal liability, 131–33

Personnel selection, 84–90

P/E (price-to-earnings) stock multiplier, 36

Pinole Valley Redevelopment Agency, 165–66

Pinole Valley Shopping Center (Pinole, California), 165–66

Plan check process, 153

Planning department policies, 153

Political dynamics, 10, 192

Political skills, 15

Predesign due diligence, 81

Predevelopment: capital, 123–25, 151; project value, 8–9

Preferred returns, 43, 138

Presentation to lenders, formats, 127

Presentation skills, 15, 126–29

Price-to-earnings (P/E) stock multiplier, 36

Primary markets for financing costs, 117

Private activity limitations, 177

Private equity capital: categories, 103–11; financing in 2010s, 194; funds and firms, 105–6; investment goals, 124; risk aversion, 125

Private REITs, 107

Problem anticipation, 78

Products. *See* Projects

Product type analysis, 79

Professional certification, 197

Professional organizations, 197

Professional services, 151

Profitability, potential, 13

Profit distribution. *See* Waterfall distribution

Profit-taking provision, 114

Pro forma preparation: cash flow, 48; financial assumptions, 13, 63, 127; hurdle rate, 61; as loan basis, 103; for mixed-use project, 74–75, *74–75*; public improvements, 158; residual land value, 63, 69

Programmatic and strategic joint venture, 135

Projects: design, 13, 60, 69, 80–81; lender concerns, 128; manager duties, 90; modifications, 151; return, 38–40, *56*; success components, 122, 172; valuation, 33–38, *34. See also* Finance; Financing for development

ProLogis, 107

Promotional returns (promote), 30–31, 138

Property characteristics, 116–19

Property management plan, 80

Property owners, 70–73

Proprietary software, lenders', 127

PSA (purchase and sale agreement), 66, 71–72

Public announcements for joint ventures, 139

Public benefits from private development, 169–70

Public improvements, 158

Public/private partnerships, 163–85; affordable housing subsidies, 179–80; application, 163–69; BIDs, 171; bond types, other, 177; co-investment, 168–69, community preparation, 169–72; deal negotiations, 173–74; deal standards, 182–85; Del Mar Station, *128,* 168; developer and community cooperation, 172–74; entitlement risk, 166; financing, 129, 174–82; grants, 179; historical preservation tax credits, 182; incentives, 179; infrastructure financing,

170–71; land assembly and conveyance, 178–79; land-secured bonds, 176–77; Low-Income Housing Tax Credit, 180–81; mixed-use development, 119; municipal bonds, 176–77; New Market Tax Credits, 181–82; partnership entity, 170; project success components, 122; public capital for private projects, 164–66, *165*; redevelopment agencies, 174–76; site access, cleanup, and reconfiguration, 167–68; sports stadiums, 177; standards for, 184–85; Stapleton Airport redevelopment, 171–72, *172, 178*; tax credits, 180–82. *See also* Mixed-use development

Public syndicates, 104

Punch lists, 19

Purchase and sale agreement (PSA), 66, 71–72

Q

Qualified Active Low-Income Community Businesses, 181

Qualified Low-Income Community Investments, 181

R

Rancho Solano golf course (Fairfield, California), 169

Real estate brokers. *See* Brokers, real estate

Real estate collapse: bond values, 95–96, 119*n*; capital markets, 93–96; cap rates, 116; CMBS and, 101–3; government credit agencies, 111; investment prospect changes, 108, 117; non-performing loans, 100–103; pension funds, 110–11; regional markets, 117; REITs, 108; risks, 8, 116; shortcomings of current practices, 118; SIVs, 119*n*

Real estate entities, 131–34; corporations, 134; limited liability companies (LLCs), 133; organizational factors, 131–32; partnerships, *132*, 132–33; REITs, 133–34; S corporations, 133. *See also* Joint ventures

Real estate evolution, 6

Real estate investment trusts. *See* REITs

Real estate operating companies (REOCs), 135

Real estate overview, 3–6

Real estate owned (REO) property, 100

Real estate–stock market comparison, *4–5,* 4–6, 36–37

Recourse, 30, 42, 137

Recoverable operation expenses, 47

Redevelopment agencies, 174–76, *175*

Regional market differences, 121–22

Regional requirements, 152–53

Regional strength, 117–18

Regulation D, 105

Reiner, David, 124

REITs (real estate investment trusts): defined, 133–34; downREITs, 108–9, 134; as equity investors, 125;

equity REITs, 107; financing in 2010s, 194–95; history and growth, 93, 107–9, *108*; Tax Reform Act of 1986, 4–5; UPREITs, 108, 134

Relationship building: capital acquisition, 99–100, 123–25, 192–93; community, 68–69, 160, 172–74, 197

Rents: cap rate and, 39; density considerations, 155; as hurdle rate basis, 60; increases, 54; overage or percentage rent, 47; project performance and, 166; recoverable operating expenses, 47; tenant strength, 118; valuation, 33

REOCs (real estate operating companies), 135

REO (real estate owned) property, 100

Request for information (RFI), 83

Request for proposal (RFP), 172

Request for qualifications (RFQ), 172

RERC (Real Estate Research Corporation), 37–38

Residential customer issues, 19

Residual land value, 59, 63–65, *64–65*

Residual tranche, 45

Resolution Trust Institute, 101

Retail project analysis, hypothetical, 45–56; developer's conceptualization, 45–46; estimating costs, 48–54, *49*; evaluating return, 54–56, *56*; loan calculations, *50–52*, 50–54; rent types, 47; revenue estimates, *46*, 46–47; tenant improvements (TIs), 47–48

Retail projects: close-out requirements, 11; rental terms, 47; risk, 19; tenants, 16, 19; valuation, 33

Return of equity (ROE), 31

Return on investment (ROI): characteristics, 19–21; evaluation, 7, 54–56

Revenue bonds, 177

Revenue distribution in joint ventures, 138. *See also* Waterfall distribution

RFI (request for information), 83

RFP (request for proposal), 172

RFQ (request for qualifications), 172

Riordan, James, 124

Risk: condominiums, 20; development process, 6–8, *7,* 19–21, 114, *115*; entitlement process, 166; high-risk investment strategies, 115; land development, 21; real estate collapse, 8, 116; retail projects, 19; risk aversion, 125; risk-reward evaluation, 119; sector risk, 102, 116, *116*; single-family housing, 19–20; term risk, 30

Ritchey, Monte, 188, 191, 193, 200–201

Riverton Houses (Harlem, New York), 110

ROI. *See* Return on investment

Rosenfeld, Dan, 8

S

San Francisco Bay Area: cap rates, *37,* 37–38, *38*; Greenbelt Alliance, 166; investment market, 117–18; Pleasant Hill BART station, 164

Santa Fe Train Depot (Pasadena, California), *128*

Savings and loans: capital markets, *99,* 99–101; 1980s crisis, 176

Schematic project design, 81

Schonbraun, Michael, 124

S corporations, 133, 134,

Secondary markets, 117

Section 1031, 104

Sectors, 16–21, 102, 116, *116*

Sector specialty organizations, 197

Securities Act of 1933, Regulation D, 105

Segmentation, loan, 42

Shadow banking, 95

Shortfall provisions, 138

Simpson, Ashleigh, 124

Single-asset joint venture, 134–35

Single-family housing: high and low end, 16; risk and return, 19–20; valuation, 33

Site access, cleanup, reconfiguration, *167,* 167–68

Site selection: analysis, 13, 67–68, 157; conditions, 10, 79; land acquisition, 66–70, *67*; lenders' concerns, 127; owners, 70–73; surveys, 67, 78; tasks, 78–79

SIVs (structured investment vehicles), 93, 119*n*

Sky Valley (Vallejo, California), 191

Small project financing, 126

Smith, Kevin H., 124

SNDA (Subordination, Non-Disturbance, and Attornment) Agreement, 43

Soil stability, 67

Solara (Poway, California), *183*

Southwest Center Mall (Dallas, Texas), 167–68

Speculation (on spec), 10

Sports stadiums as co-investment projects, 177

Staiger, Roger, III, 192, 194, 201

Stakeholder considerations, 12–15, 112–14, 116, 166, 169

Standard & Poor's Case-Shiller index, 95

Stapleton Airport redevelopment (Denver, Colorado), 171–72, *172, 178*

State requirements for entitlement process, 152–53

Stein, Debra, 159–60

Stock market–real estate comparison, *4–5,* 4–6, 36–37

Strategic/programmatic joint venture, 135

Structured investment vehicles (SIVs), 93, 119*n*

Stuyvesant Town and Peter Cooper Village (New York City), 110

Subdivision map conditions, 152–53

Subordinated debt. *See* Mezzanine debt

Subordination, Non-Disturbance, and Attornment (SNDA) Agreement, 43

Success fees provision, 113

Sun Belt cities, 117

Supported investment, 62–65, *64–65*

Sweat equity, 189

Syndicates, 104–5

T

Talent-clustering, 117

Task funding, 91

Task management, 77–91; architect selection, 85–91; community issues, 80; contractor selection, 85–91; cost and construction management, 81–84; design-bid-build model, 82; design-build model, 82–83; finance tasks, 84, *86–89*; integrated project delivery model, 83–84; market validation, 79–80; negotiated model, 82; other services, 90–91; personnel selection, 84–90; product and project design, 80–81; site tasks, 78–79; task funding, 91

Tax credit investors, 180

Tax credits, 109, 180–82, 184

Tax increment financing, 174–76, *175*

Tax Reform Act of 1986, 4–5, 194

Tax shelters, 4–5

Tax treatment: financing in 2010s, 194; joint ventures, 131–33

Team member professions, 84

Technology application skills, 15

10 Principles of Successful Public/Private Partnerships (ULI), 174

1031 Tenant in Common (TIC) investors, 104–5

Tenant improvements (TIs), 47–48

Tenant strength, 118

Terminal cap rate, 35, 39

Term risk, 30

Tertiary markets, 117

Time management, 78, 151

Timing issues: entitlement process, 154; joint ventures, 136; public/private partnerships, 172

TIs (tenant improvements), 47–48

Title issues, 67, 78–79

Townhomes, 16, 33, 63, 145

Traffic capacity, 67

Tranches, 42, 45

Transactional environments, current, 194

Transparency to stakeholders, 112–14

Triple net rents (NNN), 47
Trust building, 15

U

ULI. *See* Urban Land Institute
Umbrella partnership REITs (UPREITs), 108, 134
Under-parked projects, 158. *See also* Parking
Underwater loans, 96
Underwriting criteria, 122
Unleveraged IRR, 38, 60
UPREITs (umbrella partnership REITs), 108, 134
Urban Land (January 2009), 118
Urban Land Institute (ULI), ii, iv, 159, 197, 198, 201
Urban metabolism, 117
Urban Partners, 168
Utility availability, 67

V

Validation of assumptions, 112
Value-added opportunities, 118–19
Value creation, 114–15
Value players, 195
Values, 12. *See also* Land valuation for acquisition
Value-to-area ratio, 178
Virginia Tech Foundation, **22–23**
Visualization skills, 14

W

Waterfall distribution: capital stack position, 29–30, *44*;
    equity investors, 43; joint ventures, 131, *144,* 144–45;
    tax credit investors, 180
Web site for project, 160
Weight of capital, 95
Whole loan lenders, 99–100
Wilberding, Doug, 124
Williamson project (Charlotte, North Carolina), 188, 201

Z

Zell, Sam, 106